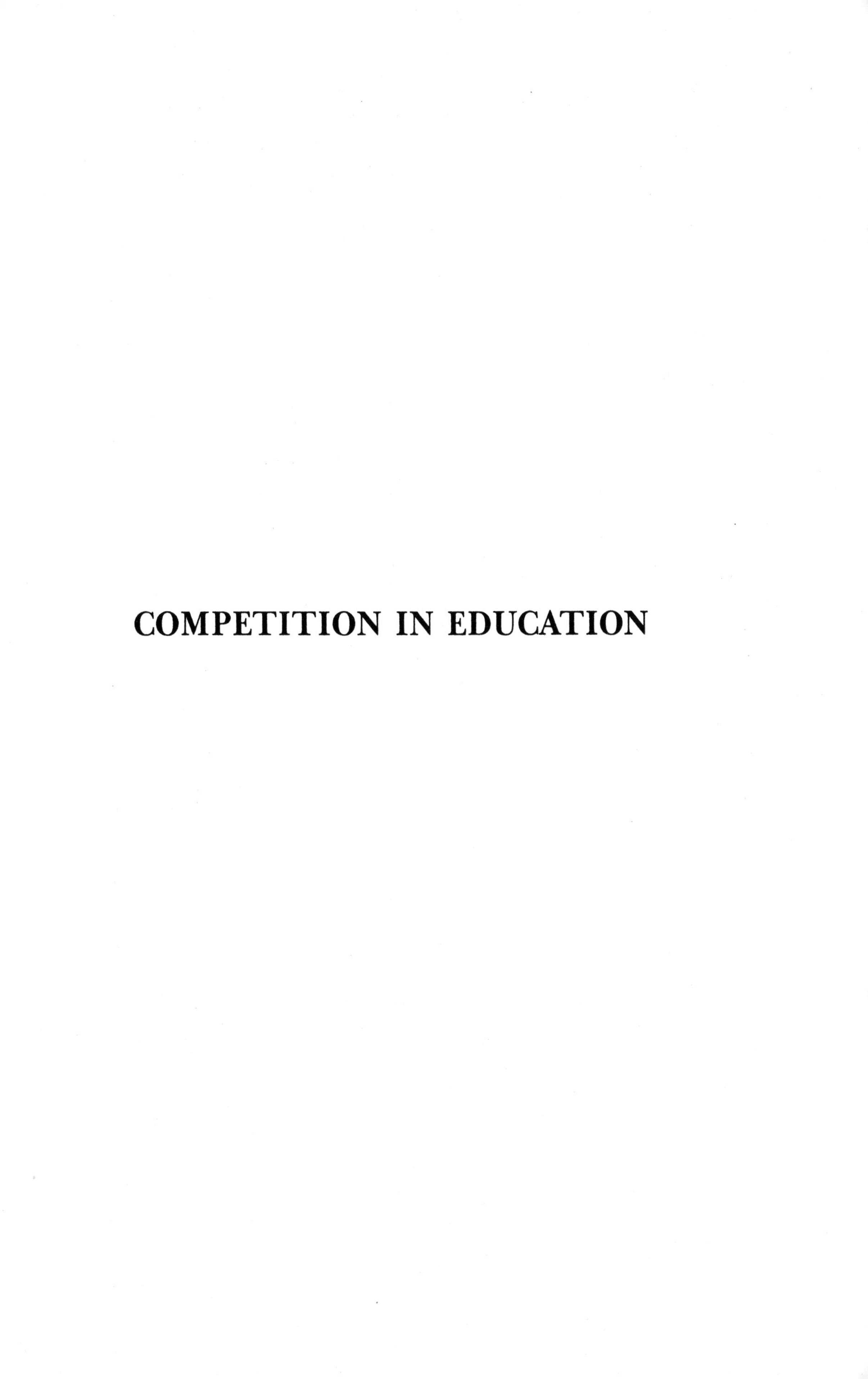

COMPETITION IN EDUCATION

COMPETITION IN EDUCATION

By

JOHN MARTIN RICH, PH.D.
University of Texas at Austin

JOSEPH L. DEVITIS, PH.D.
State University of New York at Binghamton

CHARLES C THOMAS • PUBLISHER
Springfield • Illinois • U.S.A.

Published and Distributed Throughout the World by

CHARLES C THOMAS • PUBLISHER
2600 South First Street
Springfield, Illinois 62794-9265

ISBN 0-398-05819-9

Library of Congress Catalog Card Number: 92-24758

With THOMAS BOOKS *careful attention is given to all details of manufacturing and design. It is the Publisher's desire to present books that are satisfactory as to their physical qualities and artistic possibilities and appropriate for their particular use.* THOMAS BOOKS *will be true to those laws of quality that assure a good name and good will.*

Printed in the United States of America
SC-R-3

Library of Congress Cataloging-in-Publication Data

Rich, John Martin.
Competition in education / by John Martin Rich, Joseph L. DeVitis.
p. cm.
Includes bibliographical references and index.
ISBN 0-398-05819-9
1. Education—Social aspects—United States. 2. Competition (Psychology) I. DeVitis, Joseph L. II. Title.
LC191.4.R53 1992
370. 19'2—dc20

92-24758
CIP

PREFACE AND ACKNOWLEDGMENTS

Ours is a competitive society. The roots of competition lie deep in American culture. Educational institutions reflect and reinforce competition; they also exhibit distinctive forms of competition. Some say that without competition society and education would become apathetic and stagnate. Others indict competition for engendering considerable stress, dishonesty, envy, despair, and callousness.

Though the importance of competition in American education is periodically recognized by educators, its full ramifications, significance, and dangers have not been fully explored. This book treats various major aspects of competition in education. It identifies competition within educational policies, programs, and practices, as well as the problems that certain forms of competition create. It also traces the influences on education of competitive values in American social and economic life. Noxious forms of competition are identified and measures are proposed for eliminating them while augmenting healthier forms. More cooperative programs are presented for those who seek a different approach.

The authors are indebted to a number of cherished colleagues who have helped us locate diverse sources and points of interest along our journey: Linda Irwin-DeVitis, of the State University of New York at Oneonta; Edward Burns, Robert Carpenter, Wendy Kohli, and Kenneth Teitelbaum, of the State University of New York at Binghamton; and Paul Violas, of the University of Illinois at Urbana-Champaign. We thank them for their warm spirit of cooperation.

CONTENTS

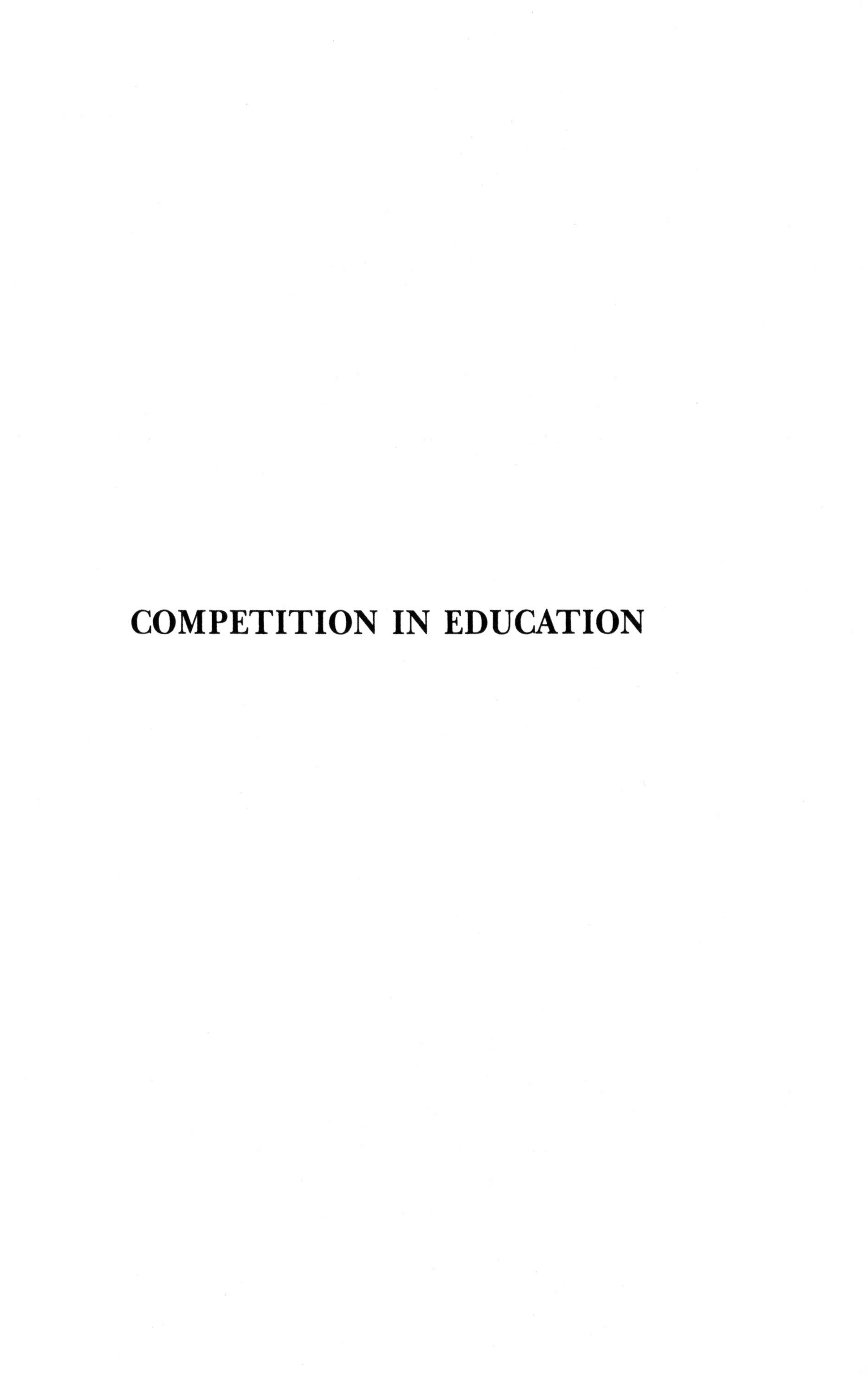

COMPETITION IN EDUCATION

Chapter One

EDUCATIONAL PROBLEMS ARISING FROM COMPETITION

Ours is a competitive society. Competition is extolled because it promotes full use of one's abilities, ensures that benefits and burdens are more fairly allocated, dispels apathy and stagnation, leads to higher standards, protects consumers and others from monopolistic practices, promotes progress, and stimulates advancements in science and other fields.

On the other hand, it is said that competition is a threat to cooperation, incites cheating and other dishonest activities, causes considerable stress, leads to a struggle for existence, stimulates rivalry, engenders shame in defeat, and is a source of envy, despair, selfishness, and callousness.

Competition in education exhibits many forms. It is found in testing, grading, promotion, class rankings, and scholastic awards. And it can be observed in the quests for college admissions, admission to graduate and professional schools, and fellowships, scholarships, and grants. Competition is also manifested in interscholastic and intercollegiate athletics, attempts to gain leadership in extracurricular activities, and students' striving against others for teacher's attention and favorable treatment. Though these are only a few of the competitive forms, it suggests the range and depth of competition in education.

Competition, according to Thomas Stauffer, exists both within universities and among them. Within institutions, students compete for grades; faculty compete for appointment, merit raises, promotion, tenure, grants, and publications; and administrators compete with different constituencies to influence academic policy. Universities compete with one another for philanthropic grants and government appropriations, for students, for recognition, and in intercollegiate sports.[1]

Greater competition in education has arisen from a concern about national preparedness. When the Soviet Union launched Sputnik in 1957, a cry of alarm was sounded and culprits were sought for the nation failing to compete effectively by falling behind in the space race. Congress decided that the schools were not teaching science and mathematics adequately and therefore in 1958 the National Defense Education Act was ratified. The Act included aid to strengthen instruction in science, mathematics, and foreign languages, funds for the preparation of school counselors, and loans to prospective teachers.

A Nation at Risk, a report in 1983 by the National Commission on Excellence in Education, also expressed great concern over national preparedness by stressing that the nation is in danger of losing its prominence as a world leader in industry and commerce by failing to compete effectively. International comparisons of student achievement were cited to substantiate the danger that American students do not fare well in such comparisons. The federal government, it said, has primary responsibility to identify the national interest in education.[2]

The Business-Higher Education Forum was invited by President Reagan to explore ways by which the nation's competitive position could be further strengthened through innovation and productivity. The Forum urged the creation of a national consensus that industrial competitiveness is crucial to our social and economic well-being. Education has given insufficient attention to developing basic skills in science and mathematics needed in an age of high technology. The Forum advocated a national strategy of education, training, and retraining at all levels to ensure that workers are adequately prepared.[3]

Thus competition is seen by some as not only a key for individual advancement but national survival. It is perceived by Andrew Colman as one of the "very foundation stones for social life" because of its basis in social behavior, whether primitive or sophisticated, simple or complex.[4]

Though the importance of competition in education is periodically recognized by educators and other citizens, its full ramifications, significance, and dangers have not been explored. This book treats various major aspects of competition in education. It identifies competition within educational policies, programs, and practices, as well as the problems that certain forms of competition create. It also traces the influences on education of competitive values in American social and economic life.

A LOOK AHEAD

This chapter provides an introductory overview of the competitive ethic in American culture as a background in which to place the problems of competition in perspective. This is followed by a statement of the functions of competition and its significance. Certain problems, however, stem from competition and therefore competition can become distorted and harmful. Subsequent chapters will address whether the noxious forms can be greatly curbed or eliminated, whether alternatives to competition should be provided, or whether competition should be eliminated in certain situations or greatly restricted overall in both society and education. But it is also important to inquire whether American education is sufficiently competitive.

A model of competition is presented in Chapter Two, and it is compared to differing interpretations of competition. Then an examination is made of the relations and differences among cooperation, competition, conflict, and aggression.

Chapter Three explores the influence of social Darwinism on ideologies of competition and advancement. It also assesses competitive and altruistic strains in sociobiology. This leads into an evaluation of competition, conflict, and aggression in the thought of Freud and Hobbes, which is contrasted with cooperative models developed by Jean Piaget and Alfred Adler.

Economic models are especially strong today. Following Max Weber, it is shown how the Protestant ethic influenced capitalism and sanctioned competition and other business practices. Adam Smith's classical economics envisioned a pivotal role for competition and, even though today's economy is more of a mixed system, competition is a central feature of the price system and markets. Business models of school management and accountability carried economic forms of competition into public education.

The glorification of athletic competition has been a hallmark of American culture despite abuses and attempts to reform or to curtail excesses. Historical and contemporary ideas about competition in American athletics are presented in Chapter Five. This is followed by an assessment of competitive athletics on education. Then an inquiry is undertaken to determine how the various proposals for athletic reform would affect competitive practices in education.

The testing movement, with its emphasis on I.Q., aptitude, and standardized achievement tests, has exerted an immense influence on education and magnified competition. The impact of this movement is assessed in terms of stimulating competitive educational programs and practices. The institutionalization of testing has promoted a competitive mentality. Other issues employed related to testing are homogeneous groupings, tracking, and the identification and development of the gifted and talented.

Chapter Seven shows that since the days of Jeffersonian democracy meritocracy has played an important role in American life. But the meritocratic ideology is under attack today with the growth of egalitarianism since the civil rights movement and the Elementary and Secondary Education Act of 1965. One outcome of employing meritocratic criteria in education is to intensify different forms of competitiveness, which may raise certain ethical questions. The conflict between meritocratic and egalitarian ideologies is explained and a modified meritocracy is outlined that avoids the more deleterious forms.

The next two chapters examine alternatives that lead to noncompetitive types of education. First it is explained why progressivism would advocate noncompetitive education and the form progressives advocate. Some aspects of libertarianism, nineteenth and early twentieth century socialism, and neo-Marxism are shown to prescribe noncompetitive features in education. An assessment is then made of these proposals.

A number of noncompetitive programs and practices are described and evaluated in Chapter Nine. These include utopian reform experiments, the free school movement, and various cooperative programs and practices. The chapter closes with an assessment of the prospects for noncompetitive education.

The final chapter summarizes and synthesizes findings from previous chapters and offers policies for augmenting healthier competition in education.

THE COMPETITIVE ETHIC IN AMERICAN CULTURE

A pervasive characteristic of American life is its competitiveness. "Competition is highly valued in American society," Stanley Eitzen claims. "Most Americans believe it to be the one quality that has made America great because it motivates individuals to be discontented with the status quo and with the second best."[5] That it is highly valued assures that it will be found in many institutions and organizations. It can be found in the economy, the business world, the professions, politics, religion, the family, sports and athletics, courtship, and various types of organizations.

Of course competition is not unique to American society: it can be found in various forms in other nations. That American society is more competitive than some other nations may stem from its heritage, economy, and government.

As a relatively young nation without the predefined and inherited social classes of Europe, social classes were more fluid and Americans could seek to gain upward mobility. With Calvinism and its sanction of hard work, religiosity, sexual restraint, and the pursuit of material advancement, a religious justification for competitive advancement was at hand. The frontier beckoned with dangers, excitement, exploration, and "get-rich-quick" schemes. Intrepid settlers blazed their way across an unchartered continent in quest of adventure, opportunities, and their fortune. The optimism of the frontier mentality carried over into American life as a whole; the American beacon attracted large-scale immigration at various periods in search of economic opportunities and religious and political freedoms.

The capitalist system is generally thought to embody the concepts of freedom of individual initiative, competition, inheritance, and the profit motive. Acquisitiveness and competition are the driving forces of the market economy. The spirit of competition and the market system are central to social organization. Though the competitive mechanism is imperfect and may be subverted through price-fixing, monopolies, and other abuses, both the ideology of economic competition and its actual practice has pervaded American life.

Democracy may promote more political competition than other forms of government: Aristocratic rule is inherited power; monarchies and oligarchies severely limit the sharing of power; and totalitarian states greatly restrict participation and exercise power through terror and force. In democracies candidates for office compete for the allegiance of various voting constituencies. Representation provides a basis for stabilizing power by a balance between the concentration and dispersion of power. Representation of interests averts threats to the power structure by attempting to fulfill diverse demands and expectations. Assuming an informed public, political candidates are accountable for serving the public interest and must compete to gain or retain office, except that incumbents may have greater resources and influence, thereby diminishing the actual competitiveness of political campaigns.

The world of work varies in competitiveness depending upon the occupation. Workers are expected to meet certain requirements in order to obtain a job and to perform at an acceptable level to retain a job. Some occupations use various forms of merit evaluation for promotion and advancement, which limits the number of workers who will advance in the system.

Professions must be able to assure the public that its practitioners are competent if the public is to retain its confidence and grant the profession the right to exercise professional judgment. Professions generally have high entrance standards that recognize only a select number of applicants as possessing the requisite abilities, aptitudes, and personal characteristics that will likely lead to a successful professional career. Some professions, such as medicine, emphasize selectivity in admissions rather than eliminating candidates after admission because of high operating costs and the great investment of faculty resources in each candidate.

Various community organizations exhibit different degrees of competitiveness. These are civic, professional, charitable, and special interest organizations. Many organizations are selective in their membership; since civil rights laws have restricted, but not entirely eliminated, previous racial, religious, and gender discrimination, selection, therefore, is made increasingly on other grounds. Election to office is usually competitive and those entrusted with leadership positions have usually gained their position by competing more effectively according to organizational rules. Some adult organizations base membership on social background, social class criteria, or income (by requiring a large membership or initiation fee). Children, too, are taught early to compete in the Cub Scouts, Boy Scouts, Girl Scouts, in contests, athletic events, projects, and for merit badges.

Courtship itself is not only a romantic ritual but a source of competition. In contrast to old-world cultures in which parents select their offspring's mate and dictate the marital arrangements, American culture endorses courtship instead. Courtship rules differ according to social class; but for middle class youth, males are expected to take the initiative and females decide to whom they will respond. This pattern has been modified with women's liberation insofar as it prescribes a more assertive and independent role for women. Nonetheless, both sexes compete against rivals for the partner or mate of their choice. Criteria for selection may include social background, manners, appearance, personality, talent, intelligence, wealth, power, and others.

Competitiveness has grown in intensity in American sports, as avid fans and alumni, big-time finances, sports salaries, and television contracts have transformed the sports enterprise. "Winning-at-all-costs," rather than sportsmanship and individual development, is increasingly the dominant mentality.

Thus competitiveness pervades many aspects of American culture. Societies differ in their degree of competitiveness, with American society probably more competitive than many others because of its heritage, economy, and government. But as will be shown in subsequent chapters, the extensiveness and intensity of competition is mitigated by a number of policies and arrangements in American life, even in those situations where competitiveness is extolled. As examples, business and industry has been guilty of price-fixing and monopolies; the Defense Department has not always exercised true competitive bidding for contracts; and tariffs restrict competition in international trade.

THE FUNCTIONS OF COMPETITION

It has already been shown that competition plays important roles in many areas of American society. Competition, it could be argued, is significant because without it a number of vital functions would probably not be fulfilled. Let us look at seven functions of competition while being mindful that they are open to dispute.

1. **Competition promotes the full use of one's abilities.** It dispels apathy and stagnation by providing individuals, groups, teams, or organizations with the incentive to strive for goals and achieve desired ends. Competition is a stimulus or spur to achievement by inciting interest in striving to outdo or surpass a competitor, opponent, or rival. Many people are not self-motivated and usually do not persist at a task merely for the joy of completing it or for its intrinsic satisfaction, except in the case of hobbies. In school and the world of work sanctions frequently need to be employed to see that individuals perform expected tasks. One strong motivating factor is to use competition to develop and channel human abilities. This can be seen in education in striving for grades, honor rolls, scholarships, college admissions, and admission to professional schools. Some would suggest that without competitive incentives individuals would not develop their full intellectual, artistic, or physical abilities.

2. **Competition leads to higher standards.** Competition encourages individuals to do their best and, under optimal circumstances, perform at their highest level. It not only promotes striving for high standards but encourages decision-makers to raise standards in light of competitive performance. Standards in track and field, baseball, football, and other sports have been elevated as today's athletes eclipse records and outperform earlier athletes. In education, as Japan outstrips the United States in certain technologies, government officials frequently seek to upgrade educational standards, both quantitatively and qualitatively, by improving basic skills, lengthening the school day and the school year, and by boosting standardized test scores.

3. **It ensures that benefits and burdens are more adequately allocated.** In systems where rewards are not competitively based, favoritism, nepotism, and power politics may prevail. Competitive systems, in contrast, are able to assess human abilities more accurately by objective standards of performance against others seeking similar goals; therefore policy makers, by gathering data on individual performance, would be able to assign responsibilities more realistically and assess burdens and benefits. Those with the highest performance would usually receive the greatest benefits, but because of their greater demonstrated abilities may be assigned heavier burdens or responsibilities. While it is true that performance could possibly be observed and assessed in noncompetitive systems free of favoritism, proponents of competition would claim that since individuals in such systems would not achieve optimal performance, such systems could not allocate burdens and benefits adequately.

4. **Protects the public from unfair economic conditions and incompetent public officials.** A competitive market system uses demand and supply to meet consumer needs through competitive pricing, quality production, and efficient services. Noncompetitive economic systems may be characterized by price-fixing, monopolistic practices, centralized and unresponsive bureaucracies, high tariffs, and other practices. In politics, those seeking public office who run against other candidates ideally vie for votes on the basis of the issues and the candidates' qualifications. Many times, however, campaigns fall far short of these standards because the issues or qualifications are obfuscated or one candidate has a far larger campaign chest than the others.

5. **Develops better qualified educators.** Through competitive preservice and inservice programs, educators become more competent than by alternate measures. Historically some educational positions were filled

by political patronage; some others were based on the candidate's religion, race, ethnicity, or gender. Affirmative Action and other regulations have sought to eliminate discriminatory practices. Norm-referenced measures would be used to indicate how an individual performs in comparison with peers. A less competitive form is criterion-referenced data that are gathered from local instructional objectives to show the extent to which the learner has achieved the objectives. Other provisions include merit pay and career ladders, which are designed to improve teacher performance by competitive means. Merit pay rewards teachers with higher salaries for doing the same or a similar job better than their colleagues. Career ladders pay teachers more for performing duties different from those of their colleagues.

6. **Helps promote learning.** It is popularly held that competition enables individuals to do their best by excelling in their studies to achieve desired objectives, rewards, and recognition. It makes their studies more stimulating and invigorating as students test their abilities against others. Moreover, advocates of competition insist that youth will have to work and live in a competitive society and therefore schools should offer competitive learning arrangements to better prepare them for future life. By this logic, competition in academic and extracurricular activities promotes transfer of training to tasks in the larger society.

7. **Competition stimulates advancements in science, education, and other fields.** Many of the advancements in the arts, sciences, and technology were goaded by competition in the search for scientific breakthroughs, new technologies to meet social needs, and the competition to find innovative modes of artistic expression. The search for the DNA molecular structure to unlock the genetic code pitted teams of scientists in England and North America struggling feverishly to be the first to make a breakthrough. A life-and-death struggle ensued in the early 1940s between allied and German scientists to be the first to develop and test the atomic bomb. In technology, different firms compete against one another searching for new technologies that will meet unfulfilled needs (as in medical discoveries) or to create a need (as with new luxury products) in order to corner a larger share of the market. Artistically, musical competition seeks out new virtuosos, and tryouts are used to select acting roles for stage and screen. In education, researchers compete for grants, to present their papers at professional meetings, to publish their articles and book manuscripts, and to garner speaking engagements to disseminate their research findings.

In concluding this section, note that some of the above functions are empirical claims that need to be established through research. Though arguments were advanced, the counter-claims have yet to be presented. Subsequent chapters will seek to determine, among other things, whether these claims and arguments can withstand careful scrutiny and investigation.

PROBLEMS STEMMING FROM COMPETITION

Competition is not an unmitigated good. Certain forms of competition can be harmful and should be restricted or eliminated. One noxious form of competition occurs when the contestants refuse to abide by the rules, thereby creating conflict. Competitors may seek to win at all costs by injuring or destroying their opponents. This may be caused by inadequate enforcement of rules by officials, improper socialization, overemphasis on gaining the reward, and the like.

Another harmful form of competition occurs when the rules themselves are unfair or unjust. *Invidious discrimination,* the principal ground of injustice connected with rules, would involve arbitrary unequal treatment in developing and enforcing rules. Thus rules that arbitrarily exclude people from benefits or treat people unequally on grounds of race, sex, ethnicity, or religion would be guilty of invidious discrimination. The quest for equality, from the *Brown* decision through Affirmative Action, was a movement, among other things, to overcome this form of discrimination.

Competition is noxious when the goals of the competition are undesirable. This occurs when the outcomes are illegal or seriously harmful to contestants. Football scholarship candidates may compete for bribes involving payments, favors, or merchandise. In some sports, the rules may be inadequate to protect the participants sufficiently from serious injury (as in auto racing, mountain climbing, hang gliding, and other sports).

Any competition that dehumanizes the participants is harmful. Dehumanization may take many forms, but a typical form found in competitive situations is humiliation in terms of one's sense of dignity. This case of humiliation occurs in many schools by the student who is embarrassed by the teacher before the rest of the class because he does not know the correct answer or told publicly he will "never amount to anything" because of his behavior.

Another form of dehumanization is a situation when one feels that she is treated as a thing or object by the teacher, thereby establishing a symbolic master-slave relationship, or acting as though students are little more than machines to be properly programmed. The former occurs with authoritarian teachers, and the latter may arise when teachers utilize a psychology of learning that employs a programming model—whether it is a narrow behaviorism or whether it views the brain as a computer. In conclusion, whenever competition is used, one must be alert to avoid these and other forms of harmful competition.

ENDNOTES

1. Stauffer, Thomas M.: Competition and cooperation in higher education. In Stauffer, Thomas M. (Ed.): *Competition and Cooperation in American Higher Education.* Washington, DC: American Council on Education, 1981, pp. 3–4.

2. National Commission on Excellence in Education: *A Nation at Risk: The Imperatives for Educational Reform.* Washington, DC: U.S. Department of Education, 1983.

3. Business-Higher Education Forum: *America's Competitive Challenge: The Need for a National Response.* Washington, DC: Business-Higher Education Forum, 1983.

4. Colman, Andrew M. (Ed.): *Cooperation and Competition in Humans and Animals.* Berkshire, England: Van Nostrand Reinhold, 1982, Preface.

5. Eitzen, D. Stanley: *In Conflict and Order: Understanding Society,* 3rd ed. Boston: Allyn and Bacon, 1985.

Chapter Two

CONCEPTS OF COMPETITION

The term competition has been defined in various ways as different concepts struggle for public allegiance. The concept also has cognate and contrasting terms that may cause confusion and misdirect inquiry unless carefully assessed. But before considering the conceptual basis of competition, it may be reasonable first to place the study of competition in a broader context that depicts it as a social process and a cultural phenomenon. This type of inquiry can be approached through the sociology of knowledge and cultural anthropology. The sociology of knowledge shows how competitive processes influence a group's thought and view of reality. Cultural anthropology depicts competitive, cooperative, and individualistic cultures and describes their different features.

COMPETITION AS CULTURAL PHENOMENON AND SOCIAL PROCESS

Karl Mannheim views competition as not only a feature of economic life but social life as a whole.[1] Competition enters into the form and content of every cultural product or movement.

Historical, ideological, and sociological knowledge is fostered by a particular group that seeks to make its view of the world universal. The "correct" scientific interpretation did not arise from pure contemplation but functioned to help some group find its way around in the world. Different interpretations of the world correspond to the particular positions different groups occupy in their struggle for power. Public interpretations of reality develop from social processes and relations.

Mannheim holds that the public interpretation of reality originated in terms of four developments. The first consists of a consensus of opinion. It is found in homogeneous societies, characteristic of primitive, archaic societies.

The second type involves a monopoly position of one particular group. It is manifest in the medieval-ecclesiastical interpretation of the world and the tradition cultivated by the Chinese *literati*.

The third type consists of competition between groups with each seeking to impose on the other group their interpretation of the world. This type corresponds to atomistic competition. It followed the period of ecclesiastical monopoly where many isolated groups bid to take over the official interpretation of the world. The Church was confronted by the rise of the absolute state that sought to monopolize education in order to dispense the official interpretation of reality. Protestant sects also arose to interpret the *Bible* in their own way. During this period science was selected as the chief educational instrument. This new type of thinking is represented by Descartes' fundamental doubt. For every group with a perspective, another sphere of reality becomes paradigmatic and acquires an ontological status. Every perspective fosters a particular cognitive attitude and a mode of thought that is appropriate for exploring the area in question. Each perspective sought to become the universally accepted set of axioms or a universally recognized hierarchy of values; it culminated instead in radically different ontologies and epistemologies.

As a consequence of increasing fragmentation resulting from atomistic competition the fourth type of competition developed, which is the dominant type in our era—concentration of competing groups and orientations. Many types of fractional conflicts tend to be increasingly interdependent and, on the other hand, polarized into extremes. This consolidation process is exemplified where different forms of irrationalism merged to form a common front against rationalism.

Mannheim states that "processes of change in the deepest strata of world interpretation, modifications of the categorical apparatus itself, can to a large extent be explained in terms of competition."[2] Doctrinal victory occurs with success in the struggle over the question whose philosophy will serve as the party's official interpretation of reality. The merging of positions occurs not by contemplation but by political processes. Today, says Mannheim, various positions seek to gain dominance but lack sufficient general validity to encompass all of reality; yet these positions tend to fuse as they seek to broaden the base of their thinking.

Opponents will be forced to adopt categories and forms of thought that are most appropriate for orientation to a given type of world order. In economics as a results of competition, a competitor is compelled to catch up with technological advances. Or a group may take from its adversary a fruitful hypothesis or anything that promises cognitive gain. As an example, Hegel's philosophy can be considered a synthesis of Enlightenment thought and conservative Romanticism and Historicism as it is oriented toward historical change. Hegel experienced a period of strict polarization from competition at the stage of concentration followed by a phase of freedom of decision leading to the first overall synthesis. The history of thought in modern times utilizes association and synthesis.

In summary, Mannheim finds competition as a basic feature of social life. Historically a struggle can be seen where each group strives to make its view dominant. Public interpretations of reality are based not strictly upon contemplation but upon social and political processes. In modern times atomistic competition has given way to a concentration of orientations. Positions tend to fuse as they broaden their base of thinking.

Mannheim seeks to study the social meanings that unite or divide people in their relation to social structures. He shows that the social process cannot be separated from social meanings. In the latter phases in the history of ideas, a struggle ensues between various social ideals and the attempt of each group to make their world view universal, which culminates in the final stages in which a growing concentration of world views develops.

COMPETITIVE CULTURES AND OTHER CULTURAL FORMS

Some cultural anthropologists have depicted preliterate cultures as competitive, cooperative, or individualistic. Sometimes they have taken some of the more extreme examples as exemplifying these terms. Competitive societies are found in many parts of the world, but Asia provides some prominent examples of such societies. One of the most competitive is that of the Ifugao of northern Luzon in the Philippines.[3] Ifugao society focuses on rice, which is their best and preferred food. Since land is limited and rice is in short supply, the social class structure centers on the acquisition and use of rice. Three classes are recognized: the lowest who do not own rice land; the middle class who owns enough rice lands to provide for themselves and their families during normal times; and the highest class who have a surplus of rice. The highest class can sell the surplus and gain income. The shortage of rice lands because of mountainous terrain leads to extreme competitiveness. Although other forms of food such as shellfish are available, it is believed that only those of low status eat such food.

Though in the Ifugao nuclear family members generally cooperate with one another, competition is nevertheless predominant in society. The acquisition of wealth is the main goal and, to demonstrate one's wealth, it is necessary to give a series of expensive feasts and make many expensive sacrifices. Wealth can only be acquired minimally through inheritance; instead, the chief means is by management of rice fields leading to a surplus that can be lent at usurious rates of interest or used to purchase land. The land can be sharecropped in which the poor will be given seeds and expected to return a large portion of the yield to the owner. Since rice is such a valued commodity, the poor will readily enter into this arrangement. Life is a constant struggle to gain rank and, once gained, to maintain it. No one can afford to relax or allow himself to show weakness in enforcing his rights or to fail to aid a kinsman in a blood feud.

Other competitive societies are less fiercely competitive. The Kachins of highland Burma seek to gain social rank by giving lavish feasts and pursuing wealth, though in a less cutthroat way than the Ifugao.[4] Once wealth is acquired a tale may be invented to validate status that one is descended from noble ancestors. To become an autocratic chieftain is a gradual process in which the chief arrogates status and wealth and emphasizes his ritual position that entitles him to material and spiritual tributes from the people. But if his demands become too great, he may be overthrown.

In competitive societies people usually seek to maximize their gains by acquiring more material goods or higher prestige than others. They may also, in some cases, see others as rivals and seek to maximize other's losses. Whereas in more cooperative societies, arrangements are more egalitarian, people are more altruistic and seek to maximize joint gains.

Two cooperative cultures are the Bushmen of the Kalahari Desert in Botswana and Namibia[5] and the Mbuti of the Ituri forest in Zaire.[6] Both are nomadic hunters and gatherers who live in small groups. Hunting is most efficiently done in cooperative groups, although the food is not divided equally but in terms of the effort expended and the hunting nets or arrows contributed. Both cultures have norms of helping and sharing. Bushmen would not eat if others present were without food. They aid one another by helping to build huts. Bushmen dislike strife and jealousy, nor do they want to accumulate goods that others may envy and would thereby prefer to give away fine possessions.

Cooperative cultures can be found in agrarian as well as nomadic lifestyles. Swaziland is a small kingdom bordered by Mozambique and South Africa. The Swazis grow crops and raise cattle more as a source of wealth and prestige rather than commodities.[7] The Chewa live in Zambia, Mozambique, and Malawi and have an economy similar to the Swazis.[8] Among Swazis, work parties are organized for large undertakings, with food, beer, and comradeship the rewards. People also work together to help a kinsman or neighbor with tasks that he cannot handle alone. The Swazis distrust competitiveness and ambition; they value good manners and obedience. For the Chewas, excessive ambition and the accumulation of unshared wealth not only is unpopular but can lead to charges of witchcraft. Kinsmen cooperate when working in the fields, and can expect assistance from others when in need. They value cooperativeness and meekness of spirit.

Individualistic cultures encourage persons to maximize their own gains without regard for what others gain, and try to minimize their losses. Among the Ik of East Africa, everyone acts largely for him or herself.[9] The government took away most of their hunting range for a game reserve, leaving an infertile mountainous homeland that, with severe droughts, destroyed their source of food and undermined their erstwhile cooperativeness. Families live together but little care is shown toward children, who are provided minimal food and instruction and are expected to be independent from the age of three. Children may take food from the weak and aged. The old are considered a burden and are helped little. Although one is expected to share food in another's presence, the tendency is to eat alone so that it will not be necessary to do so. Nevertheless, the Ik display little competition, aggression, or passion and are primarily concerned with survival. The Ik is an extreme case and other cultures that could be considered individualistic manifest some cooperative tendencies.

Characterizing cultures as competitive, cooperative, and individualistic is for purposes of analysis in which central tendencies are sought while recognizing that cultures could be placed on a continuum in terms of these tendencies. Some of the cultures cited above are more extreme examples; other cultures may have more of a mixture of traits and behavior patterns. People may behave toward others in ways that are neither cooperative nor competitive, as the individualistic cultures demonstrate. Other alternatives will be presented later in the chapter.

A MODEL OF COMPETITION

Three conditions obtain when persons are in competition with one another:

1. Two or more persons or groups strive for R (reward).
2. R is in short supply, and only one or a limited number of persons can gain it.
3. The activities are rule governed.

Let us look more closely at these three conditions. As few as two persons are involved in a competitive activity, but in other cases thousands may participate (as in the case of a marathon race or competition for scholarships). There is also the common expression "competing with oneself," and some writers believe that any conception of competition must take account of it.[10] This involves a contradiction, however, because there is only oneself to compete for R. It would be more accurate to speak of the attempt to improve oneself or to attain higher standards. That the expression has gained common usage is evidence of widespread acceptance of competition terminology and its persuasive use.

Some writers believe that competition is based on some notion of performing well. It is argued that for anyone who wants to perform well at anything, competition is inevitable because the notion of performing well is relative to other performers.[11] This is misleading since someone can seek to perform well by attempting to attain a standard independently of others, whether self-created or created by an external authority. This is a variation once again of the misnomer "competing with oneself," as the individual is seeking privately to attain something or to improve oneself. Two or more persons are not striving for R.

If R was in abundance, there would be no need to compete. But it does not mean, as some authors believe,[12] that only one person can obtain R; for this means that only one reward is available, which is not true in a number of areas, such as athletic competition or competition for scholarships.

Though competition may be a mutable concept within intellectual history, it is not necessary to claim, as some writers have done, that it is best viewed as an essentially contested concept; that is, one in which disputes are unresolvable even when contestants are aware of rival interpretations.[13] Protagonists of different ideologies and movements, however, are capable of recognizing the concept of competition in rival interpretations; disputes actually arise more over such normative considerations as what is fair competition and what are acceptable uses of competition.

Competition, it has been observed, may be voluntary or required.[14] It might be thought that if an activity is voluntary it would be more desirable than one that is required and enforced. But people do all sorts of things voluntarily that harm themselves or others: from drunken driving and snorting cocaine to cheating, stealing, and killing. And some things required—attending school or arriving at work on time—may be beneficial. Some persons may also be required to compete in an activity and later find that they are willing to compete in it voluntarily; in other words, some learn about the value of activities only by being required to participate. Thus no conclusions can be drawn about the relative desirability of voluntary and required competition without an assessment of the actual situation.

Competition can be compared to such cognate terms as rival, vie, and emulate. *Rival* suggests an attempt to outdo another, whereas competition stresses more impersonal striving. *Vie* suggests a less arduous struggle to excel but more conscious awareness of an opponent than the term *compete. Emulate* implies a conscious effort to equal or surpass someone or something that serves as a model.[15] Our approach will be to consider competition a relatively impersonal process but one with variations that periodically manifest such forms as rivalry, vieing, and emulation. These variant tendencies will be identified whenever pertinent.

The third condition in the competition model is that the activities are rule governed. A *rule* is a type of generalization used to prescribe conduct, action, or usage. Without rules, activities may degenerate into dissension, conflict, or strife in which the parties seek to gain R by any means available, including injuring or killing the other participants. Of course, this does not tell us whether the rules are fair; it only tells us that because rules exist, one can learn how to participate and not be penalized or disqualified.

The ability of an individual to participate successfully in a competitive activity depends considerably upon the person's understanding of rules. The child's understanding of rule-making functions varies, according to Piaget, with the developmental stage.[16] In the earliest stage, which is motor and individual in character, the rules are primarily those that grow out of the child's neuromuscular development. Between the ages of two and five, the child imitates the rules of others but he either plays by himself or he plays with others without trying to win. Thus he imitates rules but practices them in accordance with his own fantasy. Since at this stage the child regards rules as sacred and eternal, any attempted alteration is interpreted as a transgression.

Between the ages of seven and eight, a less egocentric and more socially-oriented outlook develops. The child now tries to win, and he also shows concern for the mutual control and unification of rules—although his ideas about them are somewhat vague.

Mastery of the rules proceeds by degrees, and between the ages of eleven and twelve, the rules of the game have become fixed and a high level of agreement can be found among the players. At this age children take pleasure in discussing rules and the principles on which they are based. They recognize the rules are formed by mutual consent and that, once agreed to, they should be observed in playing the game; nevertheless, they realize that a majority can agree to change the rules. In other words, at this age children's attitudes and practices toward rules closely resemble those of adults.

A distinction can be made, as John Searle indicates, between regulative and constitutive rules.[17] Regulative rules regulate antecedent or independently existing forms of behavior. Constitutive rules not only regulate but create or define new forms of behavior. Etiquette, folkways, mores, and student discipline codes are examples of regulative rules; whereas sports and games are based on constitutive rules because the rules make their playing possible. In other words, constitutive rules create the game, whereas regulative rules control preexisting forms of behavior.

Regulative rules generally take the form "One ought to do *X* in circumstance *C.*" These rules are usually stated in the imperative moods ("Grades in each course are due 48 hours after the final exam").

Constitutive rules take the form, *X* counts as *Y.*" Policy specifies guidelines to govern the introduction and application of innovations within organizational systems. That an innovation counts as a policy within certain contexts and that in the context there is nothing preexistent to regulate means that the innovation is an example of a constitutive rule.

Rules are one of the control structures governing student behavior. Most of these rules are of the regulative type, but some are constitutive rules insofar as they define and make possible new activities. Both regulative and constitutive rules may be found in competitive activities, except that some activities, such as athletics, may be governed by only one type of rule.

Rule-governed behavior may be thought of as rational in the sense that reasons can be offered; reasons can be given for abiding by a rule in terms of its ability to achieve the desired end and its efficacy in doing so. Dispute at this point could arise over whether the claims for the rule can be supported. The dispute is settled by reference to authoritative case studies demonstrating that following the rule achieves the stated objectives.

Another type of dispute is one in which the ends, which rule-following is designed to fulfill, are questioned. The question of the appropriateness of the rules and the reasonableness of following them is put aside until the question of ends is adjudicated.

Thus the young adult finds herself in a world proliferated with rules; however, many of the rules are not applicable because they govern occupations, statuses, and role relationships of which the individual is not a member. Thus rules applicable to immigrants, airline pilots, or recipients of social security govern the specific activities of those who fall under those categories; other rules, such as those pertaining to citizenship functions are more universal.

The growing independence of youth places them in a position from which they can in some cases develop their own rules for activities and in other cases decide whether rational grounds can be found for the rules governing the activities and, where options exist, thereby decide whether they want to participate in these activities. Although some competitive activities, such as norm-referenced testing, are required in education, other activities, such as intramural sports, may be voluntary.

RELATION OF COMPETITION TO OTHER SOCIAL PROCESSES

A number of concepts can be compared and contrasted to competition. These include cooperation, individualism, aggression, conflict, and violence. It is commonplace to consider competition and cooperation in opposition to one another insofar as one is competitive she cannot be cooperative and vice-versa. This would be to pose the terms as contradictories: that is, categorical statements that relate in such a way that if one is true, the other must be false, and if one is false, the other must be true.[18] "Either Mary is competitive or Mary is not competitive" and "Either Bill is cooperative or Bill is not cooperative." This establishes an opposition between competition and cooperation so that it is difficult to envision any reconciliation and, as a result, polarization divides people into two hostile camps: the staunch supporters of competition and the apostles of cooperative endeavors.

It would be better, however, to conceptualize the two terms as contraries. Contraries are categorical statements related in such a way that both cannot be true simultaneously, but both can be false.[19] "Sally is competing right now" and "Sally is cooperating right now," for example, are contraries. Sally may be doing neither one. She may be individualistic in the sense of attempting to maximize her own gains without regard for others' gains, and trying to minimize her losses. She is neither competitive nor cooperative at that moment. She may even have a tendency to be individualistic, but that does not mean that in the future she could not become cooperative or competitive.

Moreover, the antonym for "cooperate" is not "compete" but a host of other terms: counteract, hinder, obstruct, encumber, handicap, retard, delay, impede, disturb, annoy, and prevent.[20] It is true that in cooperation one associates with another or others for mutual benefit and to maximize joint gains and when competition turns to rivalry one seeks to outdo another, which may lead to counteracting what one's opponent is doing. Competition, however, may not have this outcome if there is more than one reward (as in scholarship competition), or if stated rules prohibit such behavior, or if tacit norms discourage it. Rules regulating scholarships, fellowships, and grants would prohibit trying to counteract or impede fellow contestants. One cooperates with contestants by agreeing to abide by the rules governing a competitive activity. And it is tacitly understood that in competing for positions or promotion that one does not seek to obstruct or impede other competitors. It is true, however, that in some sports one's action may be to counteract, impede, or obstruct an opponent, as in boxing, wrestling, the martial arts, and other sports. Yet in golf, track and field, bowling, and skiing, for instance, the rules do not permit one to impede or obstruct one's competitors. Thus only in a minority of activities would competition and cooperation be contradictories.

It may be thought that to be competitive one needs to be aggressive, but this is true only in a limited sense. *Aggression* may be considered forceful action to dominate a person, animal, or object. Some who are aggressive are hostile, quarrelsome, and start fights; yet one may also ascribe aggressiveness to one who is full of enterprise, bold and active in pursuing ends.[21] Thus aggression in the former sense is derogatory yet favorable in the latter sense. Both competition and cooperation are aggressive in the favorable sense, as one can be bold, active, and full of enterprise in cooperative groups as well as in competitive situations. Another form of aggression, limited more to competitive arrangements, is in some sports (e.g., martial arts) when one seeks to dominate the opponent. But the unfavorable form of aggression that leads to fighting and open conflict would be prohibited by the rules of most competitive activities.

Competition contrasts with such terms as discord and violence. *Discord* implies a clashing in personal relations in the form of quarreling, factitiousness, or antagonism. *Conflict* is "opposition or antagonistic struggle, the aim of which is the annihilation, defeat or subjugation of the other person or group."[22] Thus the objectives of conflict differ from competition, and conflict is not governed by rules.[23] Overtly, conflict and competition may begin with two or more parties who struggle for scarce resources or positions; however, conflict is intended to injure or annihilate the opposition. Competition could be characterized by parallel striving, while conflict is characterized by mutual interference. Competition may degenerate into conflict when competitors identify one another as enemies and strive to win at all costs, leading them to attempt to injure or destroy their opponents. When participants disdain the rules of the competitive activity and the rules are enforced irregularly or not at all, then competition has also degenerated into conflict. Force is likely substituted for rule observance. When subject to force, one does not act but is acted upon; certain things are done to the individual. Thus those who supervise competitive activities should strive to prevent them from degenerating into conflict.

Some speak of "violent competition," especially in the sports arena. Sports such as golf and tennis are competitive but not violent and other sports (football, ice hockey, boxing) are popularly considered violently competitive. All sports, when played well, could be considered aggressive in the favorable sense. When participants disdain the rules, the outcome may lead to conflict.

But what is the exact connection between violence and competition? Violence is associated with such terms as "coercion" and "force." But though it may seem that violence involves some element of coercion, it need not, as when someone sneaks up behind another and strikes him hard in the head. Coercion is found whenever constraint and/or inducement is high and choice is low. Coercion need not in any way be violent. A police office can threaten to arrest a group of demonstrators (an act of coercion) without using violence. Usually coercion involves an action by an individual, organization, or government to get an individual, group, or organization to do *X* when their intention is to do *y*. If the coercer is in a position of authority or can exercise sanctions, then success may be more likely, especially when sanctions can be applied.

Certainly violence is closely related to force insofar as a violent act would seemingly be forceful in some way. But violence need not be, as Ted Honderich has claimed, "fundamentally a use of force prohibited by law."[24] Although he is correct that laws would proscribe certain violent acts, many violent acts would not be so regulated as in cases of self-defense. Some violence (corporal punishment, for instance) may be permitted by law but prohibited by certain moral codes. Force involves the use of physical strength or power to cause one to do something. When subjected to force, one does not act but is acted upon. Force, when successful, may have strong coercive effects, but coercion itself is not force. Someone subject to force cannot be held responsible, but with coercion one can be held partly responsible, depending on the situation.

In speaking of physical violence, it would make no sense to say that an act was "violent but executed without force." Anyone making such a claim would likely be questioned about speaking in contradictions. Yet not all force is violence: one may force open a jammed door, force ahead of someone in line, and forcefully restrain someone from striking another person. Physical violence is done with considerable or great force rather than just a little force; it is also done suddenly, vehemently, and explosively. Thus violence is a type of force, but whether it also coerces depends on a number of situational factors. Violence can be and is directed toward people, animals, and things.

Thus *violence* can be defined as a sudden and extremely forceful act that causes physical harm or suffering to persons or animals. One qualification needs to be made for property. One could engage in a sudden and extremely forceful act that causes harm or utter destruction to one's property or could contract to have a demolition team destroy a building that one owns; yet owners are entitled to do whatever they wish with their property as long as it violates no law and no one is harmed in the act of destruction; the act, in other words, is thereby authorized (even though the act may be repugnant, as when a building of historical interest is destroyed). Thus violence in relation to property can be defined as a sudden and extremely forceful unauthorized act that causes harm or destruction to property.

Are conflict and competition acts of violence? Conflict has resulted in such forms of violence as wars, rebellions, riots, and feuds. But conflict is not always violent but may take the form of force or coercion where one party subjugates another. Competition cannot be intentionally violent even in contact sports because the rules proscribe inflicting intentional physical harm or suffering; if these outcomes occur, it has to be unintentional in order to remain within the rules. Even in such contact sports where physical harm more frequently occurs, rules are designed in football to protect the quarterback and eject players from the game who deliberately foul and in boxing to take points away from the boxer for low blows, butting, and other tactics. The objective of these sports is to win within the rules, not to inflict permanent harm or injury. Contact sports use force, whereas non-contact sports prohibit force. The rules, not only in sports but in most all forms of competition, are coercive insofar as constraint or regulation over free choice is high. Participants cannot compete and do whatever they want; they must compete within the rules.

In summary, competition is a contrary term to cooperation rather than a contradictory. One would likely be aggressive in the favorable but not unfavorable sense if one is competing effectively. Competition need not lead to discord and, when it does occur, it is usually thought that the competition has degenerated. Similarly, competition and conflict have different objectives and the rules of competition seek to prevent the competitive process from degenerating into conflict. Competition may become violent but it cannot be intentionally violent; in contact sports, however, force can be used according to the applicable rules and the rules are expected to have a coercive, but not necessarily a harmful, effect on the competitors.

ENDNOTES

1. Mannheim, Karl: *Essays in the Sociology of Knowledge.* London: Routledge & Kegan Paul, 1952, ch. 5.
2. Ibid., p. 211.
3. Hoebel, E.A.: *The Law of Primitive Man.* Cambridge Mass., Harvard, 1954; Barton, R.F.: *Ifugao Law.* Berkeley and Los Angeles: University of California Press, 1969.
4. Leach, E.R.: *Political Systems of Highland Burma.* London: G. Bell and Sons, 1954.

5. Thomas, E.M.: *The Harmless People.* London: Readers Union and Secker & Warburg, 1960.

6. Turnball, C.M.: *Wayward Servants.* London: Eyre & Spottiswoode, 1965.

7. Kuper, H.: *The Swazis: A South African Kingdom.* New York: Holt, Rinehart, and Winston, 1964.

8. Marwick, M.G.: *Sorcery in its Social Setting.* Manchester: Manchester University Press, 1965.

9. Turnbull, C.M.: *The Mountain People.* London: Cape, 1973.

10. Kleinig, John: *Philosophical Issues in Education.* New York: St. Martin's, 1982, p. 163.

11. Wilson, John: Competition. *Journal of Moral Education, 18:* 28, 1989.

12. Dearden, R.F.: Competition in education. In *Proceedings of the Philosophy of Education Society of Great Britain,* vol. 6. Oxford: Blackwell, 1972, pp. 119–133.

13. Fielding, Michael: Against competition. In *Proceedings of the Philosophy of Education Society of Great Britain,* vol. 10. Oxford: Blackwell, 1976, pp. 124–146.

14. Perry, L.R.: Competition and cooperation. *British Journal of Educational Studies, 23:* 129, 1975.

15. *The Merriam-Webster Pocket Dictionary of Synonyms.* New York, Pocket Books, 1972, p. 341; *Webster's New Dictionary of Synonyms.* Springfield, MA: G & C Merriam, 1968, p. 701.

16. Piaget, Jean: *The Moral Judgment of the Child.* New York: Free Press, 1965.

17. Searle, John: *Speech Acts.* Cambridge: Cambridge University Press, 1969, pp. 33–42.

18. Churchill, Robert Paul: *Becoming Logical: An Introduction to Logic.* New York: St. Martin's Press, 1986, p. 138.

19. Ibid., p. 139.

20. *Webster's New Dictionary of Synonyms,* p. 190; Devlin, Joseph: *A Dictionary of Synonyms and Antonyms.* New York: Warner, 1982, p. 58.

21. *Webster's New World Dictionary,* 3rd ed. New York: Simon & Schuster, 1988, p. 25.

22. Mack, Raymond W.: The components of social conflict. *Social Problems, 12:* 391, 1965.

23. Some writers assume that competition is a special case of conflict, and sometimes the two concepts are treated as synonymous. See: Fink, Charles F.: Some conceptual difficulties in the theory of social conflict. *Journal of Conflict Resolution, 12:* 412–260, 1968.

24. Honderich, Ted: Appraisals of political violence. In Care, Norman S. and Trelogan, Thomas K. (Eds.): *Issues in Law and Morality.* Cleveland: Case Western Reserve University, 1973, p. 4.

Chapter Three

SOCIAL THEORIES OF COMPETITION

Ideas about human nature have long played an integral part in social, political, and educational philosophy. Early political philosophers tended to establish the foundations of the state on their conception of human nature and the limitations they believed human nature imposed on human relations.

Educators, whether consciously or not, also operate out of certain beliefs about human nature, and specifically about the individual learner. Before schools can be organized and programs established, one must know something about the nature of learners—what they *are,* what they *can* become, and what they *ought* to become. One problem of speaking this way is the danger of committing the *naturalistic fallacy.* This fallacy, although it takes a number of forms, is that of deriving ethical statements from nonethical statements.[1] In the particular case of competition, some philosophers have argued that human beings possess the trait of competitiveness or cooperativeness (nonethical statement); therefore, schools should seek to develop competitiveness or cooperativeness (ethical or value statement). The problem here is that some other propositions need to be established before the conclusion can be reached. It is necessary to indicate that competitiveness or cooperativeness is good (value statement), schools should promote those good outcomes which they are most suited to foster (value statement), and schools are, more than most other social institutions, best equipped to promote competitiveness or cooperativeness (empirical statement). However, the purpose of our inquiry is not to make education and its aims conform to human nature. Rather it is to discover what in human beings can be effectively enhanced by the educational process.

Questions about human nature in education cannot be resolved solely with empirical findings, even though empirical and experimental studies of human nature have recently advanced on many fronts: biochemists have made strides in unlocking the genetic code; social scientists have provided greater understanding of social organizations and group behavior; and psychologists have ranged in inquiry from studies of unconscious forces, to the effects of conditioning, to viewing the organism as purposive and goal-directed. Educators operate with a set of values and aims, and interpretations of human nature provide only frameworks within which to view possibilities that one finds in different designs of the educational process. The educator is interested in the illumination provided by different interpretations and the educational consequences that accrue from acting on a particular interpretation. Even if widespread agreement existed today about human nature and what humans can become, these findings would provide only the broad framework or outer limits of human capacities. They would not tell us which among the many possibilities humans *should* choose. The establishment of educational programs constitutes a set of decisions about the possibilities that are best for people to realize. The ramifications of these decisions are not always carefully considered, although they have the utmost significance for the types of individuals a society produces.

PORTRAITS OF COMPETITION IN HUMAN NATURE

Thomas Hobbes

Perhaps the most classic formulation of the assumed reality of competition in human nature appears in the political philosophy of Thomas Hobbes, particularly in his seminal treatises written between 1640 and 1651. (It should be observed that he did most of his thinking on these issues during the bloody English civil wars, a circumstance that might well have skewed his vantage point in the direction of competition and more dubious human battles.) Nevertheless, Hobbes set for himself the monumental task of articulating the laws of human behavior and the conditions which are necessary for social survival and stability.

For Hobbes, the operative force of human behavior resides in the instinct of self-preservation, i.e., the ongoing maintenance of biological existence and a continual passion for power and security:

> I put forth a general inclination of all mankind, a perpetual and restless desire of power after power, that ceaseth only in death. And the cause of this, is not always that a man hopes for a more intensive delight, than he has already attained to; or that he cannot be content with a more moderate power: but because he cannot assure the power and means to live well, which he hath present, without the acquisition of more.[2]

According to Hobbes' interpretation, human beings thus lead a life which is "solitary, poor, nasty, brutish, and short." Furthermore, if they are left to their own devices, they would perpetuate an endless "war of every man against every man."

To save mortal souls from themselves, as it were, he posits that the principle of self-preservation must become more rational and move beyond mere acquisitiveness, competition, and aggression. In his use of the regulative nature of rationality, Hobbes also draws a portrait of human nature that will apply as well to later Freudian world views: human beings who are able to harbor a mirror of enlightened self-interest as a harness to their baser instinctual desires.

It is important to note that Hobbes sees humans as emerging from an original state of nature that is war-like and competitive to what he views as a more rationally constituted form of society.[3] The latter is found in a political order that is moving toward unity and cooperation. Indeed, it is arguable that his ultimate solution to societal disintegration can be summarized as follows: "peace and cooperation have a greater utility for self-preservation than violence and general competition."[4]

To obtain mutual trust from competing, self-interested individuals, Hobbes advocated that they form a covenant and subject themselves to rule by an almost absolute sovereign (leviathan). In his penchant for utilitarian individualism, Hobbes turned that concept on its head and failed to come to grips with the larger political question of balancing individual autonomy and social stability.

Of course, any society is interested in maintaining itself over extended time periods and preserving its cultural heritage. At the same time, most societies seek to improve themselves, i.e., to promote greater economic growth, advancements in technology, better international relations, higher educational standards, or in some other way. Yet, as Hobbes apparently did not fully realize, certain forms of independence and autonomy are needed among citizens to enjoy the creativity to effect these improvements. Rather than completely depending upon a sovereign, more democratic citizens seek to create a normative consensus, to develop compelling goals and consistent procedures for achieving them, and to institute effective socialization practices. Each individual who strives for independence will not likely become independent without developing certain skills and competencies that are created within various authority patterns, e.g., those of the home and school. The process of becoming independent also involves assuming some of the different authority types for oneself, to become increasingly one's own authority. Hobbes failed to grasp the role of competing authority patterns within the fuller development of individual autonomy.

Social Darwinism

"All of us are the inheritors of a tradition of thought, relating to the nature of life, which has been handed down to us from the nineteenth century," writes anthropologist Ashley Montagu. "Life, this view holds, is struggle, competition, the survival of the fittest. In the jungle, a fight with 'Nature, red in tooth and claw,' in society, the claw is perhaps gloved, and the fight is called a 'struggle' in which 'the race is to the swiftest,' in which 'the strongest survive and the weakest go to the wall'."[5]

With such a characterization of human nature, as represented by social Darwinism in the late nineteenth century, the concept of competition reached its apotheosis in American social thought and practice. F. A. P. Barnard would anoint Herbert Spencer, the champion of social Darwinism in England, as "America's Aristotle." Spencer sought to apply the grand design of Darwinian biological structures to the wider evolution of society. In the words of historian Richard Hofstadter: "Spencer's was a system conceived in and dedicated to an age of steel and steam engines, competition, exploitation, and struggle."[6]

At the forefront of Spencer's social theory was the notion of adaptation of organic constitution to environmental conditions. A reiteration of the axiom "survival of the fittest," it seemed to assure a natural process of progress and perfectability, especially for those who survived. For those who were "unfit," Spencer also had a clear, if somber, message:

> The whole effort of nature is to get rid of such, to clear the world of them, and make room for better. . . . If [humans] are sufficiently complete to live, they do live, and it is well they should live. If they are not sufficiently complete to live, they die, and it is best they should die.[7]

On reading Spencer, the industrial giant Andrew Carnegie would become rhapsodic:

> I remember that light came as in a flood and all was clear. Not only had I got rid of theology and the supernatural, but I had found the truth of evolution. "All is well since all grows better," became my motto, my true source of comfort. Man was not created with an instinct for his own degradation, but from the lower he had risen to the higher forms. Nor is there any conceivable

> end to his march to perfection. His face is turned to the light; he stands in the sun and looks upward.[8]

For Spencer, Darwinist biological concepts of society became a potent vehicle for mirroring and sustaining the dominant political ideologies of his times. Essentially a politically conservative world view which reinforced the status quo, social Darwinism permitted its proponents, then and now, to preach and practice a decidedly laissez-faire philosophy:

> Freedom to neo-conservatives means non-interference by government with exercise of individual and group preferences and "natural" social patterns and tendencies. Equality, however, in as much as it fails to evolve naturally, tends to require a government to promote it; ergo efforts to promote equality threaten freedom.[9]

Thus, social Darwinism fostered the political belief that individuals left to their own devices, without interference from government, would rise or fall according to their own abilities. The freedom to succeed was based on the presumably equal opportunity to compete, and if the individual failed, it was assumed to be his or her fault. In the hands of social Darwinism, it is questionable whether the ideal of equal opportunity was ever a viable societal goal. More likely, that hallowed ideal was used as a largely rhetorical device to maintain the existing social order.

The foregoing account of the influence of social Darwinism evidences how wider sociopolitical ideologies have drawn the attention of the American people as a whole. At this point it is important to analyze those competing ideologies that have emerged from the debate on social Darwinism.

On the one hand, American ideals seem to have been predominantly driven by the ideology of "fair play."[10] This concept of political fairness implies minimal interference with one's right to pursue happiness. Fair play emphasizes the raw opportunity to compete rather than any equality of results. As such, the doctrine represents an amalgam of classical liberalism and social Darwinism, i.e., America as the "land of opportunity" that doggedly clears the path for the "best man," or the "winner." Presumably, an absence of unfair barriers is all that is necessary to allow such "natural" consequences to occur. In modern-day parlance, fair play conjures up the perennial footrace analogy—one which is at least as ancient as the Greek Olympiad attended by Aristotle, who is usually credited with coining the notion of distributive justice. Yet the substantive core of fair play seems to stress inherently *individual* and *internal* variables about the nature of human beings and society.

On the other hand, the ideology of "fair shares" emphasizes an equality of results, especially to a reasonable share of society's resources (to the point of assuring a decent standard of human living). This ideology stresses *social, collective, cooperative,* and *external* variables which picture human nature in a radically different light than the more competitive portraiture of fair play. In effect, fair-play doctrine has tended to create specific categories of "deviance" in assessing human beings. Within such a context, the victim is often blamed for his or her condition rather than the larger social structure that may have left him or her not so blissfully free to pursue happiness—or loneliness and powerlessness. To paraphrase the present-day philosopher John Rawls, a fair shares argument would instead serve to specify what is indeed the basic structure of society, what might and should accrue from it, and how we might change that structure should it be or become adverse to the "fundamental things on which life prospects depend." All this implies ascribing "fairness with respect to the distribution of the components of [that basic social structure]."[11]

Ironically, even Spencer's major American disciple, William Graham Sumner, a Yale sociologist at the turn of the nineteenth century, would acknowledge that competitive social Darwinist ideas were not wholly sufficient to characterize the nature of being:

> It would be an error . . . to suppose that all nature is a chaos of warfare and competition. Combination and cooperation are so fundamentally necessary that even very low life forms are found in symbiosis for mutual dependence and assistance. A combination can exist where each of its members would perish. Competition and combination are two forms of life association which alternate through the whole organic and superorganic domains.[12]

Sociobiology

An intellectual inheritor of social Darwinism, the new and controversial field of sociobiology has provided more recent explanations and interpretations of human nature. Its focus is the analysis of altruism and the evolution of family systems. Its founder is Harvard entomologist Edward O. Wilson, whose *Sociobiology: A New Synthesis* has been called "one of the most important scientific works of this century,"[13] and his admirers boldly speak of him as "a worthy successor to Darwin."[14] Others see him and sociobiology in general as fostering an unwanted rebirth of social Darwinism, as well as racist and sexist views.

Sociobiology, according to Wilson, is "the systematic study of the biological basis of all forms of social behavior, including sexual and parental behavior, in all kinds of organisms, including humans."[15] It draws on evolutionary theory, population ecology, genetics, and comparative ethology. Whatever explanatory power sociobiology may possess stems from evolutionary theory, as the major advances in biology fit into the broad outlines of Darwin's ideas.[16]

Fitness in biology is a measure of one's competitive reproductive success. Thus, the most successful living things are the best reproducers. Any older species consist of individuals who are descendents of the best reproducers of previous generations.[17] However, in order to maintain family stability and to socialize the young, cooperation and altruism are needed.

In contrast to the popular view of Darwinian competition and Spencer's "survival of the fittest," sociobiology finds an important place for several forms of altruism. Altruism can be defined, in sociobiological terms, as "an act that reduces the personal reproductive success of the performer while increasing the reproductive success of the other."[18]

One form of altruism is *kin selection.*[19] Kin selection theory, which modifies natural selection, states that animals increase their inclusive fitness not only by choosing desirable mates which maximize reproductive success but by sacrificing for relatives, with priority given to the closest relatives with whom one shares the most genes. Thus, the extended family and its internal roles grew out of kin selection. But this form of altruism, since it discriminates against nonrelatives, can lead to blood feuds, tribalism, ethnocentricity, and a general lack of harmony within society and in international relations. Indeed, national and international harmony sought by some groups today may be chimerical because, according to Wilson, higher ethical values generated culturally which would point humankind to move in new directions and completely replace genetic evolution is unlikely.[20]

Reciprocal altruism, a second type, is when the return to the altruist is greater in units of inclusive fitness than its costs. Thus, the act carries a low risk to the altruist while it confers a high benefit upon the recipient. Moreover, a high probability must exist that the beneficiary will reciprocate. That is, altruists must guard against those who cheat, i.e., those who accept the benefits but refuse to reciprocate. Altruists inform one another about cheaters and sometimes punish them. Reciprocal altruism, therefore, is likely to evolve in intelligent, closely integrated social species with relatively long life spans.[21]

However, a major problem for the sociobiologist is to decide what will count as altruism. Wilson claims that most altruism is self-serving and reciprocal altruism (in contrast to kin altruism) is "calculating" and "selfish."[22] Yet there could be no absolute altruism in which the individual obliterated his own needs in order to act solely to advance the interests and needs of others without precipitating the individual's own demise. Nor is anyone likely to be absolutely egoistic where there is not even the slightest trace of altruistic feeling or action. Thus, to take care of one's health, provide the economic necessities for living, or engage in learning new things could hardly be considered selfish. To fail to care for one's health may incapacitate the individual so that she could not aid others. Consequently, acts are not morally selfish when they promote one's well-being, but only when they are unfair and fail to respect others' rights.[23] Wilson, then, may have labelled reciprocal altruism "selfish" because of a mistaken conception of altruism.

Perhaps Wilson was unduly pessimistic earlier in his conclusions that kin altruism, though it protects the family, lends to tribalism and ethnocentrism and consequently new cultural developments are kept on a leash, as it were. It is generally true that as one moves away from kin to associates and then to strangers, altruism declines; yet there are examples of people who voluntarily help strangers at some inconvenience to self without reward, recognition, or expectation of reciprocation. Such altruism may grow out of an impartial ethic or a special sensitivity to human suffering. For this type of altruism to grow, it may need to emerge from a cross-cultural ethic or theory of justice which would have wide international appeal. This universal altruism may emerge from a religious syncretism or, as some have suggested, it may simply be a creation of reason itself.[24] In short, unchained competitive impulses need not be seen as an inevitability.

Sigmund Freud

The psychoanalyst Sigmund Freud has enormously influenced personal and cultural judgments since he strode upon the intellectual scene in late-nineteenth century Austria. Theoretical constructions of personality, power, culture, child-rearing practices, even historical and literary criticism, to name only a few areas of discourse, were to be radically altered as a result. Like Hobbes, Freud was interested in balancing the often irreconcilable demands of individual versus social life.

Though most students of psychology and education are doubtless familiar with Freud's tri-partite division of personality, i.e., the Id, Ego, and Superego, it may be helpful to explicate those theoretical constructs to show how they shed light on his theory of human nature and competition.

Freud characterizes the *Id* as representative of animal-like instinctual impulses (largely of an unconscious sexual nature), the very core of human being and the repository for primary thought process. In essence, the Id signifies what we primordially desire to do if there were in fact no restrictions on our desires. These desires are most clearly demonstrable in dreams, fantasies, and similar unconscious thought phenomena. Freud further hypothesizes that the Id plays a predominant role in infancy and early childhood development, a period he considers most crucial in the overall development of the individual.

To counter-balance the Id, Freud introduces the term *Ego* to signify that self-regulating product of secondary (more conscious and rational) thought process which serves to bring the Id under some tenuous executory control. However, ego functions are refined only slowly and gradually, as the child grows and matures.

Most important for "civilizing" influence in Freud's psychology is the role of the *Superego,* i.e., the inhibiting, restraining, prohibiting standards imposed on the child by outside social forces, initially and primarily by one's parents and later by teachers and other adult authority figures. From such parental and other external social sources, the child, if she is to be "normal" and "adjusted," develops an *ego-ideal* and *conscience.* Indeed, for Freud, guilt operating via the conscience is a form of "social glue" which cements, as it were, the cultural bonds of any society. Without guilt and conscience, life would degenerate into a "tooth-and-nail" existence and attendant societal chaos.

In the end, Freud points to an optimal realization of self-control through an almost stoical exertion of rationality. He invokes such individual self-control because he contends that a substantial measure of repression is necessary to balance the individual's psychic apparatus, especially id impulses, with the demands of culture. Freud thus employs the concept of "repression" to regulate the seemingly irreconcilable conflict between personal autonomy and cultural restraint.

The term *repression* is used by Freud to express that most general, largely unconscious, defense mechanism which enables us to keep out of consciousness those thoughts, wishes, and desires too dangerous to our conscious mental processes. A form of repression, *sublimation* refers to that defense mechanism which transforms id-like excitations into more socially acceptable patterns of behavior. Indeed, for Freud, sublimation serves to build culture in the form of art, religion, literature, etc. Accordingly, he calls upon human beings to sublimate what he assumes to be primary aggressive, competitive instincts with what is deemed necessary to constitute civilization:

> Civilization thus obtains mastery over the dangerous love of aggression in individuals by enfeebling it and disarming it, and setting up an institution [superego] within their minds to keep watch over it, like a garrison in a conquered city.[25]

The demands of civilized life require human beings to struggle *with* repression, i.e., to practice a kind of frustrating, "heroic" individualism within the context of a competitive cultural ethos. To do otherwise would imperil cultural cohesion, which would, in turn, endanger individuals. This scenario summarizes Freud's version of competitive "enlightened self-interest."

However, any acceptance of such a competitive portrait depends upon whether one assumes a world of scarce resources as fundamental and immutable in human life. In the words of political theorist Kenneth Hoover:

> The purpose of the economy is to support the process of instinctual expression by organizing support and security.... This is the beginning of a formula for an intelligent allocation of resources, other than simply development for the sake of development. There is, further, the idea that a properly constructed community might well alleviate the scarcity of interpersonal expression.[26]
>
> What Freudian theory suggests is the beginning of a formula for the regulation of the market. It is predictable that an exchange system which begins as a free market will soon become a system in which those who acquire advantages will use them to structure the market so as to ensure their preeminence. Freudian theory directs us instead toward a consideration of the kinds of behavior which are acceptable in the marketplace. What kind of regulation will permit the market to operate as an exchange system for real human needs under conditions which are not degrading and repressive?[27]

CRITICS OF COMPETITION

Alfred Adler

Freud's original disciple, Alfred Adler, broke away from his teacher on the ground that Freud's psychoanalytic dependence on competitive, aggressive drives posited an overly deterministic, largely intrapsychic and biological, view of human existence. In essence, Adler proposed to avoid any such reductionism and determinism by formulating a dialectical account of social dynamics and social relationships. Adler is much more concerned with *social* influences which impinge upon thought, action, and behavior. Indeed, his overarching theory of "social interest" places the whole range of viewing human behavior in an entirely different perspective.

Adler claims that all humans enter the world from a position of "inferiority," i.e., we are all relatively helpless and dependent in infancy. From this original station in life, we gradually "strive toward overcoming" a feeling of powerlessness.[28] Adler borrowed Nietzsche's term "will to power" and coined his own term "strivings for superiority" to describe how humans could "perfect" their existence, not to depict any yearnings for power over others. In fact, on Adler's terms, any such egocentric striving would be viewed as "neurotic" and counterproductive to his own value system, which stressed "cooperation" as a prime motivating force, perhaps the most necessary human invention, in man's evolution. In some of his writings, Adler makes this point in stark fashion: "[The task of life is] to show the way in the reduction of the striving for personal power and in the education toward the community . . . and the development of social interest."[29]

In Adler's social theory, then, "inferiority" and "power," properly defined, are integral to a fuller explication of his most important principle, "social interest," which he characterizes as "compensation for all the natural weaknesses of individual human beings."[30] Social interest encompasses communal feeling, interpersonality, and empathy for others. According to Adler, the history of humankind is a movement toward more socially "superior," cooperative, and democratic directions necessitating equality in all aspects of life.[31] Indeed, he and his major disciple, Rudolf Dreikurs, use the standard of "social interest" to judge the extent to which culture and individual personality have matured:

> The degree of a person's social interest determines his ability and willingness to function socially; the lack of social interest is at the root of deficiencies, failures, and pathology. Thus, Adler found that social interest was a gauge for defining normalcy, both for the individual and for the group.[32]

Adlerians conceive of social interest as both inborn and capable of nurture and development as the child grows and matures. Accordingly, children should be given social tasks and responsibilities to perform, depending on their level of maturity. Household chores, family helping, and school duties, as examples, breed those patterns of behavior which eventually instill habits of both interdependence and independence in children. Adlerians also admonish against "pampering," a practice they regard as injurious as child abuse or neglect.[33] For instance, an isolate, self-centered "princely" child bears little mark of that indelible imprint of social interest which Adlerians insist is required for the continuous growth of humankind as a whole and for that person as a self-sustaining individual:

> The very concept of "human being" includes our entire understanding of social feeling.... [We have] always lived in groups, unless separated from one another artificially or through insanity.... In the deepest sense, the feeling for the logic of human living together is social feeling.[34]

Dreikurs notes further that "the child, at any age level, is a typical human being who wants his place in the group and rebels against being subdued."[35] He extends the notion of "social interest" to include "social equality" and democratic alignments among all persons, regardless of their station in life. Indeed, Dreikurs describes cooperative, egalitarian relationships as the "only stable basis for [any] social relationships."[36]

The Adlerian interest in addressing subordinate/superordinate relationships generates promise for growth in democratic and cooperative values, particularly in the case of the sexes. For Adler, unequal, competitive sexual relationships constituted an unwritten power struggle for both sexes. Accordingly, he advocated the equal worth of the sexes:

> Women have to suffer because in our culture it is much easier for a man to play the leading role. But the man also suffers because by this fictitious [spurious] superiority he loses touch with the underlying values.[37]

Adler coined the term *masculine protest* to express the feeling which either sex experiences in contexts involving competitive inferior/superior social interactions and distinctions. Masculine protest implied a present, but changeable, condition of "feminine" traits, principally a feeling of inferiority as a result of given, not necessary, social circumstances of male domination. Adler envisioned an evolving antithesis to this situation in the form of "strivings for superiority" which would be refined and perfected to the point of overcoming subordinate or superordinate relationships.[38] Thus, Adler viewed masculine protest as a needless, overly competitive, and culturally-biased criterion favorable to males, and not on the basis of physiological sex differentiation. His standard implied that sexual distinctions were largely the result of unnecessary *social* determinations, not biological necessities. In the final analysis, then, Adler's theory highlights *collective* and *external* references and points to possibilities for *communal* as well as merely "agentic" (self/power) development.[39]

All this is not meant to convey the impression that Adler was theorizing without moral or social blinders. Throughout much of his writing, he appears to be unaware that he is committing the naturalistic fallacy in argumentation by mixing claims for "is" and "ought." In many ways, his social theory is couched in prescriptive terms which he would like to maintain are purely descriptive:

> [Adlerian psychology]... regards as "right" that which is useful for the community.... Every departure from the social standard is an offense against right and brings with it a conflict with the objective laws and objective necessities of reality.... [It] violates an immanent social ideal which everyone of us, consciously or unconsciously, carries in himself.[40]

In addition, Adler's social analysis is lacking in rigor, depth, and precision. His account of interpersonal relationships does not elaborate fully the larger, more amorphous, power structures and sociopolitical constraints which more recent critics have observed.[41] Nor does he entirely fathom the deep-seated imponderables which might make for well-nigh irreconcilable conflict, as Freud himself recognized so well. As an example, Adler fails to distinguish adequately the boundaries between social "cooperation" and social "constraint" or "conformity."[42]

Jean Piaget

Like Adler, Jean Piaget, the famous twentieth-century Swiss psychologist, sketches out an evolutionary vision of cooperation and social equality for both the individual and society:

> One may conceive of cooperation as constituting the ideal form of equilibrium towards which society tends when compulsory conformity comes to break

> down. . . . Cooperation . . . seems to be essentially the social relation which tends to eliminate infantile phenomena. . . . [It] is the limit and norm of every human group that has ever come into being.[43]

Indeed, Piaget claims that "autonomy is a power that can only be conquered from within and that can find scope only inside a scheme of cooperation."[44]

In developing his theory of cooperation and social equality, Piaget places a heavy premium on the role of *mutuality* through *peer interaction,* particularly as it appears among older children and adolescents. He argues that the interactional "give-and-take" among such peers generates an essentially democratically-based system of values. Prior to late childhood and adolescence, the young child's immature cognitive processes are severely inhibited by a lengthy period of *egocentrism.* Piaget uses that term descriptively, not pejoratively, to characterize the relative inability to separate components of internal and external reality. In practical terms, egocentrism prevents the young child from *decentering,* or placing himself in the viewpoint of another person. Thus, Piaget postulates that maturation beyond egocentrism marks a pivotal stage in all human development.

Once the child resolves some of the difficulties inherent in distinguishing his own "reality" from the givens in external reality, Piaget foresees a more or less natural process of gradually unfolding social development (much in the manner of Rousseau's "ripe tomato" analogy). Unless one is somehow deprived of social experiences, especially with peers, Piaget assumes that such growth will occur. He argues further that peer interaction is vital because it is the only legitimately *equal* form of social participation. As such, he implies, on a broader level, that equality may likewise be the most legitimate testing ground for human development in general.

Nevertheless, the interactional "give-and-take" which Piaget extolls as the *sine qua non* of a democratically-based, cooperative morality has not been conclusively substantiated in the research literature. For example, Urie Bronfenbrenner has observed that peer interaction in American youth leads to excessive dependence on peer approval.[45] Thus, the maturing child may simply be relinquishing one form of authority for another, i.e., adult, parental authority gives way to peer authority.

SUMMARY

At base, theorists such as Freud, Adler, and Piaget are relying upon theoretical constructs—be they "aggressive instincts" (Freud, Hobbes, social Darwinists, and sociobiologists) or "cooperation" (Adler and Piaget)—which have not been conclusively warranted in either clinical or experimental studies in the social sciences. Perforce it is exceedingly difficult to prove that propensities of any sort are "built into" human nature—a monumental point of philosophical controversy at least since John Locke introduced his notion of "tabula rasa" (blank slate) in the seventeenth century and radically challenged classical conceptions of humankind's "goodness" or "evil." As the preceding discussion makes evident, future theorists and practitioners in education and the social sciences would continue to make such assumptions about the "competitive" or "cooperative" nature of human beings, however far apart their differences on such matters as "aggression" or "altruism" might take them.

ENDNOTES

1. Churchill, Robert Paul: *Becoming Logical: An Introduction to Logic.* New York: St. Martin's, 1986, p. 139.
2. Hobbes, Thomas: *Leviathan* (1651), Macpherson, C. B. (Ed.). Baltimore: Penguin, 1968, ch. 11.
3. The "state of nature" has been variously propounded by such thinkers as Plato, Hobbes, John Locke, Jean-Jacques Rousseau, and Edmund Burke. In its basic form, it refers to those natural relations among individuals prior to the formation of covenants or contracts, which imply the creation of government and statutory laws. Most of the latter served to protect property rights, particularly as evoked in the liberal individualism of Hobbes and Locke. The linkage of liberty to property has been referred to as "possessive individualism" and as antithetical to communitarian interest by such modern critics as C. B. Macpherson. See his *The Political Theory of Possessive Individualism.* New York: Oxford University Press, 1962.
4. Sabine, George H.: *A History of Political Theory,* rev. ed. New York: Henry Holt, 1958, p. 466.
5. Montagu, Ashley: *On Being Human.* New York: Henry Schuman, 1950, p. 17.
6. Hofstadter, Richard: *Social Darwinism in American Thought, 1860–1915,* rev. ed. Boston: Beacon, 1955, p. 35.
7. Spencer, Herbert: *Social Statics.* New York: D. Appleton, 1864, pp. 414–415.
8. Carnegie, Andrew: *Autobiography of Andrew Carnegie,* Van Dyke, John Charles (Ed.). Boston: Houghton Mifflin, 1920, p. 327. Cf. Henderson, C. R.: Business men and social theorists. *American Journal of Sociology,* 1: 385–386, 1896: "Competitive commercial life is not a flowery bed of ease, but a battle field where

the 'struggle for existence' is defining the industrially 'fittest to survive.' In this country the great prizes are not found in Congress, in literature, in law, in medicine, but in industry."

9. Etzioni, Amitai: The neoconservatives. *Partisan Review,* XLIV: 431–437, 1977. Cf. Steinfels, Peter: *The neoconservatives.* New York: Simon & Schuster, 1979; and Sola, Peter; DeVitis, Joseph; and Danley, John R.: Neoconservatives as social Darwinists: Implications for higher education. *Journal of Negro Education,* 55: 3–20, Winter, 1986.

10. The "fair play" versus "fair shares" argument outlined in this section is derived from Ryan, William: *Equality.* New York: Pantheon, 1981.

11. Rawls, John: *A Theory of Justice.* Cambridge, Mass.: Harvard University Press, 1971, p. 7: "The primary subject of justice is the basic structure of society, more exactly, the way in which the major social institutions distribute fundamental rights and duties and determine the division of advantages from social cooperation."

12. Sumner, William Graham: *Folkways: A Study of the Sociological Importance of Usages, Manners, Customs, Mores, and Morals.* Boston: Ginn, 1907, p. 17.

13. Wallace, Robert A.: *The Genesis Factor.* New York: Morrow, 1979, p. 11. For an ethological line of inquiry which also studies behaviors that are rooted in biology and evolution, see: Lorenz, Konrad: *Evolution and Modification of Behavior.* Chicago: University of Chicago Press, 1965; and his *On Aggression.* New York: Harcourt Brace and World, 1966.

14. Saver, Jeffrey: Edward O. Wilson: Father of a new science. *Science Digest,* 90: 84, May, 1982.

15. Wilson, Edward O.: Introduction: What is sociobiology? In Gregory, Michael S.; Silvers, Anita; and Sutch, Diana (Eds.): *Sociobiology and Human Nature.* San Francisco: Jossey-Bass, 1978, p. 2. For a more recent synthesis of the quest for sociobiological roots in intellectual history, see: Degler, Carl N.: *The Search for Human Nature.* New York: Oxford University Press, 1991.

16. Rensberger, Boyce: Evolution since Darwin. *Science,* 82: 41, April, 1982.

17. Wallace: *Genesis Factor,* p. 23.

18. Barash, David: *Sociobiology and Behavior.* New York: Elsevier, 1977, p. 77.

19. Hamilton, W. D.: The genetic theory of social behavior: I and II. *Journal of Theoretical Biology,* 7: 1–52, 1964.

20. Wilson: *On Human Nature.* Cambridge, Mass.: Harvard University Press, 1978, p. 167.

21. Some sociobiologists also mention group altruism; but since this is a more controversial form, it will not be presented.

22. Wilson: *On Human Nature,* pp. 154–6.

23. Dewey, John: *Theory of the Moral Life.* New York: Holt, Rinehart & Winston, 1960, p. 158.

24. Singer, Peter: *The Expanding Circle: Ethics and Sociobiology.* New York: Farrar, Straus & Giroux, 1981, pp. 133–4.

25. Freud, Sigmund: *Civilization and Its Discontents,* J. Strachey (Tr.). New York, Norton, 1961, p. 105.

26. Hoover, Kenneth R.: *A Politics of Identity: Liberation and Natural Community.* Urbana: University of Illinois Press, 1975, pp. 55–56.

27. *Ibid.,* pp. 72–73. Cf. Marcuse, Herbert: *Eros and Civilization: A Philosophical Inquiry into Freud.* New York: Vintage, 1962, pp. 32–34. One of Freud's major recent revisionists, Marcuse uses the concepts "basic" versus "surplus" repression to clarify those kinds of repressive measures which are necessary and unnecessary. "Basic" repression refers to that modification of the "instincts necessary for the perpetuation of the human race in civilization," e.g., provision of food and shelter and combatting of disease. "Surplus" repression refers to those additive "restrictions necessitated by social domination," i.e., layered forms of constraint over and above that which is essential to the maintenance of civilized life. According to Marcuse, surplus-repression has been caused by socio-historic conditions, which are amenable to social change.

28. Adler, Alfred: *Co-operation Between the Sexes: Writings on Women and Men, Love and Marriage, and Sexuality,* Ansbacher, Heinz L. & Rowena R. (Eds.). New York: Norton, 1978, pp. 49, 147–148, 168–169.

29. Adler: *The Nervous Character: Fundamentals of a Comparative Individual Psychology and Psychotherapy,* 4th ed. Munich: Bergmann, 1928, pp. iv–vi.

30. Adler: *Problems of Neurosis.* London: Kegan Paul, 1929, p. 31.

31. Adler: *Social Interest: Challenge to Mankind* (1938). New York: Capricorn, 1964.

32. Dreikurs, Rudolf: *Social Equality: The Challenge of Today.* Chicago: Regnery, 1971, p. viii.

33. Dreikurs & Soltz, Vicki: *Children: The Challenge.* New York: Hawthorn, 1964.

34. Adler: *Co-operation Between the Sexes,* p. 107.

35. Dreikurs: *Social Equality,* p. 80.

36. *Ibid.,* p. 115.

37. Adler: *The Education of Children.* New York: Greenberg, 1930, p. 222.

38. Ansbacher: In Adler, *Co-operation Between the Sexes,* pp. 155–156, 162–164.

39. Bakan, David: *The Duality of Human Existence.* Chicago: Rand McNally, 1966. See also: Sampson, Edward E.: Psychology and the American ideal. *Journal of Personality and Social Psychology,* 35: 767–782, 1977.

40. Adler: *The Education of Children,* p. 21.

41. Jacoby, Russell: *Social Amnesia: A Critique of Contemporary Psychology from Adler to Laing.* Boston: Beacon, 1976.

42. DeVitis, Joseph L.: Cooperation and social equality in childhood: Adlerian and Piagetian lessons. *Journal of Research and Development in Education,* 17: 24, 1984.

43. Piaget, Jean: *The Moral Judgment of the Child* (1932), Marjorie Gabain (Tr.). New York: Collier, 1962, pp. 346, 348, 371.

44. *Ibid.,* p. 371.

45. Bronfenbrenner, Urie: *Two Worlds of Childhood: U.S. and U.S.S.R.* New York: Sage Foundation, 1970.

Chapter Four

ECONOMIC MODELS OF COMPETITION AND EDUCATION

Capitalistic models of competition have influenced educational policies and practices over many generations. This was no accidental outcome but the results of a prevailing mode of thought that utilized the competitive motive as one of its basic principles. The competitive marketplace, when applied to education, seeks greater productivity, efficiency, accountability, choice, and improved vocational skills.

This chapter will examine such movements and crosscurrents as the Protestant ethic and its influence on the growth of capitalism, and the role of competition in classical economic thought and in the present economy. This inquiry then leads to the influence of business models on school management, which are expressed in terms of bureaucracy, scientific management, and accountability. It also leads to economic goals for education as well as preparing workers for business and industry and for youth to compete more effectively internationally on standardized achievement tests and in the workplace. To accomplish these goals, business has attempted to forge new relations with public education.

THE PROTESTANT ETHIC AND THE RISE OF CAPITALISM

Max Weber argued that the development of European capitalism could not be accounted for in purely economic or technical terms but was largely the result of the ascetic secular morality associated with the emphasis in Calvinistic theology on predestination and salvation.[1] Since salvation is the focus of religious life, people are interested in knowing whether they are among the chosen. Success in one's worldly calling is believed to be an almost infallible indication.

The Protestant ethic, according to Weber, regarded all work as a justified "calling" and, by treating persons in an individualistic and impersonal way, facilitated rational modes of behavior that allowed capitalistic enterprises to flourish. The maxims of action directed the believer to behave in the spirit of mature capitalism. By the term "the spirit of capitalism," Weber meant a set of attitudes and the belief that it is a good thing to make money even beyond meeting the necessities, that one should maximize wealth without much consideration for the means as long as the means are efficacious. This, in turn, sanctioned competition and other business practices.

Capitalism in general as a system of profit-making enterprises bound together by market relations can be found historically in many places. But mature capitalism is distinguished by its rational character and the rational organization of free labor. Weber indicated that in contemporary Germany areas primarily Protestant were wealthier than Catholic sections of the nation, and he showed the correlation between the growth of Protestantism and mature capitalism. He also explained that the ethical system of Confucianism in China and the belief in the transmigration of souls in India were not propitious to the rise of capitalism.

The elements in the Protestant ethic congruent with the capitalistic spirit are asceticism, a this-worldly orientation, and a compulsion to lead a well-ordered, systematic, impersonal, and individualistic life. Finally, Weber argued that capitalism, resting largely on hedonistic and materialistic incentives, no longer needs the support of the Protestant ethic. The pursuit of wealth has become stripped of its religious and ethical meaning.[2]

American capitalism began with merchant capitalism based on the activities of business people who made profits through trade and commercial activity. As industrialization proceeded, it became based more on an industrial capitalism in which business people made profits from manufacturing and production. While the flood of immigrants between 1870 and 1910 provided a source of cheap, unskilled labor for the ambitious capitalist, the schools were attempting to assimilate immigrant children into the dominant ethos of American culture. As industrial processes grew in complexity, the growth of bureaucratic organization ensued, along with the need for a managerial class. An expansion of secondary education was needed to cope with these changes. The Kalamazoo Case (1874) led to publicly supported high schools, and compulsory laws were enacted, beginning in Massachusetts in 1852 and ending in Mississippi in 1918. Nevertheless, a large number of children did not receive many years of formal schooling until the laws, after the turn of the century, were more firmly enforced and also until the passage of child labor laws.

The industrial age carried forward the Protestant ethic of hard work, cleanliness, godliness, thriftiness, and the rest of the hoary virtues. Industrialism in America emphasized social Darwinism, the accumulation of wealth, production of goods, accumulating quantities of goods in the face of scarcity, and preparing oneself vocationally in order to compete successfully. With the expansion of the high school, on-the-job apprenticeship training shifted more to the schools by instituting trade and industrial training.

The vast changes in society were also reflected in the transformation of the school from an institution for educating a select student body to one for educating all youth. Throughout American history the value of equal opportunity was ceremoniously extolled but social provisions for its full realization were seldom instituted. Even more opposed than equal opportunity has been the idea of substantive economic equality despite the promise of socioeconomic mobility. The Protestant ethic was too deeply ingrained in the American psyche to permit serious talk about economic equality. Even as the majority found that by competition and hard work alone most people did not acquire fortunes and rise to the top of the social ladder, they were saved from cynicism and any urge to rebel against the system because they were taught from an early age that everyone has an "equal" chance to rise and any failure to succeed lies with the individual and not the system. Historically public education has served as the chief agent for legitimizing the doctrine. Those who did not succeed in the academic competition were taught to accept their social position because they had been given a fair chance and could still contribute to society by putting in an honest day's work.

ECONOMIC COMPETITION

Adam Smith, the father of modern economics, provided in 1776 for readers of his masterwork, *The Wealth of Nations,* the first full account of how the economy worked.[3] Smith's theory envisioned that a free society has a tendency to grow through a hidden mechanism that operates to enlarge the "wealth of nations." This mechanism can be found in a steady rise in labor productivity that could be achieved through an ever-finer division of labor. Although the demand for workers would tend to drive up wages, this same demand would reduce infant and child mortality as wages rose and thereby increase the number of available workers and the competition for jobs.

Smith's conception of human nature postulates a "desire for betterment"—a motive that prompts manufacturers to expand their business to increase profits. The path to growth lies in "accumulation" in which capitalists, in seeking wealth, invest in machines and equipment that enables workers to produce more and thereby increases society's overall output. Individuals, he postulates, are driven by self-interest. These self-interested individuals, however, are prevented from taking advantages of their fellows by the mechanism of competition. Each individual, seeking self-gain, is faced with similarly motivated persons, and each is prepared to take advantage of another's greed should he raise the price of his goods above the level set by the market. Thus if a manufacturer charged more than his competitors for the same product, he would lose business, or if a worker asked more than the going wage, he would not find a job.

The market mechanism not only provides competitive safeguards on the price of goods but it arranges for the right quantities of goods. If the public buys out the existing supply of bread, the price will tend to rise to cover a shrinking supply; whereas if the sale of luxury boats is slow, the price will tend to fall as the merchant seeks to reduce his stock. The selfish motives of people are transmuted by the market mechanism to serve a social good. Although the individual intends only his own good, he is led by an "invisible hand" which was no part of his intention. "By pursuing his own interest he frequently promotes that of the society more effectually than when he really intends to promote it."[4] Thus the competitive market, rather than being disorderly, is a taskmaster that imposes the strictest discipline and is a self-regulating process.

In late nineteenth century America, many inventions promoted the development of capitalism. British inventors in the eighteenth century created machines for the production of textiles and these inventions found their way to America; the telegraph provided a communication link across the continent; and the use of Bessemer and open-hearth processes revolutionized steel production. Paralleling these inventions was the improvement of transportation by the steamboat and the building of a great network of canals, later to be followed by the railroads eventually linking the Atlantic and Pacific coasts. "Never before," according to economist Lester Telser, "had there been so rapid an exploitation of new knowledge in commerce and industry."[5] The steady growth of technology required massive investments that created increasingly drastic competition. As the giant businesses clashed, each sought to gain as large a share of market as possible, leading to the emergence of "cutthroat competition" that took the form of price wars with resultant heavy losses that eliminated firms until only one remained or agreement was reached to stabilize prices.[6] In the next phase of economic development the giant corporations decided not to compete. This was first done by "gentleman's agreement" to divide the market. During the 1880s trusts were established in which stockholders were asked to surrender their shares to the board of directors of the trust; in turn, shareholders would relinquish control of the companies for trust certificates by which they would share in the profits. The board would be free to absorb or eliminate competition, fix prices, and control a market. Eventually the trusts were declared illegal. Another device for limiting competition was the holding company. New Jersey passed a law permitting corporations to buy shares in other corporations and to do business in any state. Standard Oil of New Jersey used this device to acquire direct control over seventy companies and indirect control of thirty more.

But this was not the way capitalism was supposed to work. *Perfect competition* occurs when a market for a product has so many buyers and sellers that none can influence the price.[7] This means that a sufficiently large number of buyers and sellers participate in the market so that each's role is so small that any one's actions does not affect the price. The product must be homogeneous or identical so that buyers are indifferent as to the seller from whom the product is purchased. Buyers and sellers must have full information about price conditions.

In actual markets, however, the number of producers is not so large that no firm has control over price.[8] Some economists object to the perfect-competition model of economic activity because it gives excessive attention to only one competition, price competition. Thus even though competition plays an "indispensable role" in economic systems, the perfect-competition model is defective.[9]

One way that imperfect competition operates is when firms attempt to popularize brand names by differentiating the product they sell. The demand for a name brand allows the firm to move the product out of a perfectly competitive market and exert an influence on price. But the limitation here is that consumers may select other brands to meet their needs or new firms will enter the industry.

Another form of imperfect competition is *oligopoly* in which the sellers are so few that the supply offered by any of them materially affects the market price. Rigid prices are common among oligopolistic firms because their management realizes that any action upon their part will lead to counteraction by rivals. Yet in order to avoid losing customers, oligopolies are likely to match price cuts rather than price increases. Prices can therefore be set, at least within limits, by leading firms. Increasingly today a few large producers divide the market among themselves and set prices that are higher than a pure competition model would enforce. The prices set by oligopolistic firms are called *administered prices.* Usually competition among these firms means gaining business by advertising, product design, or customer service rather than price cutting. But prices in oligopolistic industries are not without control. One pressure, as noted by John Kenneth Galbraith, is countervailing power.[10] By this he means that an opposition across markets provides some compensation for an absence within a given market. The large raw-materials producer who faces little competition within his industry must sell to the large chemical or processing plant; the giant canner to the giant supermarket firm. Another restraining force is competition among different products. Since buildings are composed of glass, steel, brick or concrete and automobile engines are made of cast aluminum as well as steel, these and other different industries must compete against one another.

Oligopoly is more characteristic of the American economy than either perfect competition or monopoly. A *monopoly* exists where a single seller controls the entire supply of a good or service that has no substitute. The firm controls production and sale as well as entry of new firms into the field. Telephone and electric companies are monopolistic enterprises in most communities. The monopolist can dictate the supply of his product that will yield the most profitable price. Monopoly is at the opposite extreme from perfect competition.

As Lester Thurow has observed, a competitive economy offers many potential opportunities, but it also poses risks, income losses, and uncertainties. We want both opportunities for higher income and security for our present income. "One man's security is another man's lack of opportunity. Thus we usually end up prescribing competition for others and security for ourselves."[11]

The government establishes a legal framework to enable the price system to perform adequately. It also sees that markets remain competitive. To these ends the Congress has enacted such antitrust laws as the Sherman

Antitrust Act and the Clayton Act and has established the Federal Trade Commission. The antitrust laws prohibit collusion and attempts to monopolize the sale of a product. In addition, the government attempts to control activities in markets where competition is not expected and establishes regulatory commissions, as in transportation, communications, and electric and gas industries. Thus although monopoly is the outgrowth of competition, it annuls competition while leaving self-interest and the profit motive unchecked; hence the need for government regulation to restore competitive markets.

Of especial concern today is the decline of America's competitiveness internationally. A critical area is that of technology. Successful competition in technology requires managers with technological understanding; business traditions and financial incentives that encourage long-term investments; a well-educated work force; committed engineers and scientists; and institutions engaged in research and development.[12] America is paying an enormous price to boost its competitive position. Much of it has been initiated with borrowed funds, by selling off assets and laying off employees, or freezing workers' salaries. Worker output in Japan grew during the 1980s three times faster than in the United States.[13] What America must do, according to one report, is to "lift investments, bolster the competitiveness of small manufacturers and service companies, strengthen U.S. technology, and increase workers' skill at applying it."[14]

BUSINESS MODELS OF SCHOOL MANAGEMENT

A primary means for imposing order and efficiency—two qualities highly valued in business and industry—was through the development of bureaucracies. The term refers to complex organizations that are operated on the basis of efficiency in order to accomplish large-scale administrative tasks. The administrative hierarchy, the system of offices, and the regulations governing their operation are devised to achieve organizational goals.

The objectives of bureaucracies, according to Weber, are to eliminate irrational and emotional elements, to elevate precision, speed, continuity, unambiguity, and to encourage the subordination of personnel to the administrative hierarchy in order to reduce friction and keep material and personnel costs at a minimum.

Following Weber's interpretation, bureaucracies organize their offices according to the hierarchical principle in which each office is under the supervision and control of the higher one. The lower office has the right to appeal and issue a statement of grievance to the higher one. Qualifications for each office are specified in writing. The office is regulated by written rules that define the sphere of its authority. In order to meet qualifications for the office, one needs specialized training. The objective is to ensure that appointments will be based on merit rather than wealth, influence, or other extraneous factors. Promotion is based on seniority, achievement, or both; employment in the system constitutes a career, and the office holder is protected against arbitrary dismissal.[15]

Katz has shown in a study that school bureaucracy emerged in Boston between 1830 and 1876. The reasons for this development were the increasing complexity of school administration, political influences in school operations, successful examples from industry of managing large work forces, and the aspirations and anxieties of school administrators.[16]

Bureaucracy grew in other ways: through an expanded growth of principals and supervisors, school district consolidation, and the emergence of a large and complex state education bureaucracy. Especially dramatic was the decline in school districts from their peak in 1932 of 127,529 to less than 16,000 nationwide today.

Bureaucratic leaders were incessantly in search of greater efficiencies in operation. Interest in the process of industrial management lead to a number of studies in industry. Frederick W. Taylor advocated the scientific study of jobs based on time-studies of tasks, leading to a standard time for each job and payment of wages in proportion to output.[17] Following Taylor's study, more systematic treatments dealt with the division of labor, specialization and departmentalization of functions, and managerial supervision.[18]

American businessmen, impressed with the principles of scientific management, pressured public education, from positions of power on school boards, into adopting industrial management principles in the operation of school systems. The justification of such procedures was greater efficiency and economy. The scientific management approach, which prevailed in public education during the 1930s, viewed the teacher as an obedient servant to administrative authority.[19]

The analogy, however, between industry and education is not close and when applied too literally, leads to abuses and distortions of the teaching-learning process in the name of efficiency. Only certain aspects of education such as the business operations of school systems can operate effectively on this model.

Some bureaucracies are top-heavy organizations filled with "red tape," slavish and unimaginative bureaucrats, large-scale inefficiencies, breakdowns in effective communication between line and staff, and a tendency to alienate some teachers and students.

Despite such criticisms, not all aspects of bureaucracies have been harmful to schools. Corwin notes that the formal rules have kept schools free from the patronage of corrupt city governments, helped centralize and standardize schools that enabled them to accommodate diverse ways of immigrants, and have kept the schools from disintegrating during periods of rapid change and cultural conflict.[20]

Other efficiency models emerged more recently. Accountability, the watchword of the 1970s, developed as a result of growing public dissatisfaction over rising costs for education and the low achievement level of some students. Accountability emphasizes measurement, efficiency, system models, and competitiveness. "Outputs" in terms of student performance on standardized achievements test scores are the principal measure for determining quality. Accountability is a demand to judge students by outputs rather than inputs (e.g., percentage of teachers certified, per pupil expenditure, number of school library holdings, etc.) in order to demonstrate a positive relationship between expenditures and desired results obtained.

A program's performance objectives must first be specified in terms of instructional objectives. The program and instructional goals of school systems must be stated so that they are susceptible to measurement. Only, in this manner, some believe, can the outputs be appraised and the costs of programs assessed.[21]

No attempt is made, however, to consider the full range of educational outcomes such as aesthetic appreciation, affective changes, and the development of novel and creative approaches to problem solving. The assumptions underlying accountability may lead to a mentality alien to the educational process. Accountability overemphasizes measurement, efficiency, and competitiveness; it may usher in educational engineering: the application of technology and government cost accounting to the obdurate problems of education. Concern is not with purposes of education but with means and techniques. While means should not be ignored and a close connection should be maintained between means and ends, the technocratic model of accountability tends to shape the educational process to fit an efficiency mold and thereby may tend to become fixated upon objective data and measurable performance. Thus, in order to overcome these weaknesses, the accountability movement needs to alter some of its theoretical assumptions and broaden the range of evaluative procedures employed.

SCHOOLS OF CHOICE

Schools of choice, an emerging movement, is a central plank in the Bush administration's educational plan. Schools of choice attempt to offer parents greater options in selecting schools for their children. It is a blanket term that covers a multitude of diverse plans. Whereas the Bush administration would provide parents funds to send their children to parochial schools, other plans are limited to choices within public schools.

The schools of choice movement stems from strong dissatisfaction with public education. David Boaz asserts that "The public schools have failed because they are essentially socialist institutions: one system for the entire society, centrally directed and managed, with little use for competition or market incentives."[22] He adds that the public schools are like Soviet factories—convenient for bureaucrats, backward, overstaffed, and unresponsive to consumer demands.

William Safire claims that parental choice of schools "will introduce cleansing competition to the stolid monopoly that is now the public system.... Competition, not monopoly, is the American way; we have seen it work and produce."[23] He proposes that bad schools should be allowed to fail and be closed, while assuring their students access to successful schools. Then some failed schools should be revised, opened under new management to place "competitive pressure" on other schools.

Various earlier forms of choice in education include vouchers and tuition tax credits. These plans are related to both competition and freedom. The government has given parents the legal right to choose the type of education their child will receive, but it has largely used a negative, rather than a positive, conception of freedom. The negative form is freedom from restraint; the positive is an ability to exercise power. Thus someone not restrained is free to move about and go where she chooses (negative freedom), but she still may not be able to travel wherever she chooses because of inadequate income (lack of positive freedom). All socioeconomic classes enjoy negative freedom in parental choice (of the type of education), but only the higher classes have the economic means to fully exercise their choices. The question is whether the government should make some provision to enlarge the choices of lower-income parents. No pretension is made that the government could literally equalize in the sense of providing identical opportunities; for even if doing so were desirable—and an equal of opportunity does not demand it—the cost would be prohibitive and probably an unfair burden to the higher classes. Even egalitarians do not interpret equal as identical where the government would somehow equalize family incomes, home and neighborhood conditions, and genetic endowments. The egalitarian may want some income redistribution but would not likely believe in a literal equality, which would obviously stifle individuality, initiative, and be strongly coercive. What is sought here is that children from lower-income families are not unduly and unfairly penalized, that they are afforded basic opportunities to develop their potential in a healthy learning environment that provides some choices of programs and teachers.

The voucher plan is one proposed solution to this problem. It is based on enlarging the freedom of parental choices rather than attempting to directly equalize opportunities. Early voucher plans were essentially unregulated and posed threats of violating the separation of church and state and increasing school segregation.[24] More recent plans have sought to avoid these problems.[25]

Voucher plans purport to foster competition among schools. Parents would receive a voucher for each child in the family that can be used to send the child to the school of choice, whether public or private. Support waned in the 1980s for federally supported vouchers, but other plans have been proposed. In one plan, parents could send their child to a private school if the child had failed minimum-competency testing in public schools for three consecutive years.[26] Another plan would be a coupon similar to food stamps. Parents would purchase the coupon, with the price adjusted according to family income. The parents could purchase additional tutoring at a private or public school of choice.[27] An early plan by Christopher Jencks would create an Education Voucher Agency at the community level for receiving government funds to finance the schools. Each school would be required to take everyone who applied, except when the number of applicants exceeded the number of places, in which case a lottery would be used to fill half the places.[28]

The Office of Economic Opportunity made grants to several communities to study the feasibility of the voucher plan, but only the community of Alum Rock, California, with the aid of a federal grant, decided to try the plan. Alum Rock's plan, however, differed from most proposals by using only public schools and providing alternative programs within them, and using a board of education rather than a voucher agency. After four years of operation, it was found that teachers, students, and parents liked the plan but standardized test scores were either equivalent to national norms or had in some instances dropped below them.[29] In any case the Alum Rock program differed significantly from the original plan; it explores a new option instead.

Excluding Alum Rock, a number of basic deficiencies can be found in voucher plans.[30] A basic tenet of voucher proponents is that the public schools constitute a monopoly, and consequently, the use of vouchers would increase competition and open many new options to parents. Voucher advocates frequently use the free-marketplace analogy that vouchers would do for education what free enterprise has done for the economy and its productivity. Schools, however, are relatively decentralized and do compete with private schools and with each other: in their sports program, for teachers, appropriations, special projects, and the like. The market analogy is misleading insofar as profit-making firms sell their products to anyone who has cash or credit, whereas private schools are selective and not open to everyone. Moreover, to provide the options claimed to result from using vouchers, nonpublic schools would have to be far more innovative and experimental in their programs and organizations, as only a small number exhibit these characteristics.

Once nonpublic schools accept substantial state funds, they would likely be more thoroughly regulated. It may mean that parochial schools would not longer be able to offer sectarian religious courses, and all nonpublic schools would be subject to desegregation rulings. Voucher plans usually make no provision for eliminating discrimination in the hiring of teachers. Nonpublic schools may also be required to observe judicial standards of academic freedom.

Public schools, under a voucher plan, would unlikely receive additional tax funds but nonpublic schools would be free to increase their endowment, thereby leading to greater inequities. The voucher system would increase public costs by paying nonpublic tuitions, staffing and operation of a voucher agency, creating new buildings and facilities for private schools and underusing those of public schools (because of decreased enrollment, increased transportation costs, and inefficient use of tenured public-school teachers).

Thus, in view of the substantial shortcomings of the voucher plan, it may be wiser to offer greater curricular alternatives in public schools. Alternative schools, which are designed to provide options to the traditional model or comprehensive high school, usually have more comprehensive goals than traditional schools, greater curricular flexibility, and are smaller and less bureaucratic than the comprehensive high school. Examples of alternative schools are open schools, schools without walls, magnet schools, and multicultural schools.

A related proposal to enhance choice is tuition tax credits. Federal tuition tax credits are tax rebates to parents who pay for their children's private school tuition. These credits attempt to promote choice and greater diversity in education.

Although tuition tax credits were first proposed in the 1950s, the most significant recent bill (which failed to pass) was the Packwood-Moynihan bill (in 1978), which included tax credits for college and university costs and allowed a refund from the treasury for those claiming tuition tax credits in excess of their tax liability. The Reagan administration proposed Educational Opportunity and Equity Act of 1982 did not contain these provisions. Families would have been able to recover up to 50 percent of each child's tuition to private or parochial schools. An income cap attempted to ensure benefits go to less affluent families, and a nondiscriminatory provision precluded credits to those who sent their children to schools that discriminate on the basis of race. Thus the credits, according to proponents, would have been an aid not to nonpublic schools but to taxpaying citizens.

Proponents also believe that public schools constitute a monopoly not only over the poor but over all who cannot afford to pay property taxes for public schools and pay private school tuition. Tax credits are in the national interest, it is claimed, because it frees children of lower and middle classes to seek a more challenging environment. With a larger private sector, parents would no longer have to lobby for prayer in schools and other provisions.

Former Attorney General Griffin Bell concluded in 1978 that the Packwood-Moynihan bill was unconstitutional because it violates First Amendment guarantees against the establishment of religion. It would lead to divisive church-state entanglements and benefit sectarian schools more than nonsectarian ones.

The argument that parents whose children are enrolled in nonpublic schools have greater expenses and are thereby entitled to relief under a theory of basic fairness was rejected in 1979 by the U.S. Third Circuit Court of Appeals. Private schools already enjoy tax exempt status and receive considerable benefits under federal aid programs. The credit of

$500 per child in nonpublic schools contrasts sharply with direct federal aid of $145 per pupil in public schools.

The U.S. Supreme Court, however, ruled 5-4 in a 1983 decision that states may give tax benefits to parents to offset some of the costs of their children's school expenses.[31] The justices upheld a Minnesota law granting parents a tax deduction of up to $700 per child for their costs on elementary and secondary education, whether public or private. The Minnesota law differs from the Reagan administration proposal, which provides tax benefits only for those paying private school tuition. The majority opinion stressed that this program is available to private school parents, that it provides only attenuated benefits to private schools because it is channeled through parents, and does not involve excessive entanglement in church and state because the state's only role is the screening of textbooks to determine whether they qualified for a deduction. However, the minority opinion stated that the establishment clause prohibited both direct and indirect aid to sectarian schools.

But in the 1989 fall term, only 3,790 of Minnesota's 735,000 public school students applied to transfer schools.[32] One problem is that no agency collects basic data needed for informal decision making; another is that Minnesota provides no bus service for those electing to leave their district.

"Choice has worked," President Bush proclaimed, "almost without exception, everywhere it has been tried."[33] And Governor Bill Clinton of Arkansas added that "Choice will encourage districts to do better. Competition will improve quality."[34] Yet so far, according to Susan Chira, "there is little research to prove whether the freedom to choose schools improves them. Nor is it clear which type of choice plans work better: those that limit choice to one public school district, or those that allow money to follow children to schools, public or private."[35]

Choice plans confront some serious problems. Classroom space limits choice unless provision is made to accommodate students whose parents choose to send them. Second, unless the state is willing to provide transportation, low-income families cannot exercise their option. Third, some parents are unwilling to send their children to a distant district no matter how weak their local schools may be. Another objection is that parents do not always choose schools for educational reasons: they select schools near their home or work and sometimes withdraw their children from schools that raise graduation requirements and transfer them to schools with lower standards. A capable agency that widely disseminates information about public schools in the state may help overcome some problems of choice, but may not substantially alter misguided parental attitudes. Finally, the marketing concept applied to public schools is inappropriate because competition will not force school improvement; rather, the schools that are abandoned will lose their most vocal and influential parents. Moreover, improving schools and devising special programs requires expertise that many schools lack; thus the marketing concept fails to supply weak schools with any means of improvement; it erroneously assumes that weak schools are willfully that way and the loss of students alone will provide the stimulus needed for improvement.

Public education's problems run much deeper than insufficient choice and competition. "The problems in America's schools," says Robert Carr, "stem in large part from causes deep in the national experience: urban blight, drugs, the erosion of the family, and the long-standing failure to devote sufficient resources to schools."[36] He adds that despite these pressures the schools also have been expected to assume roles formerly handled by the family, church, and other institutions. He recommends instead to provide greater support for Head Start and other successful programs, increase teacher salaries, reduce class sizes, and improve school funding.

EDUCATION FOR ECONOMIC GROWTH AND NATIONAL PREPAREDNESS

Government officials, economists, and business executives sometimes state economic goals for education that may run counter to those of educators or parents. One example is former North Carolina Governor James Hunt's conviction that our economic future is endangered because American students, unlike those of other leading industrial nations, are not acquiring the fundamentals needed to operate effectively in a modern economy.[37] American students' test scores are low in comparison with other industrialized nations. The curriculum is less demanding than Soviet schools, and Japan has the world's highest literacy rate. Today's jobs require more than mastery of the basics but the creative use of more complex skills. Hunt insists that we must ensure that we can "continue to compete" in the world economy, as our quality of life and our children's future depend upon the quality of education. "We must act now to improve our educational system and prove that Americans can still outwork, outproduce, outinvent, and outcompete any nation in the world."[38] The fundamental belief of the Task Force on Education for Economic Growth, sponsored by the Education Commission of the States, is that education is the key to the nation's economic growth. In chairing the Task Force, Hunt helped direct it to establish state task forces to assess statewide and local needs and develop plans for school improvement. It also recommended creating closer partnerships between education, business, and government to improve education for economic growth.

Hunt seems to ignore the danger of education becoming captive to business' profit motive and national preparedness fears. Education for individual development is suppressed while blame for the economy's failures is shifted from business, industry, and government to education.

Hunt voices several influential themes that deserve further attention: national preparedness, education for economic growth, and a closer partnership between business and education. The national preparedness theme was sounded when the Soviet Union launched its Sputnik in 1957; the consequent fear that the Soviet Union was forging ahead in the space race led the following year to Congress passing the National Defense Education Act. This Act included aid to strengthen instruction in science, mathematics, and foreign languages; funds for the preparation of school counselors; and loans to prospective teachers. The Soviet Union, it was claimed, was preparing more engineers, scientists, and mathematicians than the U.S. and we were falling dangerously behind.

The National Commission on Excellence in Education, appointed by Secretary of Education T.H. Bell, reported in 1983 under the grave title *A Nation at Risk* that the U.S. stands to lose it prominence as a world leader in industry and commerce. In a "world of ever-accelerating competition," the Commission found that on international comparisons of student achievement American students never finished first or second on 19 academic tests; that 13 percent of all 17-year olds in the U.S. are functionally illiterate; and the average achievement of high school students is now lower than when Sputnik was launched. Among the Commission's recommendations are for high schools to strengthen graduation requirements; higher standards for college admission; more time devoted to learning the basics; improve teacher preparation; and ask citizens to hold educators and elected officials responsible for these changes.[39]

The Business-Higher Education Forum, a group representing corporate and university chief executives, was invited in 1982 "to explore ways in which our national competitive position could be further strengthened through increased innovation and productivity."[40] The Forum diagnosed a host of economic problems: the nation has suffered three major recessions in the past 12 years, more Americans were jobless in 1982 than any time since the Great Depression, productivity growth has declined, trade and budget deficits have risen, and many U.S. industries are less competitive than previously. It added that a nation's competitive ability depends upon productive capital investment, technological innovation, and the development of human resources. Addressing the latter deficiency, it announced that the U.S. needs a national strategy for education, training, and retraining at all levels. To this end it was recommended to develop a comprehensive national displaced worker program, tax incentives to stimulate further investment in education and worker training, new ways of attracting engineering students into teaching careers, and the upgrading of science and mathematics teachers' skills.

The National Task Force on Education for Economic Growth stated that "technological change and global competition" make it imperative to move beyond the basics to teach new skills on which technology depends. The challenge is not only to better educate an elite but to raise the floor and ceiling of achievement. The Task Force recommended, among other things, that each governor should establish a state task force on education and economic growth and develop a state plan in this area; involve business leaders, labor leaders, and members of the professions more actively in education; and improve the quality of education by using mastery for promotion, strengthen teacher certification, and reward outstanding teaching.[41]

American education, considered a decentralized system internationally, may become more centralized. President Bush and the nation's governors met in 1989 to establish national goals that can be met by the year 2000. The next year the National Governors Association met for further work on the goals and to develop a common mechanism for measuring each state's progress. Goals to be reached by the year 2000 include:

- All children will start school ready to learn.
- The high school graduation rate will be increased to at least 90 percent.
- Students will demonstrate competency in mathematics, English, science, geography and history in the fourth, eighth, and twelfth grades.
- Every school will be free of drugs and violence.

- American students will rank first in the world in mathematics and science.
- Every adult will be literate and possess knowledge and skills to compete globally.[42]

But in a 1990 Gallup poll, while more than three-quarters of the 1,594 adults interviewed attached a high priority to all six of the national goals, only 19 percent to 50 percent of the respondents believed that any particular goal was likely or very likely to be achieved in the next ten years.[43]

Moving rapidly to assess whether these goals are achieved, the National Assessment of Educational Progress (NAEP) has approved a plan to establish the first national standards for student achievement. The NAEP will seek to measure student performance against agreed-upon standards of what students should know and be able to do in grades 4, 8, and 12. Reports will be made as to the proportion of students who performed at "basic," "proficient," and "advanced" levels at each grade. The NAEP cited its statutory authority to set "appropriate achievement goals" for each grade and subject tested.[44]

A movement to create national examinations for elementary and secondary school students is gaining momentum. Supporters include President Bush's Education Policy Advisory Committee and a diverse group of businessmen and educators that has endorsed national testing in grades 4, 8, and 12. Testing advocates claim that students will only study harder when parents know how they rank on a reliable test taken by all students. Test scores should affect high school graduation and job opportunities. Schools, districts, and states, according to proponents, could be ranked using national test data.

Critics have pointed out that such a testing plan would constitute a radical break with two centuries of American traditions of local control and would represent a de facto national agreement on what should be taught and thereby diminish curriculum variety. It also raises the possibility that a person's career options will be decided at an early age. In addition, critics say that the nation is already overtesting students.[45]

Turning to the second theme—education for economic growth—it is not surprising that business and government leaders should look to education to increase productivity and competitiveness. Business historian Alfred Chandler Jr. has stated that "The past two decades is the greatest crisis of American industry ever, by far."[46] Industry had to restructure because of overdiversification and, while restructuring, "the competition was getting tougher." Germans and Europeans and Japanese would have given U.S. industry competition earlier if World War II had not intervened. Chandler observes that "It first hit us in the 1960s and our response was very poor."[47]

Education provides a significant means for making industry more productive. The Organization for Economic Cooperation and Development argued that education facilitated economic growth by fostering technological innovation and by increasing the productivity of labor.[48] Edward Denison's influential study showed that investment in education brings higher returns than investment in physical capital and that an increase in education expenditures is a highly effective means of increasing the Gross National Product.[49] Some other economists, while differing in details, have also concluded that investment in education has a positive effect upon economic growth.[50]

Nevertheless, some questions could be raised without negating these conclusions. Denison's approach focuses rather exclusively upon formal education and tends to ignore the effects of on-the-job training.[51] Also since individuals' educational programs and the type of job that they take are not always closely related, the upgrading of positions in industry may not always be related to educational prerequisites but to such factors as the employer's desire to hire high school graduates rather than dropouts. One effect of increased education is that it makes better decision makers in the allocation of resources, including the use of time. The greater the decision-making functions associated with a job, the greater the potential effect of education on productivity.[52] An alternate explanation by Herbert Gintis is that education's contribution to productivity is indirect not so much through technical training but that it socializes for docile and efficient adaptation to bureaucratic and industrial hierarchies.[53]

The third and final theme to consider is building a closer partnership between business and public education. Concern about the nation's economic condition and the quality of the workforce has led to partnerships between educators and business executives. These arrangements involve much more than the usual work/study programs and cooperative learning arrangements. Some corporations have "adopted" schools or disadvantaged students in schools and provided technical, managerial, and financial aid and exposure to successful adult role models. As an example, the Boston Compact was formed in 1982 in which business leaders agreed that they would hire graduates of Boston public schools and provide employment for students; in turn, school officials agreed upon higher competency levels for graduation, higher percentages of graduates entering college, and lower absenteeism and dropout rates. By 1987, over 350 companies were participating in the program and thousands of Boston students have been involved in summer job programs. Examples elsewhere of the partnership include providing resource people for schools, laboratory assistants, curriculum advisors, hardware and software, scholarships, and volunteer mentors. Today there are more than 1500 such partnerships nationwide.

The Committee for Economic Development emphasizes the need to redesign vocational training by providing both strong academic programs and on-the-job training in the best cooperative education programs. The Committee stated that "economic productivity and the quality of education cannot be separated."[54]

Business involvement has now moved well beyond the "adopt a school" programs that marked the 1980s to an even larger role. The Business Roundtable, composed of chief executive officers of the nation's 200 largest corporations, began a long-term effort in which each state would be paired with at least one corporation to enlarge political and financial resources for educational reform. About one-third of the states have taken up the Roundtable's agenda that includes creating an outcomes-based system, strengthening assessment measures, rewarding school success and punishing failure, using site-based management, and establishing prekindergarten programs for all disadvantaged children.[55]

Yet all is not entirely well between business and education. A study in 1988 by the New York state comptroller's office called for a national study to control governments' use of tax breaks to lure new businesses or to assure that old ones do not leave. The practice has been overused, thereby draining government resources. The National School Boards Association is attempting to revise state and local tax systems to ensure that tax incentives do not adversely affect funding for schools.[56]

Moreover, small business owners oppose increased state spending on education. The National Federation of Independent Business reported that many small firm owners believe they are not receiving a good return on their public school investment and, although funding for public education has climbed sharply in recent years, test results should improve before spending is increased. Small-business groups favor greater accountability and more emphasis on basic competencies in reading and mathematics.[57] Thus rather than enter into a "partnership" with public education (as the case with some large corporations), small business owners are resisting higher state expenditures until certain desired outcomes are demonstrated.

In conclusion, business can help bridge the gap between the financial burden taxpayers are willing to bear and the need to improve educational standards. But a danger exists that the relationship will lead to a restricted curriculum that excludes subjects such as music and art that might be deemed unnecessary for producing competent workers. Business involvement may therefore increase disparities in the quality of education by pouring resources into some programs at the expense of others. School systems should have their own philosophy, and interaction with businesses should not infringe on those goals.

ENDNOTES

1. Weber, Max: *The Protestant Ethic and the Spirit of Capitalism.* trans. Talcott Parsons. New York: Scribner, 1930.
2. Though scholars have disputed Weber's thesis by arguing that the spread of capitalism in Holland was from economic causes and that the use of capitalism in Catholic countries was inhibited by the Counter-Reformation, Weber's thesis has been one of the most influential ideas in contemporary social science.
3. Smith, Adam: *The Wealth of Nations.* London: Routledge, 1900.
4. Ibid., p. 345.
5. Telser, Lester, G.: *A Theory of Efficient Cooperation and Competition.* New York: Cambridge University Press, 1987, p. 11.
6. Leiter, Robert D.: *Modern Economics,* 2nd ed. New York: Barnes & Noble, 1976, p. 185; Heilbroner, Robert L.: *The Making of Economic Society,* 5th ed. Englewood Cliffs, NJ: Prentice-Hall, 1975, p. 113.
7. Mansfield, Edwin: *Principles of Macroeconomics.* New York: W.W. Norton, 1974, p. 50.
8. Ibid., p. 42.
9. Demsetz, Harold: *Economic, Legal, and Political Dimensions of Competition.* Amsterdam: North-Holland Publishing, 1982, pp. 2–4.
10. Galbraith, John Kenneth: *American Capitalism: The Concept of Countervailing Power.* Boston: Houghton Mifflin, 1952, pp. 115ff.
11. Thurow, Lester C.: *The Zero-Sum Society.* New York: Penguin Books, 1981, p. 126.
12. Lipson, Joseph I. and Fisher, Kathleen M.: Technologies of the future. *Education & Computing* 1: 11–23, (1985).
13. Steward, Thomas P.: The new American century: where we stand. *Fortune* 123: 12–23, (Spring/Summer-Special Issue, 1991).
14. Ibid., p. 16.

15. Gerth, H.H. and Mills, C. Wright, trans. & eds. *From Max Weber: Essays in Sociology.* New York: Oxford University Press, 1958, ch. 8; Weber, Max: *The Theory of Social and Economic Organization,* trans. A.M. Henderson and Talcott Parsons, New York: Free Press, 1957.

16. Katz, Michael B.: *Class, Bureaucracy, and Schools: The Illusion of Educational Change in America,* Expanded Ed. New York: Free Press, 1957.

17. Taylor, Frederick W.: *Scientific Management.* New York: Harper, 1911.

18. Monney, James D. and Reiley, Alan C.: *Onward Industry.* New York: Harper, 1931.

19. Callahan, Raymond E.: *Education and the Cult of Efficiency.* Chicago: University of Chicago Press, 1962.

20. Corwin, Ronald G.: *Education in Crisis.* New York: Wiley, 1972, pp. 7–12.

21. See: Lessinger, Leon, and Associates: *Accountability: Systems Planning in Education.* Homewood, IL: ETC Publications, 1973; Van Haden, H.I. and Glass, K.M.: *Accountability for Results in Education.* Swarthmore, PA: A.C. Croft, 1972.

22. Boaz, David: The big flaw in school reform. *New York Times* (May 30, 1991): A15.

23. The President's plan: A sampling of opinion. *Education Week* (May 29, 1991): 24.

24. For some of the early plans, see Blum, Virgil C.: *Freedom of Choice in Education.* Macmillan, 1958; and Friedman, Milton: The role of government in education. In Solo, Robert A., ed. *Economics and the Public Interest.* New Brunswick, NJ: Rutgers University Press, 1955.

25. Jencks, Christopher, et al. *Education Vouchers, A Preliminary Report on Financing Education by Payments to Parents.* Cambridge, Mass: Center for the Study of Public Policy, 1970; Hertling, James: Bennett emphasizes benefits of choice, rigor, and character. *Education Week* 4: 15 (April 15, 1985).

26. Lerner, B.: Vouchers for literacy: Second chance legislation. *Phi Delta Kappan* 63: 252–254 (1981).

27. Garms, W.I.: Commentary: Striking a balance between individual choice and the interests of the state. *Education Week* (April 1983): 24.

28. Jencks, Christopher: *Education Vouchers.*

29. Warren, Jim: Alum Creek voucher project. *Educational Researcher* 5: 13–15 (March 1976).

30. LaNoue, George R.: Vouchers: The end of public education? *Teachers College Record* 73: 304–319 (December 1971).

31. *Mueller v. Allen,* 463 U.S. 388 (1983).

32. The uncertain benefits of school choice: *U.S. News & World Report* (November 6, 1989): 79–82.

33. Ibid.

34. Fiske, Edward H.: Choice of public schools may be wave of future. *New York Times* (June 4, 1989): Y13.

35. Chira, Susan: The rules of the marketplace are applied to the classroom. *New York Times* (June 12, 1991): A1.

36. Carr, Robert W.: Markets can't fix schools' problems. *Wall Street Journal* (May 12, 1991): A19.

37. Hunt, James B.: Education for economic growth. In Noll, James Wm.: *Taking Sides,* 4th ed. Guilford, CT: Dushkin, 1987, pp. 116–122.

38. Ibid., p. 118.

39. National Commission on Excellence in Education: *A Nation at Risk: The Imperative for Educational Reform.* Washington, DC: U.S. Government Printing Office, 1983.

40. The Business-Higher Education Forum: *America's Competitive Challenge: The Need for a National Response.* Washington, DC: The Forum, 1983, p. v.

41. Task Force on Economic Growth: *Action for Excellence: A Comprehensive Plan to Improve Our Nation's Schools.* Denver, CO: Education Commission of the States, 1983.

42. Smothers, Ronald: Efforts to revamp nation's schools spur dispute at governor's meeting. *New York Times* (July 29, 1990): 12Y.

43. Olson, Lynn: Gallup poll finds doubts goals can be met by 2000. *Education Week* (September 5, 1990): 12.

44. Rothman, Robert: NAEP to create three standards for performance. *Education Week* (May 23, 1990): 1, 8.

45. Putka, Gary: National test for students gains support. *Wall Street Journal* (September 4, 1990): B1, B6.

46. A chat with the dean of American business history. *Financial World* (June 25, 1991): 42.

47. Ibid.

48. OECD: *Policy Conference on Economic Growth and Investment in Education.* Paris: OECD, 1962.

49. Denison, Edward F.: *Measuring the Contribution of Education (and the Residual) to Economic Growth.* Paris: OECD, 1964.

50. Benson, Charles S.: Economics of education: U.S. experience. In Boyan, Norman J., ed. *Handbook of Research on Educational Administration.* New York: Longman, 1988, pp. 360–361.

51. Koulourianos, Dimitri T.: *Educational Planning for Economic Growth.* Berkeley: Center for Research in Management Science, University of California, 1967, p. 39.

52. Welch, F.: Education in production. *Journal of Political Economy* 78: 35–59 (January–February, 1970).

53. Gintis, Herbert: Education, technology, and the characteristics of worker productivity. *American Economic Review* 61: 266–279 (May 1971).

54. *Investing in Our Children: Business and the Public Schools.* New York: Research and Policy Committee of the Committee for Economic Development, 1985.

55. Weisman, Jonathan: Be willing to fund education reform with tax hikes, business leaders told. *Business Week* (June 19, 1991): 12.

56. N.S.B.A. survey to seek data on effect of business tax breaks, ibid.

57. Schellhardt, Timothy D.: Small business seeks curb on state education spending. *Wall Street Journal* (May 22, 1991): B2.

Chapter Five

THE GLORIFICATION OF ATHLETIC COMPETITION

Sport increasingly looms larger in everyday life by occupying interests and shaping ideals of youth and adults. Athletic competition exercises an inordinate influence in both reflecting and shaping mass behavior and values of males and, to a lesser extent, females. It begins as early as Little League and continues through high school and college sports to the world of professional athletes.

This was not always the case. Athletic movements were initiated after the Civil War by students in higher education. They began as spontaneous games and sports apart from or in opposition to college authorities and later were placed under the control of faculty advisory councils. Athletic regulation began with the earliest intercollegiate athletic competition. In 1870, rowing was the first intercollegiate sport to be regulated, followed by football in 1873, and track in 1875. The early athletic associations were composed of student representatives who established rules for each sport. Not until the 1880s did college faculty representatives impose regulations upon athletics.[1]

Mass media coverage of sports in the United States did not begin until 1895 when William Randolph Hearst purchased the New York *Journal* and expanded its sports pages two to four times over his rivals.[2] The rise of football and the emergence of the daily press' sports pages were contemporaneous and for the first time provided popular news about the American college, which encouraged college administration's promotion of football. Almost all alumni became hearty supporters of intercollegiate athletic competition, and athletic victories were more important than anything else in convincing legislators to provide colleges with greater funding.[3]

High schools emulated college athletics by initially regulating rules of play but not standards of eligibility. Teachers, principals, and janitors were eligible to compete on teams and, in turn, held contests with college teams. Some players only attended school during football season. Supervision began through state associations, with the first in Wisconsin in 1896 and other states following closely behind.

Baseball was the first professional sport to gain favor, with the Cincinnati Red Stockings team that made a national tour in 1869, followed by the formation of the National League in 1876 and the rival American League in 1900. The rise of professional baseball encouraged the growth of baseball in high schools, colleges, YMCAs, clubs, and sandlots.[4]

PLAY, GAMES, AND SPORT

Such basic processes as play, games, and sport exhibit a family resemblance. Johan Huizinga observed that play is a voluntary and superfluous activity. It is engaged in freely and at leisure. It is not "ordinary" or "real" life but a world of "only pretending" which, despite a consciousness among the players that it is pretending, does not prevent them from taking it with the utmost seriousness. Play, according to Huizinga, extends within certain limits of time and space and has its own meaning. Play creates order; it is order. The aesthetic factor in play is the impulse to create orderly form, investing itself even with rhythm and harmony. Play is rule governed and circumscribes the play world. Engaging in play means a mutual withdrawal from the larger world and rejecting its norms. Play involves no material interest and no profit can be gained from it. It promotes social groups that tend to distinguish themselves by secrecy and disguise.[5]

Though games contain a vital play element, the two have been differentiated from one another by Roger Caillois' model of games. His model classifies games into four types: *agôn* (competition); *alea* (chance); *mimicry* (pretense); and *ilinx* (vertigo). Within each categories different examples of games can be listed; these specific games fall within a range of *paidia* (free improvisation and fantasy) to an inverse tendency called *ludus* (games governed by convention to obtain a determinate result).

Those games of greatest interest here are competitive ones (*agôn*) in which Caillois envisions an equality of chance prevails in order that antagonists will confront one another under ideal circumstances. Equality of chance is sufficiently important that a handicap is assigned to superior players. The basis of the game is the desire to excel and win recognition for one's ability. Competitive games presuppose discipline, perseverance, appropriate training, concentration, and assiduous effort.

The *paidia* element is highest in unregulated competition, while the *ludus* tendency prevails in regulated games.[6]

Sport can be distinguished from play and games. John Loy does not subsume sport under play because to do so would eliminate professional sports. Instead he contrasts games and sport on numerous criteria. Sport has a larger number and variety of formal norms and sport can therefore be conceived as an institutionalized game. By this he means that sport exhibits distinctive, enduring patterns of culture and social structure, the elements of which include norms, sanctions, knowledge, and social positions. Other differences between sport and games include the selection of teams (selected carefully in sport; more spontaneously in games); greater role differentiation in sport in contrast to the frequent performance of identical activities in games (contrast poker with football); and establishment in sport of permanent sponsoring bodies. In addition, game rules are transmitted by oral tradition while sport rules are formally codified and enforced by a governing body; sport requires greater knowledge and physical skills; and training for games is casual but for sport it is acquired through institutionalized formal instruction.

Loy distinguishes four levels of social organization in sport: primary, technical, managerial, and corporate levels. At the primary level, face-to-face relations prevail and administrative leadership is not formally delegated (as in a sandlot baseball game). Simultaneous face-to-face relations no longer prevail at the technical level but members still know one another. Administrative leadership is officially designated. This level is characteristic of scholastic and college athletic teams. Some of the large professional ball clubs would represent the managerial level in which members may not know everyone but would know one or more of the professional leaders. The corporate level is characterized by bureaucratic organizations consisting of major governing bodies of amateur and professional sport at the national and international levels.

Kinds of involvement, according to Loy, can be assessed in terms of relations to the production of a sport in terms of producers and consumers. Producers are primary (contestants); secondary (those who do not compete but perform tasks that have sport consequences, as owners, coaches, and trainers); and tertiary (those involved in a sport situation whose activities have no direct technological consequences as cheerleaders, band members, and concession workers).

Consumers as well can be divided into three groups: primary (those in attendance at a sport competition); secondary (those who vicariously involve themselves in sport through television or radio); and tertiary (those involved with sport other than as spectators, as in sport conversation or reading about sports).[7]

The institutionalization of sport results in social activities becoming organized in a relatively enduring way. Sport is therefore organized distinctively based on a unique form of social activity. These social activities provide a basis for the participants' social identity and serve as a link to other social structures (media, family, government, and education). The institutional qualities embody regulations and standards that serve as agents of social control. Modern sport differs from earlier sport by the extent to which it has become rationalized; that is, its formerly expressive and nonutilitarian activities have been transformed into instrumental and utilitarian activities (with the shift from *paidia* to *ludus*). Sport has become a formal ludic activity. These changes are signified by bureaucratic organizations, formalized procedures, specialized personnel, professionalized training, technologized equipment, and commercialized sponsorship.[8]

IDEOLOGY AND SPORT

Sport can be better understood by comprehending its underlying ideologies. An *ideology* is a system of beliefs, opinions, and attitudes. The beliefs and opinions may or may not be true; the attitudes may be realistic or unrealistic, undistorted or distorted. The prevailing ideology undergirding a sport provides a rationale, explanation for behavior, and a sense of direction and purpose. Four ideologies may be especially useful in explaining sport activity: functionalism, interactionism, neo-Marxism, and the American Dream.

Functionalism views society as an entity in which all the parts function to maintain one another as a whole, with the disruption of one part provoking readjustment among the others. A functionalist approach to sport seeks its structural relationship to the larger culture. Organized sport has expanded with industrialization and technology. Parallels can also be found between religion and sport ritual. While some attempt has been made to relate the Protestant ethic to the growth of sport, this hypothesis is not supported internationally because of high sport achievement in many non-Protestant nations. What can be found in all societies where sport holds an important place is that the achievement motive is basic. The greatest emphasis on achievement can be found in the upper-middle class. In addition to the achievement motive, other value orientations are the exertion of power, obedience in team sports, and asceticism in individual sports.

The main functions that sport serves within culture and society are pattern maintenance and integration. Functionalism observes that sport socializes the young, and in primitive societies socializes towards adult and warfare skills as well. Sport is structured in modern societies according to subsystems of social class and gender; it thereby serves to integrate these systems. Social dysfunctions may develop when competitive values conflict with cooperative values in the larger culture. Another conflict may occur between the values of affiliation and achievement. The relation between affiliation and achievement may be strong or weak depending on the social control imposed on the sport (comparatively strong in golf; weak in professional boxing). Sport has also functioned to diffuse technical inventions such as the bicycle and the automobile and has influenced fashion and health practices. Sport serves different functions depending upon the cultural level. In primitive cultures, sport's function is universal, frequently religious, collectively oriented, and related to adult and warfare skills; whereas in modern society sport's function is pattern maintenance and integration, individual oriented and specific in skill training.[9]

Functionalism, while it provides a better understanding of system maintenance, views the structure of society as the normal way modern societies function. Thus if sport is viewed as an input to societal maintenance, conflict in sport, such as violence among players or fans, is simply defined as deviance or antisocial behavior and research becomes preoccupied with ways to eliminate it. But what may appear to the dominant group as deviance or social disorganization may not be so perceived by minority groups because they adhere to different norms. Functionalism overlooks the complexities of power in society, the relation of culture to hegemony, the role of sport in this relation, and the conflicting values among different social groups.

A second ideological approach to sport is interactionism. Its tenets are that human beings act toward things according to the meanings that the things have for them. These meanings are the product of social interaction and are modified by each individual through an interpretive process used in dealing with signs.[10]

Erving Goffman has used interactionism to gain a greater understanding of sport. He explores an "encounter" or "focused gathering," which involves a single visual or cognitive focus of attention, an openness to verbal communication, and mutual relevance of acts. Encounters can be found in card games, dancing, jury deliberation, love-making, and boxing. What becomes significant in encounters is what is attended to and how the situation is defined. With games, "rules of irrelevance" are employed, as in checkers when participants will accept bottle tops, gold figurines, or uniformed men standing on colored flagstones as suitable for playing the game. A set of rules informs players what should not be given relevance and what should be treated as real. A game generates roles and identities, as in baseball by identifying the third baseman's role and establishing a meaning for the event "grounding out to third." A game creates a world of meaning different from all other worlds except when the same game is played at other times. Each encounter has its own resources and roles that Goffman calls "realized resources." In each encounter, the problem of how to allocate these resources must be solved. The attributes of the participants will have to be considered in deciding on allocation, as in skills that lead to the selection of partners or in awarding prizes. The basic activity in a game is a "move," which is not communicated like a message or performed like tasks or deeds, but is simply made or taken. Each move is selected from a small number of possibilities, largely determined by the previous moves of the other team. To be at ease in an encounter is to be subject to its rules, so as to be entranced by the meanings they generate. Not everyone plays by the rules. One reason that cheaters are resented is that they shortcircuit the game's outcome and destroy its reality-generating power.[11]

While interaction gives greater attention to the transactions among sport participants and their symbolic meanings than do other theories, it fails to explain the larger social structure in which these encounters occur. Many problems found in sport encounters may stem partly or entirely from the larger social order, such as illegal betting, graft, use of illegal drugs, hooliganism, and the attitude of "winning at all costs." Thus by ignoring the larger social structure, interactionism cannot address issues of power, conflict, and change. Interactionism offers the beginnings of a teleological, rather than causal, explanation of human action but without placing it within the context of a theory of society.

A third ideology is neo-Marxism. Sport, for the neo-Marxist, is a mere extension of capitalistic imperialism. International organization of sport is tied to imperialist international organizations, and close links can be found between civilian and military sport insofar as Western military sport is connected directly to NATO. The Olympic sports ideology is hypocritical by seeking to hide the reality of class struggle behind the so-called "brotherhood between peoples." Sport has always been linked to the international class struggle and the Olympic movement is an important ideological element in the struggle. Bourgeois sport is a class institution integrated into capitalist production and class relations. Sport is mediated by the state which coordinates the structures of society as a whole. Many national movements—German nationalism under Prussian rule, the work of Mao Tse-Tung, and colonial nations—have struggled for the establishment of nation states and have used physical activities and sport to create a national identity. In this type of state, sport is a para-state institution for regimenting youth. This is accomplished by the state controlling youth activities, using leading athletes for propaganda purposes, and imposing competitive sport in schools as the compulsory form of physical education. Performance, competitiveness, and the seeking to eclipse records in sport are carried over from capitalism's emphasis on productivity, the search for profits, rivalry and competitiveness. The repressive techniques of capitalism are reproduced in sport: stereotyped movements, the parcelling up of the body, measurement, stopwatch timing, and the abstraction of space and time. Thus sport treats the participant as a machine just as the worker becomes a machine appendage in the capitalist system. Sport as an ideology strengthens the ideology of alienated labor and thereby sport conditions people for oppressive factory work. Sport is also tied to the financial network of monopoly capitalism, as trusts, banking groups and monopolies use international competition to reinforce their domination. In addition, sport develops its equipment and sporting goods on a capitalistic basis. Spectator sport is a commodity to be sold, and athletes are bought and sold according to supply and demand. Sport is a means of regimentation and dehumanization to be used for maintaining law and order.[12]

While neo-Marxism highlights exploitation and class conflict more effectively than other ideologies, the neo-Marxist views sport as appropriated by one class and therefore rules out conceiving it as an arena of uneasy accommodation among classes. Instead of investigating the range of evidence from the different types and levels of sport, neo-Marxism is exclusively preoccupied with the highest levels and an assumption that the pattern at the top determines all sports activity. Moreover, bourgeois ideology is equated with extreme conservatism, which is a gross oversimplification that ignores progressive and liberal elements. Sport is also said to strengthen the ideology of alienated labor. But this does not explain why sport, in contrast to work, continues to be very popular. If, on the other hand, people are so unconscious of their alienation, compensatory mechanisms like sport would be unnecessary. Additionally, if the bourgeois ideology purveyed in sport is so extensive, then how did neo-Marxists escape its influence? Thus the neo-Marxist ideology, while calling attention to some important areas neglected in other ideologies, is excessively deterministic, relies too greatly on an economic model, and fails to establish an incontrovertible correspondence between the economic model and all major forms of sport.

A fourth and final ideology is the American Dream, perhaps the most potent ideology in both sport and American life. Americans generally believe in achievement, success, and materialism. This combination of values in conjunction with equal opportunity, ambitiousness, and hard work and the means of attaining it could be considered the American Dream. Sport is an accessible way of understanding the American Dream because achievement and success are openly emphasized and rags to riches stories about sports figures abound in the mass media. Some of the core beliefs underlying the ideology are to work hard in order to succeed in competition; those who work hard gain success and are rewarded with fame, power, money, and property; since there is equal opportunity, those who fail are guilty of insufficient effort or character deficiencies.[13]

While sport may lack the social influence of society's central institutions, sport is significant symbolically by dramatizing and ritualizing the problematics of achieving respectability in a society obsessed with status, advancement, and success.[14] It captures a number of contradictions and potential sources of tension in American society—cooperation and competition, individualism and group loyalty, equality of opportunity and inequality of rank and rewards, winning and losing, success and failure—and makes them seem to fit together and thereby enables its followers to adjust to American life.

Harry Edwards conducted a systematic investigation about the nature and consequences of sport as found in leading publications; this lead to his uncovering a sports creed whose ideology seeks to convince people of the benefits and virtues of sports participation. Popular acceptance of the creed may be expected to reflect or reinforce the American Dream. The creed is expressed in seven central themes in which it is claimed that sport: (1) builds character; (2) teaches discipline; (3) provides competition and teaches competitiveness; (4) enhances physical fitness; (5) enhances mental fitness; (6) contributes to religiosity by encouraging acceptance of traditional religious precepts of American Christianity; and (7) contributes to nationalism by encouraging acceptance of patriotic values and patriotic symbols.[15]

Let us look more closely at the evidence for these beliefs (competition and sport will be presented in the next section). As for sport promoting good character, one study found in successful competitors both admirable qualities (openness, sociability, humor, and self-discipline) and less admirable ones (a need for grudge matches, inability to accept defeat, and unquestioning acceptance of the coach's authority).[16] Another study showed that as one continues in organized sport, sportsmanship diminishes in favor of the desire to win.[17]

As for teaching discipline, sport requires fortitude but Edwards believes that it selects athletes who have fortitude rather than developing it in those who do not.[18] Research investigating midwestern high school athletes found a lower delinquency rate for athletes than nonathletes.[19]

As for enhancing physical fitness, it is true for participants in minor sports who develop lifelong habits of exercise; however, Edwards indicates that with major contact sports college and professional athletes are high insurance risks because few participants finish their careers without some lifetime disability. And as for enhancing mental fitness, Edwards concludes that there is no evidence pro or con.[20]

Edwards claims that there is no hard evidence that sport promotes or detracts from formal religiosity.[21] As for contributing to nationalism, sport is an instrument of national policy in Communist and Third World nations. Whether sport in democratic societies creates long-term national loyalty is still open to investigation.

Thus, overall, the sports creed with its link to the American Dream, is more significant for its symbolic value and its ability to motivate and compel devotion rather than any hard evidence of its general validity. It functions as an integrative force in a society that reflects similar values. Of the four ideologies presented, no single one is able to explain all major aspects of sport, but each provides us with a greater understanding of a more limited range of sports phenomena.

SPORT COMPETITION

Competition in sport is of three types: first, direct competition where two opponents (individual or team) confront each other (e.g., in all contact and nearly all court sports); second, parallel competition, an indirect form, where contestants take turns competing with one another by taking turns or competing in separate areas (e.g., golf, swimming, bowling, track); and third, competition against a standard (as in archery, figure skating, trap shooting, diving, and gymnastics).[22]

A number of explanations can be offered about the compelling nature of sport competition on some contestants. One explanation is that of a differential reinforcement; that is, the winner of a competition receives more reinforcement than the other contestants. To understand competitive behavior, one would need to know the basis on which the reward is made.[23] Another view holds that competition stems from two basic drives: the drive to constantly improve one's abilities and the drive to constantly evaluate one's abilities, opinions, and emotions. An individual's competitive sport behavior, therefore, results from a desire to become better in athletic ability and a desire to discover one's performance level by comparisons with teammates and opponents.[24] The effects the audience has on competitive behavior varies. Whether the audience will have a significant effect depends upon the contestant viewing the audience as an important and relevant referent and her concern about how the audience is evaluating her.[25]

An individual's competitiveness depends upon her genetic endowment, past environmental history, and specific features of the current situation. Children who grow up in a family and social environment where competition is minimized need explicit stimuli in which they can learn to respond competitively. Continuous reinforcement enhances the learning of a particular skill; but once the skill is learned, reinforcement is more effective when introduced intermittently than continuously. Moreover, competitive behavior is shaped by the consequences it produces. In other words, competition must produce satisfaction for the child to reinforce itself. Considerable competition before the child receives positive feedback may likely discourage the child.[26] Children are not competitive in tasks with which they are unfamiliar or have not mastered. The child's competitive behavior increases with the realization that other people are present. A major surge of competitiveness begins with school attendance and the presence of other children.[27] The standards that the child pursues are decisively influenced by significant adults, peers, and the mass media. But the standards of performance may not always be realistic for the skill and developmental level of the child.[28]

Girls at one time were expected to participate in swimming, diving, ice skating, and other "graceful" activities. They learned that after about the age of twelve sport participation brings little glory; rather, they should belong to a booster club or become a cheerleader. The bias against women's athletics stems considerably from the Victorian era in which it was believed that a woman's duty was to attract a mate, bear and rear children, and serve her husband. The arguments to support this ideal were based on biological and medical opinions that sport is harmful to women and on a cultural ideal of feminine dress and behavior. The myth of the fragile female was shattered in World War II when women played important roles in the military and civilian labor force. The women's movement of the 1960s, the fitness movement of the 1970s, and the growth of women's role models in sport contributed to a wider recognition of women's role in athletics. Since passage of Title IX of the Higher Education Act in 1972, athletics and fitness have become more socially acceptable and available for women of all ages.[29] According to R.B. Alderman, "There is absolutely no reason to believe that women are not as competitive as men if subjected to the same cultural conditioning relevant to competitiveness in sport."[30]

Competition can be both frustrating and create anxiety among the contestants. When two contestants or two teams are attempting to achieve the same reward and the outcome is so defined that a disproportionate share will result, then frustration will automatically occur in the loser. Further frustration may occur when the loser is required to conceal his frustration and act like a sportsman.[31] Even for the winner the contest may be frustrating because one's opponent is attempting to block or thwart goal-directed behavior.

Anxiety is also common in competitive sport. Experimental and experiential evidence indicates that anxiety is common in competitive situations and its effect on sport performance is extremely debilitating. This anxiety has been explained by using a model in which an objective demand—a particular contest—serves as an aroused stimulus. The situation is interpreted by the athlete as being physically or psychologically dangerous and therefore a threat. As a response, an anxiety reaction occurs. Tests have been developed to assess anxiety levels in contestants.[32]

Much of the frustration and anxiety may stem from the ideology of winning. Infrequently subscribed to today is the Grantland Rice adage, "It isn't that you win or lose but how you play the game." In terms of success, a non-zero-sum type competition allows varying degree of partially winning and partially losing. If success can be evaluated in terms of satisfaction, enjoyment, and athletic improvement, then a non-zero-sum type competition prevails. But the prevailing sport competition in the United States today is a zero-sum type competition wherein one competitor wins and the other loses. This attitude was conveyed by Vince Lombardi's remark that "Winning isn't everything, it's the only thing." George Allen added, "Every time you win, you're reborn; when you lose, you die a little." Bill Musselman of Minnesota took it one step further: "Defeat is worse than death because you have to live with defeat."[33]

The "winning at all costs" attitude may be a prominent factor in the increased violence and cheating in organized sports that threaten the basic rationale for sport and its ideology founded on the American Dream. "Winning at all costs" has often led to discord and conflict. As noted in chapter two, discord implies a clashing in personal relations in the form of quarreling, factitiousness, or antagonism. Conflict is opposition or antagonistic struggle, the aim of which is the annihilation, defeat or subjugation of the other person or group. A principal form of conflict is violence, which is a sudden and extremely forceful act that causes physical harm or suffering to others.

Learning how to use violence begins early in the sport socialization process. The process begins by observing the behavior of role models and significant others engage in such behavior. Albert Bandura has found that children will repeat adult aggression seen live, on film, or on television.[34]

Hockey is unique among sports in legitimating fistfighting. Intentional assaults to injure or intimidate an opponent have been found in some situations to have a positive effect on the culprits' performance. A study of the types of penalties assessed during four seasons of the National Hockey League found a positive relationship between the incidence of aggressive penalties (e.g., slashing, spearing, charging, fighting) early in the game and winning the game.[35] The "win-at-all costs" carries within it the seeds of its own destruction by operating outside the rule structure. Though it was once assumed that sport violence was unique to males, increasingly the same behaviors are observed among female athletes.[36] As for the fans, a study of 68 newspaper accounts of crowd violence during or after sporting events found 75 percent of the episodes incited by game violence.[37] Other investigators have found that some combination of ethnic, political, economic, or religious strains underlie sport-related riots.[38] Competitive sport has been used to demonstrate cultural, ideological, racial, or ethnic superiority, thereby serving to link sport to societal problems.

Another form of sport deviance is cheating, which involves bending the rules of interpretation or breaking the rules of a sport in order to control the outcome. Some forms of cheating have become routinized or institutionalized (e.g., intentionally falling in hockey, faking an injury to pressure an official to award a penalty, or hitting an opponent after a whistle to draw a retaliatory penalty). But other forms of cheating, if detected, may be severely punished (e.g., fixing games, falsifying transcripts, awarding unearned credits, playing ineligible athletes). Cheating is regulated in sport by an elaborate set of rules observed by officials and fans, and also by the knowledge that cheating by one side may be matched by the other side and thereby neutralize one another.

Other serious problems afflict the sports world. The Knight Foundation Commission on Intercollegiate Athletics observed that many high school athletic programs are beginning to emulate the worst features of college programs by emphasizing financial and athletic outcomes at the expense of the educational value of sport. The Commission recommended that athletes spend as much time preparing themselves academically as they do athletically. Athletes, they said, should be guided toward institutions that will place their welfare as students and their personal maturation ahead of their athletic performance. In too many cases, the educational context for collegiate athletics competition is pushed aside because of institutional indifference, presidential neglect, the growing commercialization of sport, and the desire to win at all costs.[39] The Southern Association of Colleges and Schools urged colleges and universities to assume clear authority through the president of each institution for the administrative and financial operations of athletic programs, and also require student athletes to meet the same academic standards and curriculum requirements as other students.[40] The Knight Commission, in addressing coaches, urged them to make the student-athlete understand that fewer than one in a hundred will ever make their living from their athletic ability, and to emphasize the value of a college degree and the importance of the athlete's behavior on and off the field.[41] Of greatest importance, the Commission should stress that winning at all costs is never acceptable.

ENDNOTES

1. Van Dalen, Deobold B. and Bennett, Bruce L.: *A World History of Physical Education: Cultural, Philosophical, Comparative* (2nd ed.), Englewood Cliffs, NJ: Prentice-Hall, 1971, pp. 408–409.

2. Ibid., p. 408.

3. Rudolf, Frederick: *The American College and University: A History.* New York: Vintage Books, 1962, pp. 384–85; Veysey, Lawrence R.: *The Emergence of the American University.* Chicago: University of Chicago Press, 1970, p. 351.

4. Van Dalen and Bennett, *A World History,* p. 411.

5. Huizinga, Johan: The nature of play. In Morgan, William J. and Meier, Klaus V. (eds.). *Philosophic Inquiry in Sport.* Champaign, IL: Human Kinetics Publishers, 1988, pp. 3–6.

6. Caillois, Roger: The structure and classification of games. In ibid., pp. 7–15.

7. Loy, John W., Jr.: The nature of sport: A definitional effort. In Hart, Marie and Birrell, Susan (eds.) *Sport in the Sociocultural Process.* Dubuque, IA: Wm. C. Brown, 1981, pp. 21–37.

8. McPherson, Barry D.; Curtis, James E.; and Loy, John W.: *The Social Significance of Sport.* Champaign, IL: Human Kinetics Books, 1989, pp. 18–19.

9. Luschen, Gunther: The interdependence of sport and culture. In Hart and Birrell, *Sport in the Sociocultural Process,* pp. 92–106.

10. Blumer, Herbert: *Symbolic Interactionism: Perspectives and Method.* Englewood Cliffs, NJ: Prentice-Hall, 1969, ch. 1.

11. Goffman, Irving: Fun in games. In Hart and Birrell: *Sport,* pp. 40–91.

12. Brohm, Jean-Marie: Theses toward a political sociology of sport, ibid., 107–113.

13. Nixon, Howard L. II: *Sport and the American Dream.* New York: Leisure Press, 1984, pp. 10, 17.

14. Loy, John W.; McPherson, Barry D.; and Kenyon, Gerald: *Sport and Social Systems.* Reading, MA: Addison-Wesley, 1978, pp. 413–414.

15. Edwards, Harry: *Sociology of Sport.* Homewood, IL: Dorsey Press, 1973.

16. Ryan, Francis: An investigation of personality differences associated with competitive ability, and further observations on competitive ability in athletics. In Wedge, B.M. (ed.): *Psychosocial Problems of College Men.* New Haven: Yale University Press, 1958, pp. 113–139.

17. Webb, Harry: Professionalization of attitudes towards play among adolescents. In Kenyon, G.S. (ed.): *Aspects of Contemporary Sports Sociology.* Chicago: Athletic Institute, 1969, pp. 161–178.

18. Edwards, *Sociology of Sport.*

19. Schafer, Walter E.: Some social sources and consequences of interscholastic athletics: The case of participation and delinquency. In Kenyon: *Aspects,* pp. 29–44.

20. Edwards, *Sociology of Sport.*

21. Ibid.

22. McPherson, Curtis, and Loy, *Social Significance,* p. 16.

23. Church, R.: Applications of behavior theory to social psychology. In Samuels, R.A., et al. (eds.): *Social Facilitation and Imitative Behavior.* Boston: Allyn and Bacon, 1968.

24. Festinger, Leon: A theory of social comparison processes. *Human Relations,* 7, 1954, 117–140.

25. Cottrell, N.B.: Performance in the presence of other human beings. Mere presence, audience, and affiliation effects. In Samuels, R.A. et al. (eds.): *Social Facilitation.*

26. Alderman, R.B.: *Psychological Behavior in Sport.* Philadelphia: W.B. Saunders, 1974, pp. 88–89.

27. Ibid., pp. 98–99.

28. Sherif, Carolyn W.: The social context of competition. In Hart and Birrell, *Sport,* pp. 132–155.

29. McPherson, Curtis, and Loy: *Social Significance of Sport.* ch. 9.

30. Alderman, *Psychological Behavior,* p. 100.

31. Layman, E.: Aggression in relation to play and sports. In *Contemporary Psychology of Sport.* Chicago: Athletic Institute, 1970.

32. Martens, Rainer; Vealey, Robin S.; and Burton, Damon: *Competitive Anxiety in Sport.* Champaign, IL: Human Kinetics Books, 1990, ch. 1.

33. Quoted in Michener, James A.: *Sport in America.* New York: Random House, 1976, pp. 420–21.

34. Bandura, Albert: *Aggression: A Social Learning Analysis.* Englewood Cliffs, NJ: Prentice-Hall, 1973.

35. Widmeyer, W.N. and Birch, J.S.: Aggression in professional ice hockey: A strategy for success or a reaction to failure? *Journal of Psychology* 117(1): 77–84.

36. Bredemeier, B.J.: Moral reasoning and the perceived legitimacy of intentionally injurious sport acts. *Journal of Sport Psychology* 7(2): 110–124.

37. Calhoun, Donald W.: *Sport, Culture, and Personality,* 2nd ed. Champaign, IL: Human Kinetics Publishers, 1987, p. 292.

38. Smith Michael D.: Sport and collective violence. In Ball, Donald W. and Loy, John W.: *Sport and Social Order: Contributions to the Sociology of Sport.* Reading, MA: Addison-Wesley, 1975, pp. 281–330.

39. Pitsch, Mark: High schools urged to assist in reform of collegiate sports. *Education Week* (March 27, 1991): 1, 17.

40. Weiss, Samuel: Southern college group seeking tougher supervision of athletics. *New York Times* (May 19, 1991): 1, 14.

41. Knight Commission tells presidents to use their power to reform the 'fundamental premises' of college sports. *Chronicle of Higher Education* 37 (March 27, 1991): A1, A33, A36.

Chapter Six

THE TESTING MOVEMENT IN EDUCATION

Educational Testing can be viewed as either an honorific or pejorative term, depending upon one's interpretation of the relative merits or deficiencies in its development, use and abuse in American society. On the one hand, proponents of increased use of testing tend to assume a meritocratic argument for their ends and means. In their view, if education is based on equal access so that students with the potentials most valued by society are to be in a better position to develop them, then testing needs to be implemented and refined in order to assure that those talents can be identified, nurtured, and rewarded. On those terms, tomorrow's leaders will be sorted through the competitive system of grading, promotion, honors, and awards. Those who fail will be notified that they were given a fair chance and must now assume societal roles consonant with demonstrated abilities. On the other hand, egalitarians, who seek fraternity and solidarity as social goals, would contend that the talents so rewarded would most likely be those which the advantaged already possess, leading to a crass hierarchy of social values that is highly conservative, e.g., undesirable social relations that are quite aggressive in nature.

There is no question that the testing movement, with its emphasis on intelligence quotients (I.Q.), aptitude, and standardized tests, has exerted an enormous influence on education and, in the process, has served to magnify competition in schools and society. This chapter provides a general assessment of the impact of the testing movement, particularly in terms of reinforcing competitive educational programs and practices, e.g., grading, ability grouping, tracking, standardized testing, and international comparisons of educational systems.

GRADING: PARAMETERS AND PITFALLS

In the early days of one-room common schools in mid-nineteenth century America, dividing pupils into grade levels and administering grades to them were almost unheard of practices. As the number of classes and students increased, however, grade levels were established to promote greater instructional effectiveness. Pestalozzian instruction and more effective divisions of labor that better used the special abilities of teachers also encouraged the use of grades. Thus, in theory, grades and grade levels were introduced to assure improvement in instruction. Yet the onus of grading clearly shifted the responsibility for achievement to the *student;* it also placed her in a much more competitive system in which success or failure was measured by grades.

Since the origins of systematic grading practices, a certain invidious mythology has sustained itself over the years despite what research has had to say about the inefficacy of grades. Charles Hargis, a researcher in special education, has ably and succinctly summarized many of the myths surrounding the administration of grades, particularly as they relate to competition in education:

(1) Grades motivate pupils to strive for better grades. To the contrary, Hargis argues that "failure and failing grades are negatively motivating. They contribute to the condition called 'learned helplessness' . . . [and] make students do worse."[1] Motivation through grading would appear to stimulate only some pupils who are already achieving at high levels.

(2) Grades constitute satisfactory indicators of learning. According to Hargis's research, they indicate very little about specific educational attainment. Indeed, "they say nothing of strengths, weaknesses, readiness, deficits or achievement. Grades are only comparative and normative."[2] Put another way, they serve mainly the function of sifting and sorting students within the microcosmic world of inner classroom walls, a sanctum providing no real proof of promise or achievement outside its sheltered confines.

(3) Grades do provide helpful information for redesigning instructional activities. Hargis questions even that conventional piece of wisdom because grades, in themselves, do not respond to the myriad kinds of assistance that individual students might require. In fact, not even standardized achievement tests reveal such specific information.[3]

(4) Grades are objective. That statement is filled with mythological assumptions. Actually, there are many external and internal variables that can influence grading practices to the point that "objectivity" becomes a mere charade, e.g., teacher and pupil sex variables;

racial, class, and cultural differences; personal characteristics; how well the teacher likes the individual students, etc.[4]

(5) Grades prepare students for life's harsher realities. If one accepts a more or less competitive view of social reality, Hargis concedes that grades establish a competitive classroom ethos; however, he also urges us to consider that cooperative pedagogical activities might be sacrificed in the process.[5]

(6) Grades afford concrete feedback on instruction from the teacher to students. Yet "grades are not specific . . . [and] without specific information about what is wrong, students are kept demoralized and confused."[6]

Libertarian critic, John Holt, pushes the antigrading argument to its ultimate extreme: "I do not believe that testing and grading perform any inherent or useful function in learning; in fact, they corrupt and impede the learning process."[7] A slightly more moderate viewpoint is taken by Edward Burns, himself a recognized critic of the uses and abuses of educational tests:

> Grade equivalents are said to be used for several reasons including the following: (1) determining a child's strengths and weaknesses, (2) planning instruction, (3) grouping pupils, (4) maintaining a record of a child's academic progress, and (5) for the many grants, reports, and documents requiring information pertaining to a school or a school district's academic status. Grade equivalents are used because of their apparent simplicity and because they are believed to be easily understood. However grade equivalents are used or whatever benefits grade equivalents might yield, these indices should be regarded as only a superficial reflection of a child's academic progress.[8]

THE EDUCATIONAL TESTING MOVEMENT IN AMERICA

Recent revisionist historians have hypothesized that the widespread use of educational testing emerged in the first decade of this century as the United States sought to ameliorate growing social, economic, and political problems resulting from vastly increasing industrialization, urbanization, and immigration. A far more complex society presumably demanded new efforts at social engineering which crosscut ideological lines and public/private barriers: "The testing movement, financed by corporate foundations, helped meet the need for 'continuous measurement' and 'accountability.' It also served as a vital part of the hand which helped fashion the peculiar meritocracy within that state."[9]

Two strands of testing dominated the search for meritocracy: the development of "intelligence" tests and the growth of "achievement" tests.

The intelligence testing movement was spurred by Alfred Binet, a French psychologist who, in 1904, worked with a special commission to initiate testing techniques to identify "children whose lack of success in normal classrooms suggested the need for some form of special education."[10] Binet's testing consisted of a compilation of short tasks tied to everyday life problems and rudimentary reasoning processes. Age levels were assigned to each task so that the relationship between the child's chronological age and her "mental" age became her "intelligence quotient" (I.Q.). Interestingly, Binet himself recognized some of the inherent limitations and pernicious social consequences of his own test device: " . . . if reified as an entity, [it] could be perverted and used as an indelible label, rather than as a guide for identifying children who needed help."[11] Binet's admonitions went largely unheeded and IQ testing became a commonplace mechanism for universal measurement of school-aged children.

In the United States, Henry Goddard, psychological director of a training school for the "feeble-minded" in New Jersey, popularized Binet's measurement scales and techniques, but in far cruder, more injurious, fashion. Inventing the label "moron" for what he termed "high-grade defectives," Goddard was heavily affected by the eugenics movement of the early 1900s. He advocated the deployment of IQ tests to "recognize limits, segregate and curtail breeding to prevent further deterioration of an endangered American stock, threatened by immigration from without and by prolific reproduction of its feeble-minded within."[12] Indeed, Goddard's testing recommendations were used to classify immigrants at Ellis Island and as justifications for restrictions on immigration through the 1920s.

Lewis Terman, a Stanford psychologist, further legitimized the Binet test throughout the United States in the form of the Stanford-Binet IQ instrument. A particular nuance in Terman's reformulation was to cast the test as a "sorting machine" for classifying people into various and sundry occupational categories:

> The time is not too far distant when intelligence tests will become a recognized and widely used instrument for determining vocational fitness . . . When thousands of children who have been tested by the Binet scale have been followed into the industrial world, and their success in various occupations noted, we

> shall know fairly definitively . . . the minimum "intelligence quotient" necessary for success in each leading occupation.[13]

In the groves of academe, Carl Brigham, of Princeton University, used the IQ instrument for his work with the College Board and the development of the Scholastic Aptitude Test (SAT) in 1925. According to Brigham,

> the tests have proved most useful in the office of the Supervisor of Freshmen [at Princeton]. For the first time we have been able to locate with some certainty, the men of good intellectual ability, who are neglecting their studies and are not realizing their maximum capacities along academic lines.[14]

Brigham also extolled the Nordic race and its presumed superiority, fearing that it would be made inferior if intermingled with Alpine, Mediterranean, or Negro blood: "We must face a possibility of racial admixture here that is infinitely worse than that faced by any European country today, for we are incorporating the Negro into our racial stock, while all of Europe is comparatively free from this taint."[15]

At the level of manpower needs for the armed services, another IQ psychologist, Robert M. Yerkes, of Harvard University, developed the Army Mental Tests which the United States military used to recruit for over one million personnel during World War I. Yerkes' tests also purported to show the "meagre intelligence" of immigrant groups and "to establish the relation of inferior intelligence to delinquency and crime."[16] His work was closely tied to that of Brigham in terms of its impact on limiting immigration.

The achievement testing movement, pivotally influenced by psychologist Edward L. Thorndike of Columbia University, has been integrally related to societal equations of competition and meritocracy. For the full first half of this century, Thorndike lectured literally thousands of educators on such notions as:

> To him that hath a superior intellect is given also on the average a superior character.
>
> The abler persons in the world in the long run are the more clean, decent, just, and kind.[17]

Claiming the genetic superiority of the white race, Thorndike argued that "mental and moral inheritance from near ancestry is a fact" and that "racial differences in original nature are not mere myths."[18] Accordingly, he advocated a systematic plan of eugenics, including the legal sterilization of "dull or vicious epileptics and for certain sorts of dull and vicious sex perverts."[19]

In specific terms of educational testing, Thorndike's works had a profound impact on school teachers and school systems throughout the nation. His theoretical studies and statistical procedures lent "scientific" credence to the social agendas buried beneath his disciplinary efforts. Indeed, his meticulous attempts to quantify nearly everything he touched added a certain air of "objectivity" to his myriad criteria for classifying, evaluating, and standardizing pedagogical content and methods, as well as those students engulfed in his wide-reaching "sorting machine." For example, Thorndike's achievement testing network included his famous Handwriting Scale, "the first calibrated instrument for the measurement of an educational product,"[20] and a broad assortment of *norm*-referenced tests for all grade levels. ("Norm" refers to "normal," "average," or "typical" in the sense that students are measured against each other, rather than in terms of their absolute knowledge of a particular body of content material. On the other hand, *criterion*-referenced measurement deals with how pupils master a specific set of academic knowledge.) Thus, by definition, Thorndike's test methodologies reinforced an implicit system of competition in schools across America.

In more recent times, Berkeley psychologist Arthur Jensen and Nobel Prize laureate William Schockley, a physicist, have applied their theories of racial psychology to blunt the impetus of compensatory education programs for black students in the 1960s and 1970s. Shockley specifically used the phrase "raceology" to characterize his contributions. In particular, his social agenda called for:

> a voluntary sterilization plan for those with low IQ's and, therefore, presumably inferior genes. His proposal incorporated a bonus plan which was graduated so that the lower the IQ, the greater the material reward one would receive for submitting to the operation. By the early 1970's, some state legislatures were seriously considering Shockley's proposal or a variant of it.[21]

Jensen's studies, presented in a controversial 1969 issue of the *Harvard Educational Review,* generated a proverbial storm of debate on the issue of nature (genetic determinants) versus nurture (environmental determinants). According to Jensen, fifty years of IQ testing had disclosed that American blacks tended to score 15 points below their white counterparts—even though Jensen, himself, took scant account of the cultural bias of the tests themselves. Nevertheless, he argued that any failings in anti-poverty programs were due to the "fact" that "they were trying to do the impossible, i.e., raise IQ which was 80 percent genetically determined."[22] Thus, using his logic, any deficiencies in compensatory education could be readily explained and justified. Moreover, any need for increasing their availability could just as easily be curtailed.

In addition, another modern-day IQ psychologist, Richard Herrnstein, has written extensively on the presumed correlation of genetic intelligence and social class in an attempt to reinforce Jensen's arguments. Herrnstein insists that American citizens should resign themselves to the "cold facts" of such an assumed, but unproven, correlation:

> Greater wealth, health, freedom, fairness, and educational opportunity are not going to give us the equalitarian society of our philosophical heritage. It will instead give us a society sharply graduated, with even greater innate separation between the top and the bottom, and even more uniformity within families as far as inherited abilities are concerned.... When people can freely take their natural level in society, the upper classes will, virtually by definition, have greater capacity than the lower.[23]

In effect, Herrnstein's claims serve to justify an almost "pure" form of meritocracy in which hierarchical leadership patterns are accepted as givens.

RECENT DEVELOPMENTS IN EDUCATION TESTING

In the 1960s, and then again in the 1980s, a new wave of educational testing moved the operative thrust of measurement and assessment from the local school level to wider state policy initiatives. By 1985, some 39 states were involved in some form of minimum competency testing (MCT) of students.[24] In most cases, pupils in those states were required to pass such tests before receiving a high school diploma.

States have the right to establish standards for high school graduation and minimum performance standards for students. Courts have also approved the right of local school boards to use standards higher than the minimum in testing for promotion.[25] They generally have upheld the use of MCT unless the test is found to be discriminatory or unconstitutional. Students are entitled to notice of test standards and an opportunity to satisfy those standards before a school can withhold diplomas. Courts have prohibited the use of MCT as a graduation prerequisite until all students subject to the requirement have entered first grade under desegregated conditions.[26] Also, courts have ruled that pupils with disabilities need more notice of the MCT requirements than nondisabled students to ensure them adequate opportunity to prepare for the test.[27]

Plaintiffs in Florida claimed that the state's competency test violated the due-process and equal-protection clauses of the Fourteenth Amendment. The Fifth Circuit Court of Appeals placed the burden of proof on the state of Florida to show that the test actually covered instructional material presented to students.[28] The court found that the test was valid in terms of both the curriculum and instruction, and that any causal link between the disproportionate failure rate of black students and past discrimination had been severed. Consequently, Florida was allowed to deny diplomas to those who failed the test, beginning with the 1983 class. However, critics contend that there is a danger that teachers will teach to the test to make the test valid, which reduces the teacher's discretion and flexibility, narrows the curriculum, and might cause the minimum requirements to become the maximum.

Teacher competency tests have also been in vogue since the late 1970s and early 1980s. At present more than half the states mandate admission tests for entrance into teacher education programs, and nearly all the states require tests (e.g., the National Teacher Examination) for teacher certification. Some states require prospective teachers to pass a test of teaching competence or mastery of subject matter. To ensure fairness and relevance, developers of such tests must be certain their test questions are valid and that test scores accurately reflect a prospective teacher's achievement. Research into the usefulness of state-devised teacher competency tests is limited, and studies of the NTE have yielded mixed findings. One study showed that student teachers who scored well on the NTE generally had received high ratings from their supervisors during practice teaching.[29] On the other hand, an earlier review of NTE found no evidence of validity.[30]

Competency testing has also proven to be controversial in American jurisprudence. In 1971, the United States Supreme Court held in *Griggs v. Duke Power Company* that tests used to screen applicants must clearly be related to the job and its tasks, a ruling that also applies to the use of screening tests for teachers. The Court, however, upheld South Carolina's right to use the NTE to determine pay scales and eligibility for certification, even though blacks scored lower than whites, because the proportion of black teachers approximated the proportion of black citizens.[31] Such court decisions have spawned enormous debate, particularly concerning whether they, in effect, serve to limit the number of minority-group members who might enter the teaching profession. As educational historian Joseph Newman observes:

> At a time when the percentage of minority students in elementary and secondary schools is increasing, the percentage of minority teachers is decreasing. . . . In the public schools, the percentage of black students has risen more than 16 percent, yet the percentage of black teachers has fallen, slowly but steadily, for three decades—from 8 percent in 1970 to 6 percent in 1990. If this trend continues, only 5 percent of America's teachers will be black in the year 2000. The outlook for Hispanic teachers is similarly bleak.[32]

Another contentious issue in law and education is the practice of tracking, i.e., the subdividing of students by ability or achievement level within and among curriculum groups. Typically, these groups are academic (college preparatory), general, and vocational curriculums. In 1967 the use of tracking in a Washington, D.C., case was ruled unconstitutional in federal district court (*Hobson v. Hansen*).[33] The plaintiffs contended that some children were erroneously assigned to lower tracks and had little opportunity to advance to higher tracks because of the limited nature of the curriculum and the absence of remedial instruction. The court ruled that the plan denied equal opportunities for students in lower tracks. The court also emphasized that it was not abolishing the use of track systems; classifications reasonably related to educational purposes were constitutionally permissible unless they discriminated against identifiable groups of children.

The Fifth Circuit Court of Appeals struck down a tracking plan in Jackson, Mississippi, and held that students could not be placed in classes on the basis of standardized test scores until a desegregated school district had been developed to the court's satisfaction.[34] In a Louisiana case the federal district court held that the classification of students on a nondiscriminatory basis is permissible, but that tracking could not be used to perpetuate racial segregation.[35] The Fifth Circuit Court of Appeals concluded in an Alabama case than an ability grouping, which had been initiated shortly after a court desegregation order and resulted in a continuation of segregated schools, violated protected rights.[36] Not all grouping plans are struck down, as seen in a San Francisco case involving the assignment of students to an academically elite senior high school based on student achievement. Blacks, Hispanics, and students from low socioeconomic backgrounds were underrepresented, resulting in a lawsuit. The Ninth Circuit Court of Appeals found that there was no clear evidence of an intent to discriminate and deemed the use of ability grouping to be educationally justified.[37]

In cases of tracking and grouping the courts generally appeal to the due-process and equal-protection clauses of the Fourteenth Amendment. They are concerned that tests used for assignment purposes are unbiased and valid; that scores on both standardized reading and mathematics tests are used; and that the grouping plan help the school achieve its educational objectives rather than foster racial discrimination.

Above and beyond judicial rulings, there is research evidence that clearly runs counter to the advisability of ability grouping and tracking. Studies disclose that such grouping appears to heighten the academic differences that children bring to kindergarten and first grade. Those differences seem to be rather meagre when they begin school. According to Newman,

> The studies most favorable to ability grouping show that it offers only slight advantages to students in the top groups—their achievement tends to be as high in ungrouped classrooms. The studies least favorable to ability grouping show that it does significant harm to the achievement of the students in the bottom groups.[38]

Jeannie Oakes, perhaps the most perceptive critic of tracking and ability grouping, has argued that such grouping arrangements actually make the teacher's tasks more difficult and burdensome. Instead of grouping children, she advocates wider use of cooperative learning models, which she views as especially helpful to students who seem to need more assistance, monitoring, or coaching.[39] Whereas ability grouping sets students apart from one another, cooperative practices bear more propensity for bringing them together.

Other studies reveal additional pernicious effects of tracking and grouping within the very ethos of classroom instruction. A self-fulfilling prophecy may be at work in any explanation of the following findings: teachers appear to be less focused on instruction of academic skills and perspectives when dealing with lower-track youth; the latter pupils are seldom able to mingle with peers who may be headed for college and achievement-oriented professions; and lower-track students seem to disclose a lessened sense of self-esteem.[40]

TESTING AND ACADEMIC PERFORMANCE: SOME INTERNATIONAL COMPARISONS

It should not be surprising that students who pursue a more rigorous academic curriculum tend to perform better on standardized tests of achievement. The American College Testing (ACT) Assessment Program has recently shown that completion of a core curriculum (four years of English and at least three years of mathematics, science, and social studies) puts students in good position to score higher on ACT college entrance examinations. Conversely, "The best way for educators to insure that working-class students will never have a serious chance at jobs that require a college degree is to encourage or simply allow them to take the easy way out of high school."[41]

Such conventional wisdom has caused some critics to urge that American schools need to adopt models and methodologies that are more akin to the relatively elitist educational systems practiced in Germany and Japan. However, as Michael Kirst has pointed out:

> About 75 percent of our students graduate from high school, and some 44 percent go on to higher education. In most other Western nations, students are diverted into vocational and technical programs at age 14 or 15, and only 15 to 30 percent are graduated from a secondary school. Considering the large percentage of teenagers the U.S. schools enroll, the level of attainment of these students is surprisingly high.[42]

Comparative educator Torsten Husén, of the University of Stockholm, has similarly argued that the value orientations of American and European schools are so different that any international comparisons are tantamount to comparing apples with oranges. From his extensive studies of high school seniors in the United States and Europe, he concludes that

> The international surveys of both mathematics and science demonstrated that the top 5 percent to 10 percent at the end of secondary education (i.e., the elite) tended to perform at nearly the same level in both comprehensive and selective systems of secondary education. Thus the elite among U.S. high school seniors did not differ considerably in their performance from their age-mates in France, England, or Germany. The comprehensive systems, where the net is cast more widely, result in a bigger "talent catch." In addition, those who are less able get a better opportunity to develop their potential than in the selective systems of the traditional European type.[43]

As for comparisons with Japan, it is noteworthy that college-bound Japanese students do tend to pursue a more rigorous college preparatory curriculum, particularly in the sciences and mathematics, than their American counterparts. Moreover, Japanese youth concentrate their energies on academic tasks to a far greater degree than their U.S. contemporaries. The emphasis on academic learning time is augmented by a longer school year in Japan (roughly one-third longer than that in the United States). Japanese students do more homework and compete more strenuously for college admissions since the latter are linked to career success with the best companies and industries.[44]

However, there are negative trade-offs and palpable hazards in the overly competitive nature of Japanese education. Continuous, seemingly endless, cramming sessions mark the daily routine of Japan's adolescents. Suicide rates among their youth have been escalating in the 1980s and 1990s. The school years become a "pressure-cooker" period in the lives of children while, ironically, the college years become more a "safety valve" in which undergraduates lead a more or less carefree existence prior to entering the competitive world of business and industry. Such relief from the customarily traumatic experiences of late adolescence is seen as a "moratorium" period—a psychosocial, culturally accepted delay of adulthood.[45] In American culture, extended forms of education, miliary service, and living at home with one's parents afford outlets for such a moratorium. (Of course, this moratorium might also be welcomed by society as a benevolent way to cool off the economy, i.e., keeping youth out of the labor market.)

Pedagogically, there are also distinctive differences in Japanese and American schools, some of which make the United States appear to be more progressively attuned to learning processes. In Japan, teachers tend to use imitation by rote learning as their principal instructional techniques; such methods emphasize memorization of factual information rather than conceptual understanding, critical analysis, or artful creativity.[46] While this pattern is certainly not uncommon in U.S. schools, the rigidity of their classroom formats seems somewhat less striking and more susceptible to at least piecemeal changes.

Yet problems abound in American pedagogy and attendant measures of assessment as well. Linda Darling-Hammond and Ann Lieberman, co-directors of the National Center for Restructuring Education, Schools, and Teaching, pose the crucial issues succinctly and forcefully:

> In contrast to that in most other countries, testing in America is dominated by multiple-choice instruments designed to rank students cheaply and efficiently. Initially created to facilitate tracking and sorting of students, these instru-

> ments were not intended to support or enhance instruction. Because of the way in which the tests are constructed, they place test takers in a passive, reactive role, rather than a role that engages their capacities to structure tasks, produce ideas, and solve problems. The tests thus exclude many kinds of knowledge and types of performance . . . [47]

Such practices also tend to minimize higher-order cognitive processes and analytic, open-ended forms of expression. That is to say, American schools, like their Japanese counterparts, must still face—and eradicate—the all too facile proclivity to emphasize rote learning at the expense of active discourse, critical reading and analysis, overarching syntheses, and lively application of learning to vital life situations. For example, the National Assessment of Education Progress (NAEP) has recently concluded that "only 5 to 10 percent of students can move beyond initial readings of a text; most seem genuinely puzzled at requests to explain or defend their points of view. . . . [Thus] it is not surprising that students fail to develop more comprehensive thinking and analytic skills."[48] Even more pointedly, these tendencies need to be rechanneled and overhauled for those who are most needy within our school systems: those students who have been victimized by misplaced tracking mechanisms and remedial programs.

Accordingly, a number of schools, school districts, and states have begun to adopt alternate, "authentic" kinds of assessment which stress institution-specific and pupil-specific modes of evaluation. Such states as California, Connecticut, Maryland, New York, and Vermont are constructing assessment models that include a wide variety of multifaceted methodologies, e.g., exhibitions in the arts, scientific experiments, essay examinations, and portfolios of students' work. The latter usually require individual or group investigation and often highlight higher-level cognitive processes. Preliminary results of the pilot program in Vermont indicate that portfolio assessment has worked exceedingly well in developing students' writing skills; however, the same students appear to do less well in mathematical problem-solving. Currently, more than 35 states have expressed some interest in studying and perhaps adopting some form of portfolio evaluation.[49]

THE TESTING INDUSTRY: ITS IMPACT AND CONSEQUENCES

The vast impact and consequences of the testing industry in the United States can be glimpsed from the fact that, since 1978, close to two million prospective college students in the Northeast and Middle Atlantic states have taken the Scholastic Aptitude Test (SAT) and its related achievement tests each year. The latter are administered by the College Entrance Examination Board (CEEB). In the South, Midwest, and West, a similarly large number of precollege students take the ACT examination conducted by the American College Testing Program. Beyond their collegiate experience, undergraduates headed for law, medical, business and graduate school can look forward to the LSAT (Law School Admission Test), the MCAT (Medical College Admissions Test), the GMAT (Graduate Management Admission Test), and the GRE (Graduate Record Examination). All of these tests are generated by the CEEB.

The competitive nature of such examinations can cause many students to "get ill, lose sleep, and worry constantly over their prospective encounter with the SAT or ACT. The kids who worry too much about the tests are prone to choke on the day of the test because of the additional pressure they put on themselves. A bad day, produced by anxiety or illness, can lower an applicant's score on the test and lessen her prospects for that 'right' college she wants to enter."[50]

Even though many selective colleges and universities claim that test scores are only one indicator of potential for college success and employ other criteria for admissions as well (e.g., high school grades, class rank, rigor of the student's academic program, leadership qualities and extracurricular activities, etc.), there is conflicting evidence about cut-off scores from the College Board itself. On the one hand, in 1979, Fred Hargadon, then chairman of the CEEB, contended: "The College Board discourages the use of score cut-offs or the use of scores in isolation from a variety of other considerations in evaluating candidates for admission."[51] At the same time, he added: "I don't happen to agree with cut-off scores, but if they're set low enough there's probably good reason for doing that.... This is a matter of allocating resources. Colleges do have a conscience, and there's no need to recruit and admit a student who at the cheapest college will still be spending a fair amount of money, if they're not going to succeed in the program."[52]

According to a study by Wing and Wallach (1971), some 76 percent of college admissions decisions can be accounted for by surveying candidates' SAT scores.[53] Yet there is ample data to indicate that the value of SAT scores as a predictor of first-year college grades is paltry at best. High school grades have generally been found to be a more reliable index to such success.[54] In addition, students who prepare for the SAT through commercial coaching courses have also been able to increase their scores by approximately 25 points on both its verbal and mathematical sections.[55]

Given these dubious circumstances, scores of critics, both within and outside the gates of academe, have seriously questioned the need for standardized scholastic aptitude tests in college admissions. As Banesh Hoffman sees it: "Why should there be a standard of 'scholastic aptitude' when, for all we know, there is no such specific thing as 'scholastic aptitude' in the first place? Is it not a numerical invention? If by 'scholastic aptitude' we mean some combination of relatively superficial, numerically measurable, verbal and arithmetical traits that are correlated with professional grades with all their crotchets, idiosyncrasies, and exceptions, are we not talking of a smoothed-out, carefully sandpapered, statistical monstrosity?"[56]

Other educational observers echo Hoffman's pointed criticism of the tests in different ways:

> [Once upon a time] only those young men who could read and write Latin could get into [the learned professions] and if tests had been given in Latin, I am sure they would have shown that professionals scored higher in Latin than men in general, that sons who grew up in families where Latin was used would have an advantage in those tests compared to those in poor families where Latin was unknown, and that these men were more likely to get into the professions. But would we conclude we were dealing with a general ability factor?[57]

And, ultimately, such tests show very little, perhaps nothing, about what the college student will do once she enters the outside world after graduation, either in terms of individual achievement or her contributions to social responsibility. Such legitimate concerns about the ACT, SAT, LSAT, MCAT, GMAT, and GRE have caused some institutions of higher learning to re-look the necessity of entrance examinations. For example, such prestigious liberal arts colleges as Bard, Bates, and Bowdoin no longer require any admissions test for prospective undergraduates; and such illustrious medical schools as Johns Hopkins and the University of Rochester have abandoned the MCAT.

In closing, educators and the public at large would be wise to ponder Hoffman's grim admonition: "Testing is no game. It is in deadly earnest. If tests are misused, the consequences can be far from trifling. Lives can be warped and careers ruined—as much by unwarranted promotions as by misguided guidance and lack of recognition of ability.... The strength and vitality of a nation may be jeopardized."[58]

CONCLUSION

In the long run, will the head-long push for even more widespread, systematic testing actually diminish the level of school instruction? At present, standardized tests are required in nearly all of our nation's 15,367 public school districts, including more than 100 million tests per year at an astounding price tag of $700 to $900 million dollars.[59] As one school principal, Arthur Laughland, puts it: "I read recently that our children's lives are far too precious to entrust them to professional educators. How much more foolish to entrust our judgments about quality education to the cheap panacea of easily administered tests?"[60] Finally, in the words of Paul Pottinger: "We must learn if tests are contributing to the loss of our ability to think, analyze, understand, and write.... We must know if we are decreasing the intellectual nourishment of our youth by seducing them into memorizing facts or using phony analytical skills on trivial multiple-choice problems."[61] The choice of moving beyond the testing mystique and demystifying its omnipotence is in our hands and remains vital to the future interests of our children and their society. If we begin to argue about what an education might mean rather than how to raise test scores, perhaps the reform of American education will be pointed in more fruitful directions.

ENDNOTES

1. Hargis, Charles H.: *Grades and Grading Practices: Obstacles to Improving Education and to Helping At-Risk Students.* Springfield, IL: Charles C Thomas, 1990, p. 22. Cf. Grimes, L.: Learned helplessness and attribution theory: Redefining children's learning problems. *Learning Disability Quarterly,* 4: 91–100, 1981.

2. Hargis: *Grades and Grading Practices,* p. 23.

3. *Ibid.* Cf. Shriner, J. and Salvia, J.: Chronic noncorrespondence between elementary math curricula and arithmetic tests. *Exceptional Children,* 55: 240–248, 1988.

4. Hargis: *Grades and Grading Practices,* p. 24. Cf. Smith, A. and Dobbin, J. E.:

Marks and marking systems. In Harris, C. W. (Ed.): *The Encyclopedia of Educational Research.* New York: Macmillan, 1960, pp. 783–791.

5. Hargis: *Grades and Grading Practices,* p. 25.
6. *Ibid.,* p. 26.
7. Holt, John: *The Underachieving School.* New York: Pitman, 1969, pp. 204–205.
8. Burns, Edward: *The Development, Use, and Abuse of Educational Tests.* Springfield, IL: Charles C Thomas, 1979, pp. 66–67.
9. Karier, Clarence J.: Testing for order and control in the corporate liberal state. *Educational Theory,* 22: 158, 1972. Cf. also Wiebe, Robert H.: *The Search for Order.* New York, Hill and Wang, 1967; and Baritz, Loren: *The Servants of Power.* New York: John Wiley, 1960.
10. Gould, Stephen J.: *The Mismeasure of Man.* New York, W. W. Norton, 1981, p. 149. The subsequent treatment of intelligence and achievement testing movements in this section has been substantially informed by the excellent synopsis in Corbett, H. Dickson and Wilson, Bruce L.: *Testing, Reform, and Rebellion.* Norwood, NJ: Ablex, 1991.
11. Gould: *The Mismeasure of Man,* p. 151.
12. *Ibid.,* p. 159.
13. Owen, D.: *None of the Above: Behind the Myth of Scholastic Aptitude.* Boston: Houghton Mifflin, 1985, p. 183.
14. *Ibid.,* p. 184.
15. Brigham, Carl C.: *A Study of American Intelligence.* Princeton, NJ: Princeton University Press, 1923, p. 209.
16. Yerkes, Robert M.: Testing the human mind. *The Atlantic,* p. 358 (March 1923).
17. Thorndike, Edward L.: Intelligence and its uses. *Harpers,* pp. 233, 235, January, 1920. For an enlightening biographical portrait of Thorndike, see: Karier, Clarence J.: *Scientists of the Mind: Intellectual Founders of Modern Psychology.* Urbana, IL: University of Illinois Press, 1986, pp. 89–105.
18. Thorndike: *Individuality.* Boston: Houghton Mifflin, 1911, pp. 36–40.
19. Thorndike: *Human Nature and the Social Order.* New York: Macmillan, 1940, pp. 455, 957.
20. Linden, K. W. and Linden, J. D.: *Modern Mental Measurement: A Historical Perspective.* Boston: Houghton Mifflin, 1968, p. 26.
21. Karier, Clarence J.: *Shaping the American Educational State: 1900 to the Present.* New York: Free Press, 1975, p. 408.
22. *Ibid.,* pp. 279–280. Cf. Jensen, Arthur R.: How much can we boost IQ and scholastic achievement? *Harvard Educational Review,* 39: 1–123, 1969.
23. Herrnstein, Richard: I.Q. *Atlantic Monthly,* p. 64, September, 1971.
24. Marshall, J. C.: *State Initiatives in Minimum Competency Testing for Students.* Bloomington, IN: Consortium on Educational Policy Studies, 1987, p. 6.
25. *Sandlin vs. Johnson,* 643 F. 2d 1027 (4th Cir. 1981).
26. *Debra P. v. Turlington,* 644 F. 2d 397 (5th Cir. 1981).
27. *Brookhart v. Illinois State Board of Education,* 607 F. 2d 179, 187 (7th Cir. 1983).

28. *Debra P. v. Turlington,* 644 F. 2d 397 (5th Cir. 1981).

29. Andrews, J. W., Blackman, C. R., and Mackey, J. A.: Preservice performance and national teacher exams. *Phi Delta Kappan,* 12: 358–59, 1980.

30. Quirk, T. J., Witten, B. J. and Weinberg, S. F.: Review of studies of the concurrent and predictive validity of the National Teachers Examination. *Review of Educational Research,* 43: 80–113 (1973).

31. *Griggs v. Duke Power Co.,* 401 U.S. 424 (1971).

32. Newman, Joseph W.: *America's Teachers: An Introduction to Education.* New York: Longman, 1990, p. 72. Cf. Graham, Patricia Albjerg: Black teachers: a drastically scarce resource. *Phi Delta Kappan,* 68: 598–605, 1987.

33. *Hobson v. Hansen,* 269 F. Supp. 401, 492 (1967).

34. *Singleton v. Jackson Municipal Separate School District,* 419 F. 2d 1211, 1214 (5th Cir. 1969).

35. *Moore v. Tangipahao Parish School Board,* 304 F. Supp. 244 (E. D. La. 1969).

36. *United States v. Gadsen County School District,* 572 F. 2d 1049 (5th Cir. 1978).

37. *Berkelman v. San Francisco Unified School District,* 501 F. 2d 1264 (9th Cir. 1974).

38. Newman: *America's Teachers,* p. 191. Cf. also Oakes, Jeannie: *Keeping Track: How Schools Structure Inequality.* New Haven: Yale University Press, 1985; Oakes: Keeping track, part 1: The policy and practice of curriculum inequality. *Phi Delta Kappan,* 68: 12–17, 1986; Oakes: Keeping track, part 2: Curriculum inequality and school reform. *Phi Delta Kappan,* 68: 148–154 (1986); and Persell, Caroline J.: *Education and Inequality: The Roots and Results of Social Stratification in America's Schools.* New York: Free Press, 1977, p. 92.

39. Oakes: *Keeping Track.* Cf. Rosenbaum, James E.: *Making Inequality: The Hidden Curriculum of High School Tracking.* New York: John Wiley, 1976; and Powell, Arthur G., Farrar, Eleanor, and Cohen, David K.: *The Shopping Mall High School: Winners and Losers in the Educational Marketplace.* Boston: Houghton Mifflin, 1985.

40. Oakes: Keeping track, part 1, pp. 16–17. Cf. also Peterson, Penelope L., Wilkinson, Louise Cherry, and Halliman, Maureen (Eds.): *The Social Context of Instruction: Group Organization and Group Process.* Orlando: Academic Press, 1984, chs. 8–10.

41. Newman: *America's Teachers,* p. 192. Cf. *ACT ISSUEgram,* 6: 3–5, 1986.

42. Kirst, Michael W.: *Who Controls Our Schools?: American Values in Conflict.* New York: W. H. Freeman, 1984, pp. 73–74.

43. Husén, Torsten: Are standards in U.S. schools really lagging behind those in other countries? *Phi Delta Kappan,* 64: 458, 1983. Cf. also Husén: *The School in Question.* New York: Oxford University Press, 1979.

44. Kirst: *Who Controls Our Schools?,* pp. 81–82. At the same time, some American critics would question the prudence of a longer school calendar and the adverse effects of excessive, unproductive homework.

45. See: Erikson, Erik H.: *Identity: Youth and Crisis.* New York: W. W. Norton, 1968.

46. Kirst: *Who Controls Our Schools?,* pp. 86–89.

47. Darling-Hammond, Linda, and Lieberman, Ann: The shortcomings of standardized tests. *The Chronicle of Higher Education,* pp. B1–2 (January 29, 1992).

48. National Assessment of Educational Progress: as cited in *ibid.,* p. B2.

49. DeWitt, Karen: In Vermont schools, test on how well students think draws new interest. *New York Times,* p. I–18 (September 1, 1991).

50. Strenio, Jr., Andrew J.: *The Testing Trap.* New York: Rawson, Wade, 1981, p. 124.

51. Hargadon, Fred: as quoted in *ibid.,* p. 128. Testimony on the Educational Testing Act of 1979, U.S. House of Representatives 4949, before the Subcommittee on Elementary, Secondary, and Vocational Education of the House Education and Labor Committee, July 31, 1979, p. 6.

52. *Ibid.* Hargadon's comments on the "MacNeil/Lehrer Report," broadcast on November 2, 1979.

53. Wing, Jr., Cliff and Wallach, Michael: *College Admissions and the Psychology of Talent.* New York: Holt, Rinehart and Winston, 1971.

54. Perrone, Vito: as cited in Strenio, Jr.: *The Testing Trap.* Testimony on the Educational Test Act of 1979, U.S. House of Representatives 4949, before the Subcommittee on Elementary, Secondary, and Vocational Education of the House Education and Labor Committee, September 10. 1979, p. 10.

55. Federal Trade Commission: Effects of coaching on standardized admission examinations. Revised statistical analyses of data gathered by Boston Regional office, Federal Trade Commission, Bureau of Consumer Protection, March 1979, Executive Summary, p. 1.

56. Hoffman, Banesh: *The Tyranny of Testing.* New York: Collier, 1962, p. 136.

57. McClelland, David: Testing for competence rather than for "intelligence." *American Psychologist,* 6 (January, 1973).

58. Hoffman: *The Tyranny of Testing,* p. 103.

59. Toch, Thomas and Wagner, Betsy: Schools for Scandal. *U.S. News and World Report,* 112: 66–72 (April 27, 1992). Accompanying the widespread use of standardized testing is the reported spread of cheating on such examinations. In 1990, one in eleven teachers surveyed nationally claimed that administrators had pressured them to cheat on tests in order to improve their school districts' "image." In North Carolina (1990), 35% of teachers surveyed admitted that they had tampered with tests for similar reasons. *Ibid.*

60. Laughland, Arthur: In Houts, Paul L. (Ed.): *The Myth of Measurability.* New York: Hart, 1977, p. 335.

61. Pottinger, Paul: as quoted in Strenio: *The Testing Trap,* p. 293. Testimony on the Educational Testing Act of 1979, U.S. House of Representatives 4949, before the Subcommittee on Elementary, Secondary, and Vocational Education of the House Education and Labor Committee, September 10, 1979, pp. 13–14.

Chapter Seven

MERITOCRACY AND COMPETITION

Since the days of Jeffersonian democracy meritocracy has played an important role in American life. Post-industrial societies increasingly seek mechanisms by which a highly trained work force can be screened and developed, and a meritocratic system is designed to be fairer and more impartial than an ascriptive system. Such a system would be executed through public education usually under the rubric of "equal educational opportunity."

Meritocracy and competition are connected insofar as competition is a necessary feature of all meritocratic systems. One would expect that as systems become increasingly meritocratic, they would become more highly competitive. What form does this competition take? Is the type and degree of competition in meritocratic systems desirable? And if not entirely desirable, what policy changes are needed?

Despite the alleged superiority of a meritocracy over previous systems the meritocratic ideology is under attack, especially since the growth of egalitarianism during the civil rights movement and the Elementary and Secondary Education Act of 1965. What are the consequences of the use of meritocratic criteria in American education today? What would be the outcomes of extending these criteria to the entire educational system? Can meritocracy be successfully defended against the numerous criticisms leveled against it? Should there be a trade-off between meritocracy and some form of egalitarianism so that these two ideologies could coexist, or are they so unreconcilable and conflictual that either one or the other must ultimately be accepted as the guiding ideology?

A PROFILE OF MERITOCRACY

A meritocratic system is based on achievement rather than ascription. In a meritocracy, awards, recognition, and the apportionment of goods and services would be based on demonstrated ability rather than seniority, race, religion, nationality, sex, and other artificial distinctions that are used to mete out the perquisites of life. Instead, the abilities and skills deemed most desirable and worthy of rewards would be determined by the priorities and values of the institution.

Meritocratic values include competitiveness, willingness to learn and adapt quickly to new situations and tasks. Devalued are gregariousness and advancement through political manipulation, even though these traits may not be entirely eliminated. Education is of vital importance because one would no longer be able to depend upon artificial distinctions for advancement.

"The partial triumph of the meritocracy," says Jencks and Riesman, "brings with it what we call the national upper-middle class style: cosmopolitan, moderate, universalistic, somewhat legalistic, concerned with equity and fair play, aspiring to neutrality between regions, religions, and ethnic groups."[1] It is a system, according to Daniel Bell, that advocates the elimination of "social differences in order to assure an equal start, but it justifies unequal results on the basis of natural abilities and talents."[2] A meritocracy is a "credentials society" in which certification through degrees and licensing becomes a condition for employment. But a technocracy should not be confused with a meritocracy, as a technocratic mode emphasizes technological efficiency and credentials that specify minimum achievement. Meritocracy, Bell emphasizes, is more than a technocracy because it stresses individual achievement and earned status confirmed by one's peers.[3]

The university, which once reflected the social system, has now become the arbiter of social status by determining the future stratification of society.[4] In a postindustrial society, technical skill becomes a condition for achieving power and higher education the means for obtaining such skill. The shift in power involves the replacement of family capitalism by managerial capitalism; patronage in government is replaced by civil service; and the WASP domination of the Ivy League colleges yields to the inclusion of ethnic groups. Thus the postindustrial society, in this aspect of power and status, is a logical extension of meritocracy: "it is the codification of a new social order based, in principle, on the priority of educated talent."[5]

The meritocrat advocates institutions that enable individuals to develop their talents and that distribute such goods as education, specialized jobs, and high income in a manner consistent with demonstrated ability. Since talents are unequally distributed and standards are developed with reference to human abilities rather than a priori, the outcomes will be unequal. The aim is to establish equal opportunity in the form of equal political and legal rights. The meritocrat is opposed to an equality of condition based on income, wealth, position, power or influence in society; as anything more than equal opportunity would threaten our fundamental liberties and would be based not on fairness but envy and resentment. The extension of equality of condition would violate equal liability and the impartiality of universalism and shift society to unequal burden and administrative determination.[6] Some inequalities of result are unavoidable and desirable. The critical point is to determine which inequalities are fair; this assessment is made by ascertaining "which have been earned . . . and which kinds of equalities are necessary to preserve the natural rights of men and the social rights of citizenship."[7]

A meritocratic system is based on equal access to education so that those students with the potentials most valued by a given society would be in a better position to develop them and subsequently be rewarded for their use. Tomorrow's leaders will be sorted out through the competitive system of grading, promotion, honors, and awards. Those who fail will be notified that they were given a fair chance and must now assume societal roles consonant with demonstrated abilities. Programs for the gifted and talented would be encouraged, but the meritocrat would unlikely support competency education if programs are based only on minimum competencies.

THE CASE AGAINST MERITOCRACY

The arguments against meritocracy are numerous and cut across a wide range of issues. Our purpose here is to state each of the most significant criticisms persuasively and to show in what way a meritocrat could possibly respond meaningfully to them.

Michael Young, in an influential work of futuristic fiction, depicts what results from a consistent meritocracy unfettered by conflicting moral considerations.[8] Jobs and material rewards are distributed strictly according to ability and no one has any special claims on occupations on the basis of age, membership in a professional class, or other considerations. A multitrack school system is established and students are sorted on the basis of intelligence testing. Power shifts from the people to administrators and those who demonstrate socially desired abilities. The upshot of this scenario is that class divisions widen, those with greater ability develop a contempt for those of lesser ability, and social contact between the classes is reduced. The technocratic society displaces many skilled workers and they are left with the most menial jobs in order to survive.

Although the futuristic meritocratic society that Young describes is clearly objectionable, many of its features stem from organizational change and technological complexity rather than meritocracy. Moreover, the type of merit cultivated is restricted to a narrow technological talent that contributes to the bureaucratic state rather than a wider range of abilities. In the scenario, technical proficiency leads to political control by an elite; yet there is really nothing inevitable about this development even when technological ability is exclusively prized, as politics could remain in the hands of politician and/or other groups. That a technological elite would aggrandize the material rewards is not necessarily the case since a society may provide those who perform distasteful but essential tasks substantial rewards as incentives. It might also be assumed that a career as technologist or a scientist brings with it many of its own rewards and pleasures; consequently, political leaders may see no reason to provide greater material inducements for such careers. In a democratic society—and it is assumed so far that meritocracy need not be inconsistent or in conflict with democracies—each person is to be respected as a person and enjoy his/her civil rights; therefore, menial jobs need not deprive persons of their overall dignity.[9]

Another problem with meritocracies, according to Schaar, is that the formula should read: equality of opportunity for all to develop talents that are highly regarded by a given people at a given time.[10] Every society has a system of values and these are organized in a hierarchy with the system of evaluation varying from one society to another. The upshot is that the formula is highly conservative. Before one subscribes to this formula, Schaar insists, one should be certain that the values, goals, and institutions of society are the ones actually desired.[11]

Although Schaar's critique of meritocracy is primarily directed to conditions in the United States, if his criticisms are accurate they would apply not only to capitalist but socialist countries as well. As Husén noted, "in the Soviet Union a meritocracy of scientists, engineers, party bureaucrats, and intellectuals of the arts has emerged and is with regard to both prestige and remuneration a privileged group."[12] This group, which has developed for more than half a century, has been able to pass its privileges on to their offspring.

Schaar admits that every society, whether meritocratic or not, chooses only certain values and talents to reward and excludes or discourages others. But it cannot be known in advance that a meritocratic society will endorse a harmful set of values; it is necessary to examine the society itself, since the adoption of a meritocratic approach does not commit one to a certain set of values or talents to reward. That meritocratic societies are essentially conservative is not inherently the case since new and neglected talents can be identified and rewarded and thereby lead to social change. Those who determine and enforce meritocratic standards can decide whether they wish to preserve values or innovate; their only constraint is that the system be based on equal opportunity and demonstrated performances arising from competitive situations.

Critics also cite undesirable interpersonal relations likely to ensue in a meritocratic system. Schaar believes that such a system promotes cruelty and competitiveness.[13] It is not generous to tell persons whose talents are limited that they can go as far as their talents will take them. He cites a footrace in which nine persons who are physical ill-prepared for the race compete with a track star, with the same rules for all. "But life," according to Nozick, "is not a race in which we all compete for a prize which someone has established; there is no unified race, with some person judging swiftness... No centralized process judges people's use of the opportunities they had; this is not what the process of social cooperation and exchange are *for.*"[14]

That a meritocracy is competitive is not to be denied. But competition is not necessarily undesirable while cooperation is inherently good: firms can compete to develop new safety and health products; a gang of thieves can cooperate with one another to swindle others. Competition and cooperation, moreover, are not polar opposites (as explained in Chapter Two) but may be juxtaposed in various types of activities, as in cooperation to establish rules for a game before competing with one another, or when competing firms in a particular industry seek agreement on certain trade policies. What is more important is whether the competition is fair and is designed to achieve an acceptable set of purposes. In a meritocracy one can also compete in professions designed to serve others and the public interest.

Other writers, however, believe that a meritocracy has more serious related weaknesses. "It [meritocracy] is a dehumanizing society," observes Nielsen, "because it destroys any notion of fraternity or solidarity or even belonging to a common community of which we are all members: as equal members of a Kantian kingdom of ends."[15] Related to this criticism is Rawls' charge that a meritocracy discounts self-respect and thereby neglects one of the more important primary goods of its members.[16]

These are serious charges that can only partly be mitigated in a strict meritocracy. But overlooked is the likelihood that a society is not necessarily better off where the satisfaction of the less talented is increased at the expense of limiting the more talented from realizing their abilities. Even the less talented will probably achieve more under a system, such as a meritocracy, that encourages them to excel. A meritocracy dispels complacency, provides incentives to improve oneself, promotes self-discipline, and encourages lifelong effort.

It might appear that if people feel inferior in one area because they perform poorly, then by de-emphasizing that area they will no longer feel inferior. Yet there is the likelihood that other areas would replace the one de-emphasized with the same or similar effect. "If after downgrading or equalizing one dimension, say wealth, the society comes generally to agree that some *other* dimension is most important, for example, aesthetic appreciativeness, aesthetic attractiveness, intelligence, athletic prowess, physical grace, degree of sympathy with other persons, quality of orgasm, then the phenomena will repeat itself."[17]

But critics claim it is a fallacy that meritocratic competition can be genuinely fair. Frankel asks if it is unfair that a person cannot take a test because he cannot afford to travel to the testing center, why is it not unfair for the person to be deprived of an education needed to prepare for the test? If it is unfair to be deprived of such an education, is it not also the mark of unequal opportunity to permit the person to remain in an environment that discourages the individual from seeking such an education?[18]

To push the argument further, each person would not only need similar resources and educational opportunities for self-improvement but would need to come from a similar type of home environment. Moreover, the size of the family and the quality of interpersonal relations among its members would likely have a significant effect on learning and thereby would need to be regulated to remove inequalities. But even this may not be enough because of genetic differences; consequently, breeding would need to be controlled to ensure that marked genetic differences would not arise. Unless the family and genetics are controlled, it may be necessary for egalitarians to resort to measures similar to those that Kurt Vonnegut sketched for a society in the year 2018. People who were outstanding in various ways were given handicaps: those who could dance well had to wear sandbags on their feet, those with comely features wore a mask, and those with high intellectual ability were required by law to wear radios in their ears that would emit noise every twenty seconds to prevent such people from taking unfair advantage of their brains.[19]

Societies that espouse equal opportunity nevertheless place certain limits upon it in terms of which circumstances are, for practical purposes, modifiable, and is believed to be worth modifying. Unless the policy-maker is prepared to deny the institution of the family protections that is now enjoys, some inequalities will persist. An attempt to eradicate these inequalities would likely involve removing children at an early age from families altogether and raising them in state nurseries. But even state nurseries may be unable to eradicate inequalities unless all babies would receive equal treatment and attention. Yet such provisions are unlikely because different people with different abilities would supervise the babies. Moreover, even in the highly unlikely event such plans could be successful, genetic differences that create inequalities would still exist. Not only would such genetic and environmental engineering run counter to the norms of most cultures but would raise serious moral issues.

Thus the pursuit of equality would be at the expense of other principles; and since equality is neither a sole or absolute principle in most philosophies and social systems, its extension must yield in certain contexts where its application infringes upon other values. In other words, the above plans to reduce inequalities would likely infringe liberty, cause people to suffer, and may fail to respect persons. Since most egalitarians believe in other principles in addition to equality, they would likely accept some restrictions on policies to eliminate inequalities; in doing so, however, they may have to answer the meritocrat's questions about the reasons why the egalitarian places limits at certain points rather than others.

A final serious weakness of equality of opportunity, according to Schaar, is that even though it is frequently defended as a democratic principle, it is not connected with and even contradicts democracy.[20] It leads to hierarchy and oligarchy and encourages citizens to believe that political authorities have superior rights on the basis of special merit by which they make their policy; these superior rights thereby absolve citizens from taking an active citizenship role.

Schaar, however, does not demonstrate that the principle of equal opportunity leads inevitably to hierarchy, and, if he did, he does not establish that such a hierarchy cannot coexist with democracy.[21] It is true that specialized knowledge does not require a hierarchy; but once goals are established, the specialized knowledge that contributes to the achievement of goals provides a basis for hierarchy in terms of rational authority (as found today in various disciplines and professions in democratic societies).

That some thinkers have defended equal opportunity in undemocratic systems does not mean that it is incompatible with democracy but that it is not specific to democracy. Instead, the principle itself is largely formal and instrumental; its basic impact would be determined by the dominant values of a particular society. Thus it is important not to equate equal opportunity exclusively with the form that it takes in the United States, as it could be connected with different types of societies that have greatly different outcomes. Nevertheless, a central and invariant feature of meritocracy is the use of competition to ascertain ability and talent and thereby apportion the rewards, recognitions, and key positions of society.

MERITOCRACY AND EGALITARIANISM

Egalitarians of diverse backgrounds generally reject meritocracy. Bowles and Gintis believe that meritocracy reinforces inequalities and maintains significant class and race differences in educational achievement.[22] Meritocracy, according to Hurn, not only purports to select rationally the talented but perpetuates inequality and convinces the lower class of their inferiority.[23] Schools are thereby driven by the needs of an elite rather than the welfare of the whole society. Meritocracy seeks to convince people that those in high-status positions deserve these positions because they are more talented and harder workers. Schools, then, accord legitimacy to this view.[24]

Egalitarians find a number of obstacles in creating a meritocratic society in the United States: (1) there is a surplus of unemployed or underemployed degree holders; (2) no correlation exists between college grades and occupational status or future earnings;[25] and, (3) school performance is not a predictor of job performance.[26] Educational credentials are used to ration access to high status occupations. As the percentage of the population with higher levels of educational credentials rises, admission standards to a particular occupation increase but not in response to the growing complexity of the job itself.

Ogbu claims that the public schools prepare minority children for their inferior role in the caste system, one in which children grow up with the "appropriate" attitudes and values to serve more effectively in their future inferior roles in society.[27] Researchers have documented the connection between students' socioeconomic status and the quality of education received.[28] The sorting system equates children's socioeconomic status with their academic placement.

Egalitarians claim that schools of today replicate earlier class divisions. One example is the use of tracking. Oakes states that tracking is a very salient feature of secondary schooling.[29] Students may be tracked according to curriculum: college preparatory or academic, general or business, and vocational track. Minorities may be discouraged from selecting the college preparatory program. Students are also sorted according to ability groupings through intelligence tests, achievement tests, grades, reading scores, and teacher evaluation.

Mastery learning proponents claim that sorting students according to ability is a way of creating unnecessary and unneeded groups in grade levels because under appropriate instructional conditions more than 90 percent can mastery course material.[30] Studies have found that although homogeneous groupings may benefit the more able student, they may negatively influence achievement among average and slow learners.[31]

The meritocrat would be able to counter these arguments with varying degrees of success. The effects of education on future life chances is greater than egalitarians earlier suggested. A positive correlation between education and income has been demonstrated in more than thirty countries.[32] Earlier it was claimed that an excessive supply of candidates exists and, as a corollary, this expansion adds little to worker productivity, it merely leads to upgrading of qualifications required for entry into a range of professional and technical occupations. But even if this hypothesis is accepted, it does not mean that upgrading paper qualifications will continue indefinitely, as relative earnings of the more highly educated would decline because employers would not upgrade pay to match paper qualifications. The fall in earnings would thereby act as a signal to deter some entrants in pursuing programs for entry into these fields. Thus the self-adjusting mechanism is that some students would make different career choices.

While the meritocrat would insist that advancement not be based on social class, race, ethnicity, and other extrinsic variables, egalitarians claim that these variables have been used to sort students for educational placement. Though legal and policy decisions in recent years have limited arbitrary restrictions based on race and ethnicity, social class is more difficult to separate except under special programs for the poor and disadvantaged children. Egalitarians would claim that providing the poor equal access, as the meritocrat would do, is insufficient; rather, compensatory education, parent education, and other programs are essential. Meritocrats, however, may ask whether egalitarians are consistent in their principles. If one really believes in equality, why limit one's proposals to these programs? Other measures are needed to bring about a genuine equality: A national policy of income distribution could be established through significant changes in the tax structure. Families could be more stringently regulated through marriage laws that would determine who could marry, which married couples could have children, whether the parents may rear them or should be required to send them to a state nursery.

Meritocrats would likely support tracking and ability grouping so long as these arrangements are not based on race, ethnicity, social class, and other extraneous factors. They would question the alleged superiority of heterogeneous groups. Individualized instruction in heterogeneous groups is extremely difficult to implement effectively and would require such costly changes in school practices as to be a virtual "economic impossibility."[33] Teachers confronted with heterogeneous classes in working-class schools have generally not been able to individualize instruction or work effectively with low achievers. One possible solution is to group low achievers homogeneously for reading and language arts instruction in small groups taught by skilled teachers.[34]

FACULTY ADVANCEMENT AND MERITOCRACY IN HIGHER EDUCATION

Faculty advancement includes salary raises, new and greater responsibilities, promotion in rank, and the granting of tenure. Colleges and universities usually employ a merit system in which faculty compete on annual evaluated performance in teaching, research, and service, with research of greater weight in the leading research universities and teaching and service of primary importance in the smaller colleges and universities.

In view of past discrimination based on race, ethnicity, religion, and sex, is a meritocratic system appropriate in higher education? Should it be combined with another system that would have promise of overcoming alleged weaknesses of meritocracies? Or should it be dispensed with altogether?

As seen earlier, objections to meritocracies are numerous and varied. Objections to meritocratic standards can be distilled into two general types: objections on principle and on implementation. Those who disapprove on the latter grounds believe that the system has proven or will prove to be a failure when put into practice. Far too many vagaries and personal biases arise, they contend, for such a system to work successfully. Evaluators may use inappropriate standards or apply them incorrectly; favoritism and politics are prone to enter any evaluation. This line of argument is common against the use of merit raises in public schools, but it can also be heard in higher education.

Objectors on principle frequently claim that a meritocratic system is essentially unfair until greater equality prevails; otherwise those who have not been denied opportunities will have a decisive advantage over others who were not so fortunate. Other than a small number of exceptional cases, persons who rise to the top are those whose opportunities were not denied.

To deal with objections on principle, the application of a notion of justice is needed. Underlying the rules governing faculty advancement is the principle of distributive justice, which is concerned with how scarce resources are to be fairly allocated. In terms of particular acts, Aristotle said that justice consists in treating equals equally and unequals unequally but in proportion to relevant differences.[35] This does not mean that people are to be treated alike: only that the burden of proof falls on those who would treat people differently to identify *relevant* differences. But what actually counts as "relevant differences"? Rescher has identified many candidates for relevant differences: need, merit, effort, productivity, social utility, supply and demand, and others.[36] Of these relevant differences, merit is the operative criterion in faculty advancement. But what is meritorious differs according to observers, historical periods, and contexts. In the larger society, some have historically viewed wealth as meritorious; others have selected aristocratic excellence; and still others prefer athletic prowess. Prior to the Civil War, the American college was not involved in research and hence research counted for nought in faculty advancement; but since many colleges were church-affiliated, good character traits among faculty were expected and generally rewarded. Today teaching, research, and service are the relevant differences on which advancement decisions are made, with the relative weight accorded each criterion dependent on the type of university, its mission, and the composition of the student body.

Increasingly, market conditions of supply and demand are becoming arbiters of faculty advancement, with technology and business administration enjoying a wide advantage over other disciplines. "But," asks Daniel Bell, "as economic decisions become politicized, and the market replaced by social decisions, what is the principle of fair reward and fair differences? Clearly this will be one of the most vexing questions in a postindustrial society."[37]

One argument against meritocratic criteria is that rewards may be allocated solely on the basis of innate abilities or inherited aptitudes; and since the individual has no hand in the matter, it thereby would be unfair to reward or blame the individual. Yet many cultures do reward the youth who inherits a strong and vigorous physical constitution that can be converted into athletic success. Musical prodigies and children with high IQ's and scientific aptitude are also usually rewarded. Perhaps, then, merit should be based strictly upon acquired skills and abilities, such as skill in reading or learning to speak a foreign language. Yet to what extent is progress in acquiring these skills based on genetic differences? Whatever the skill, if the above plan is followed, genetic and acquired differences would have to be separated (which with most skills would be difficult to do). But there may be some skills or abilities that derive solely from practice, perseverance, and drill; these skills or abilities would be the object of merit. Now, however, the relevant differences have shifted from merit to effort. Perhaps effort should be rewarded or rewarded more than it currently is rewarded, but it would not be the primary consideration in faculty advancement because effort alone, without native talent and a nurturing environment, is no assurance of acquiring a requisite level of competency, even though without a minimum level of effort few would succeed. Thus with effort as the sole or even primary criterion, the university may advance incompetent or mediocre faculty members to the highest rank and into key decision-making positions.

But that leaves us with the recognition that merit programs for faculty and administrators may actually be rewarding a combination of native abilities, capitalizing on a nurturing environment, and effort. The nurturing environment or lack thereof, especially in childhood, is something over which the individual has little or no control; whereas in adulthood one can attempt to arrange an environment that will help to promote desired abilities. Thus merit is awarded by using one criterion not under an individual's control and a second not under individual control until the important formative years have passed. Consequently, one is partly rewarded for a favorable genetic endowment and being reared by a family that wisely utilizes educational resources. Since the provision of such an environment is partly a function of family income, the poor are usually disadvantaged by the use of merit criteria. The poor and minorities, however, have been aided by recruitment goals designed to interview and seek out more qualified applicants from these groups.

Though not always formally stated, merit criteria may also reward those individuals with effective interpersonal relations who work harmoniously with the administration, faculty, staff, and students. Thus the merit process, especially tenure decisions, considers these informal, less tangible factors in long-term appointments in addition to formal criteria.

Critics of meritocratic systems persistently speak of their unfairness. That leads us to consider a principle of justice. This is not a question for a judge because the principle already regulates his or her professional functions. But it is less evident why others should adopt such a principle. Rawls has argued that we are committed to adopt the principle because we are engaged with others in joint activities designed to promote common and complimentary interests; thus we cannot expect others to respect our interests if we do not respect theirs.[38] Peters takes a different approach to justification. He finds justice a limiting principle that stipulates the desirability of making categories on relevant grounds and the undesirability of expectations on irrelevant grounds. The principle, he claims, is presupposed in attempts to justify conduct or answer the question "What ought I to do?" Any answer to the question could not be accepted or rejected unless there were grounds of relevance for doing so. Moral discourse would make no sense without rules for relevance, and justice is built into the concept of a general rule. Those who tell others that there is no need to justify conduct are using practical discourse to do so; and since rules of relevance are built into practical discourse, such persons are presupposing the principle of justice while seeking to ban it or avoid it.[39]

One way to avoid acting unjustly is to know what the principal injustices are. ***Invidious discrimination,*** one ground of injustice, would involve arbitrary unequal treatment in developing and enforcing rules or in distributing burdens or benefits. Thus rules that arbitrarily exclude people from benefits or treat people unequally on grounds of race, sex, ethnicity, or religion would be guilty of invidious discrimination. The difficulties that women earlier encountered in gaining tenure in some departments, the unwritten prohibition by some universities in employing Jews, and segregated faculties that historically brought about all-black colleges and all-white colleges are cases in point.

This means that it may be legitimate for institutions to establish goals to recruit more women and minorities but less warranted to establish quotas. If a university department or business firm mandates hiring only women and minorities or a certain percentage from the two groups, it connotes that whites or white males should be punished as a group and are equally guilty of discrimination. This means that one would subscribe to a notion of collective guilt. Of course, if certain white males are guilty of discrimination, they should be punished as individuals as the law provides. Moreover, if a university department was adjudged guilty of discriminating against minorities and quotas were mandated, how would such quotas be determined? Should the measure be the proportion of minorities in the local community, the state, region, or the nation? Or should it be the percentage in the discipline itself? But if the discipline has discriminated against minorities, then using it as a measure would be improper; yet to use one of the other measures may create a need for a much higher proportion of qualified minority applicants at a given time in the population, leading thereby to unqualified applicants. Thus the use of quotas would abandon merit criteria despite the fact that the discovery of discrimination was made possible by applying the principle of merit.[40]

Judgmental injustice is a second type of injustice. It consists of making unfair judgments of other persons—as individuals, and their activities and achievements. The American Association of School Administrators warns the administrator that his or her judgment should not be clouded by any member of the school staff because of their rank, popularity, social standing, or position so as to conceal or condone unethical conduct. Nor should the administrator permit strong and unscrupulous persons to seize power and responsibility which is not their own.[41]

An earlier version of the NEA Code of Ethics enjoined teachers to "Speak constructively of other teachers, but report honestly to responsible persons in matters involving the welfare of students, the school system, and the profession."[42] The current NEA Code of Ethics obliges teachers not to intentionally expose students to embarrassment or disparagement, and urges teachers not to knowingly make false or malicious statements about a colleague.[43]

Exploitation is a third type of injustice. It involves making improper use of another for one's own advantage by violating another's trust, manipulation of another's natural handicaps, or deliberately disadvantaging them in some competitive of joint undertaking.

One of the most significant forms of exploitation is sexual harassment. Sexual harassment, according to the Equal Opportunity Commission, is "unwelcome sexual advances, requests for sexual favors and other verbal or physical conduct of a sexual nature." Such actions become illegal whenever a person's reaction to such conduct is made a basis for employment decisions or substantially interferes with work performance or creates an intimidating or offensive work environment. Sexual harassment is a violation of many state laws as well as Title VII of the Civil Rights Act.

But what is to count as "unwelcome sexual advances"? The aggrieved party would need to demonstrate that the advance was sexual in intent and caused physical, social, or psychological harm. Although beyond the scope of our inquiry, what is needed is an elucidation of a general theory of harms to apply to cases of alleged sexual harassment.[44]

In considering other problems of faculty advancement, faculties are becoming older and a majority in most institutions are tenured. To find a place for younger talent, tenured vacancies in many universities are not maintained but dropped to the rank of assistant professor. Particularly acute are the tensions that arise during retrenchment between tenured and nontenured faculty.

The AAUP's guidelines for financial exigency affirms the importance of meaningful faculty participation in such decisions.[45] Those whose programs are likely to be affected should be heard. Tenured professors, according to the AAUP, should not be terminated in favor of nontenured professors who at a particular moment seem to be more productive. Criteria used in termination should include age and length of service. Tenured faculty should be given an opportunity to readapt within the department or elsewhere within the institution. Earlier retirement may be feasible for older tenured faculty by the institution investing additional funds in the individual's retirement income.

Other recommendations for faculty facing financial exigencies are that they should be involved in preexigency planning, resist unfounded administrative attempts to declare states of exigency, develop careful guidelines to handle retrenchment, and accept a proper share of responsibility for determining necessary terminations.[46]

A form of discrimination that is arbitrary and deceptive pertains to publication. It is important that stated criteria for faculty advancement actually be used in decisions rather than as a cloak for a hidden agenda. Lewis reviewed numerous studies of publication productivity in various disciplines and concluded that the "publish or perish" dogma is largely a fraud. Although to publish nothing at a major university will bring downward mobility, those who publish frequently in reputable journals will receive some rewards—these rewards, however, could be marginal. For 80 or 90 percent of academics, except for those in a dozen or so prestige institutions, the publish or perish threat is empty. About 90 percent of all major publications come from the top 25 doctorate-granting institutions.

The use of the publish or perish dogma, Lewis concludes, derives from a number of reasons: to conceal complicated institutional decisions about the true reasons faculty were terminated; maintain control over persons by the fear of losing their positions; help maintain the status quo by diverting attention from department affairs; and convey to faculty that objective standards of evaluation are being used when actual decisions are subjective.[47]

In conclusion, to answer our original question about the appropriateness of a meritocratic system in faculty advancement, it has been shown that an unmodified meritocratic system is in danger of failing to correct certain injustices. Thus it has been suggested that a modified meritocratic system be employed that is grounded not only in merit but in a viable principle of justice that seeks to eliminate the three major types of injustice. By doing so the interests of all faculty are more likely to be served and the future of the university enhanced.

MERIT RAISES AND CAREER LADDERS

A number of national commission reports have expressed concern about teacher performance. The National Commission on Excellence in Education emphasized paying higher teacher salaries based on performance.[48]

Merit pay rewards teachers with higher salaries for doing the same or a similar job better than their colleagues. *Career ladders* pay teachers more for performing duties different from those of their colleagues. Both plans require systematic, periodic assessment of faculty. In contrast, most school systems today base salary on formal education completed and the amount of teacher experience.

In a 1986 Louis Harris poll, of the 72 percent of teachers who said that they were familiar with merit pay, 71 percent were opposed to such systems; 55 percent of principals concurred. Teachers were split in their views of career ladder programs, with 49 percent in favor and 46 percent opposed.[49] Thus it can be seen that unless teacher attitudes change dramatically, teacher morale may decline under merit pay plans. Less threatening is the career ladder plan, which is being tried in a number of states and involves different levels of responsibility and pay for different jobs (such as probationary teacher as a classification for starting teachers, and master teacher for those who have demonstrated superior performance).

A study of nine local school districts in eight states with successful merit pay and other teacher incentive plans found that 67 percent of the administrators believed that school-wide and district-wide plans would be a better alternative to state plans. District-wide plans were seen as allowing more diversity, addressing the district's needs more effectively, and enabling teachers to identify more closely with the plans. Support from the state level, administrators said, should take the form of resources and grants; whereas the federal government government should be involved in research and evaluation.[50]

Proponents of merit pay argue that it stimulates individual improvement, rewards deserving teachers, promotes greater student achievement, and is consistent with practices in industry. Other reasons to support merit pay are that it is the main way to gain public support for higher salaries, and that such plans, when carefully developed, can be feasible.

Opponents suggest that merit pay will lead to politics and patronage rather than improved instruction, there are not generally accepted criteria of teacher merit, there are great difficulties in evaluating which of two good teachers is better, and that evaluative judgment could be subjective and arbitrary. It is also claimed that the cost may be prohibitive if paid personnel are to do the rating, and that it may create serious morale problems. Silk charges that "Merit raises will introduce more competitiveness into teaching. Average and below-average performance is inherent in a competitive arrangement. No matter how highly selected and trained the participants, some are always more competent than others."[51] McCracken and Vold claim that merit pay emphasizes techniques and skills over formal education and reduces teaching to the level of craft. It assumes that teaching is little more than a skill learned through supervised repetition rather than based on theoretical disciplines.[52]

Career ladders differ from merit plans by designating different teacher teacher categories—such as beginning teachers, senior teachers, and master teachers—while merit plans have only one category. Usually a certain percentage of teachers can advance in a given year on a career ladder, with master teachers sometimes used as consultants or trainers of beginning teachers. Beginning teachers may remain for three to five years on the first rung of the ladder, and it may require up to five years before being eligible to apply for the next level of the career ladder. Teachers who reach the two top rungs of the career ladder may be employed 10–12 months annually and supervise beginning teachers, evaluate other teachers, and develop curricula.

Florida, Tennessee, and Texas are among the states that have enacted comprehensive legislation detailing the structural elements of the plan. According to Robinson, the following features should be part of every career ladder plan: adequate basic salary level, sufficient financing for the plan, availability to all who qualify, well-defined educational objectives, board and administrative commitment, faculty involvement in program development, assessment measures which are objectively and consistently applied, and continuous review of the plan.[53] Hawley points out, in order to stimulate good teaching, the rewards associated with a career ladder must not put teachers in competition with one another.[54]

The career ladder is designed to improve the teaching-learning process, enhance quality of the teacher work force, improve educational institutions as organizations, and regain community confidence in schools. Other objectives are to reward outstanding teachers, utilize faculty more effectively, provide incentives throughout a teaching career, and promote better teacher preparation and professional development.

Career ladder plans are opposed on grounds that they would include favoritism and local politics in evaluation, insufficiently consider formal education and teaching experience, and fail to address the needs of teachers but the evaluation needs of administrators instead. They also would not allow all those eligible to advance because of insufficient funding, likely promote competition and divisiveness among teachers, use funds for administering programs rather than for increasing teacher salaries, and create difficulties in evaluating and comparing teacher performance.

A different type of criticism focuses on the rationale for work itself. Hertzberg claims that job satisfaction and dissatisfaction are not polar opposites but different concepts. Job satisfaction lies in the work itself, achievement, and responsibility; whereas job dissatisfaction is related to working conditions, salary, and how workers are treated. Hertzberg calls the former motivation needs and the latter hygiene needs. Thus career ladder plans address the needs of the system but not the motivation needs of teachers, as only the hygiene needs are considered. Motivation needs are fulfilled through psychological growth, psychic rewards, and professional autonomy.[55]

In conclusion, while career ladder plans are likely to be used more widely in public education than merit raise systems because of less resistance from administrators and teachers, the career ladder is likely to flounder, among other reasons, because states and local districts are unable to fully fund them. In the meantime, measures for improving instruction will likely focus instead on reforming teacher education and establishing national standards for teacher certification.

ENDNOTES

1. Jencks, Christopher and Riesman, David: *The Academic Revolution.* Garden City, NY: Doubleday Anchor, 1969, p. 12.
2. Bell, Daniel: On meritocracy and equality. In Schaefer, David Lewis (Ed.). Port Washington, N.Y.: Kennikat Press, 1979, p. 41.
3. Bell, Daniel: *The Coming of Post-Industrial Society.* New York: Basic Books, 1973, pp. 414, 453.
4. Ibid., p. 410.
5. Ibid., p. 426.
6. Bell: On meritocracy and equality, p. 47.
7. Bell, Daniel: A 'just' equality. *Dialogue* 8 (1975): 3.
8. Young, Michael: *The Rise of the Meritocracy.* New York: Random House, 1959.
9. Galston, William A.: *Justice and the Human Good.* Chicago: University of Chicago Press, 1980, pp. 178–79.
10. Schaar, John H.: Some ways to think about equality. *Journal of Politics* 26: 867–895.
11. Ibid., p. 871.
12. Husen, Torsten: *Talent, Equality, and Meritocracy: Availability and Utilization of Talent.* The Hague: Martinus Nijhoff, 1974, p. 105.
13. Schaar, John: Equality of opportunity, and beyond. In Pennock, J. Roland and Chapman, John W. (Eds.). *Equality.* New York: Atherton Press, 1967, p. 233.

14. Nozick, Robert: *Anarchy, State, and Utopia.* New York: Basic Books, 1974, pp. 235–6.

15. Nielsen, Kai: *Equality and Liberty.* Totowa, NJ: Rowman & Allanheld, p. 161.

16. Rawls, John: *A Theory of Justice.* Cambridge, MA: Harvard University Press, 1971, pp. 106–8.

17. Nozick, *Anarchy,* p. 243.

18. Frankel, Charles: Equality of opportunity. *Ethics* 81: 203–4 (April 1971).

19. Vonnegut, Kurt: *Welcome to the Monkey House.* New York: Dell, 1950, p. 7.

20. Schaar: Equality of opportunity, and beyond. pp. 245–47.

21. Stanley, John: Equality of opportunity as philosophy and ideology. *Political Theory* 5: 73 (February 1977).

22. Bowles, Samuel and Gintis, Herbert: *Schooling in Capitalist America.* New York: Basic Books, 1976.

23. Hurn, C.J.: *The Limits and Possibilities of Schooling,* 2nd ed. Boston: Allyn and Bacon, 1985, p. 31.

24. Ibid., p. 66.

25. Jencks, Christopher: *Inequality.* New York: Harper, 1973.

26. Berg, Ivar: *Education and Jobs.* New York: Praeger, 1970.

27. Obgu, J.U.: *Minority Education and Caste.* New York: Academic Press, 1978.

28. Oakes, J.: *Keeping Track: How Schools Structure Inequalities.* New Haven: Yale University Press, 1985.

29. Ibid.

30. Bloom, Benjamin S.: *All Our Children Learning.* New York: McGraw-Hill, 1981.

31. Froman, R.D.: Ability grouping: Why do we persist and should we? Paper presented at the annual meeting of the American Research Association, Los Angeles, 1981; Esposito, D.: Homogeneous and heterogeneous ability grouping: Principal findings and implications for designing more effective educational environments. *Review of Educational Research,* 43: 163–79, 1973.

32. Psacharopoulos, George: *Returns to Education: An International Comparison.* Amsterdam: Elsevier, 1973.

33. Scriven, Michael: Problems and prospects for individualization. In Talmadge, Harriet (Ed.): *Systems of Individualized Instruction.* Berkeley, CA: McCutchan, 1975, pp. 199–210.

34. Slavin, Robert: How ability grouping affects student achievement in elementary schools. CREMS *Report* (June 1986): 2–4; Levine, Daniel U.; Levine, Rayna F.; and Eubanks, Eugene E.: Successful implementation of instruction at inner-city schools. *Journal of Negro Education* (Summer 1985): 313–332.

35. Aristotle: *Nichomachean Ethics* (transl. Martin Oswald). Indianapolis: Bobbs-Merrill, 1962, bk. 5.

36. Rescher, Nicholas: *Distributive Justice.* Indianapolis: Bobbs-Merrill, 1966.

37. Bell, *Post-Industrial Society,* p. 451.

38. Rawls, John: Justice is fairness. *Philosophical Review* 67: 164–194, 1958.

39. Peters, R.S.: *Ethics and Education.* Atlanta: Scott, Foresman, 1967, pp. 49–54.

40. Bunzel, John: Rescuing equality. In Kurtz, Paul (Ed.): *Sidney Hook: Philosopher of Democracy and Humanism.* Buffalo: Prometheus Books, 1983, pp. 178–80.

41. American Association of School Administrators: *AASA Code of Ethics.* Washington, D.C.: The Association, 1966, p. 25.

42. National Education Association: *Opinions of the Committee of Professional Ethics.* Washington, D.C.: The Association, 1958, Opinion 11, pp. 26–28.

43. National Education Association: Code of ethics of the education profession. In *NEA Handbook 1979-80.* Washington, D.C.: The Association, 1979, Principles I: 5 and II: 7, pp. 285–286.

44. See: Feinberg, Joel: Harm and self-interest. In his *Rights, Justice, and the Bounds of Liberty.* Princeton, NJ: Princeton University Press, 1980, pp. 45–68.

45. American Association of University Professors: On institutioal problems resulting from financial exigency: some operating guidelines. *AAUP Policy Documents and Reports.* Washington, DC: The Association, 1977, pp. 48–49.

46. Strohm, Paul: Faculty rights and responsibilities during retrenchment. In Mingle, James K. and Associates: *Challenges of Retrenchment.* San Francisco: Jossey-Bass, 1981, p. 151.

47. Lewis, Lionel S.: *Scaling the Ivory Tower.* Baltimore: Johns Hopkins University Press, 1975, pp. 31–42.

48. National Commission on Excellence in Education: *A Nation at Risk: The Imperative for Educational Reform.* Washington, DC: Government Printing Office, 1983.

49. Rich, John Martin (Ed.): *Innovations in Education: Reformers and Their Critics,* 5th ed. Boston: Allyn and Bacon, 1988, p. 191.

50. Inman, Deborah: Merit pay and other teacher incentive plans. *School Business Affairs* 50: 50–52, October 1984.

51. Silk, David Neil: Are merit raises meritorious? In Rich: *Innovations,* p. 197.

52. McCracken, Kenneth D. and Vold, David J.: Merit pay: resurrection of an unworkable past. In Vold, David J. and DeVitis, Joseph L. (Eds.): *School Reform in the Deep South: A Critical Appraisal.* Tuscaloosa: University of Alabama Press, 1991, pp. 65–72.

53. Robinson, G.E.: *Incentive Pay for Teachers: An Analysis of Approaches.* Arlington, VA: Educational Research Services, 1984.

54. Hawley, W.D.: The limits and potential of performance-based pay as a source of school improvement. In Johnson, H.C. Jr. (Ed.): *Merit, Money and Teachers, Careers Studies on Merit Pay and Career Ladders for Teachers.* New York: University of America Press, 1985.

55. Chandler, T.J.L.; Lane, S.L.; Bibik, J.M.; Oliver, B.: The career ladder and lattice: a new look at the teaching career. *Journal of Teaching in Physical Education* 7: 132–141, 1988.

Chapter Eight

NONCOMPETITIVE THEORIES OF EDUCATION

Those who strongly object to our competitive society and desire a different approach for their children should have the option of alternative socialization processes based on noncompetitive values. The objective of this chapter is to present various theoretical models of some recent important formulations of noncompetitive approaches to teaching and learning. The theories of education which we have chosen for this analysis are romanticism, progressivism, libertarianism, Marxism, and feminism. Any of these models could be used, with varying results, in efforts to foster more noncompetitive forms of education. The first three models, however, would need to reduce greatly the impact of the mass media and other sociocultural constraints which instill and extol competitive values; whereas Marxism and feminism, since they seek to develop a new society, will likely have to develop new media forms and different cultural dispositions.

ROMANTICISM

The Romanticist French philosopher Jean-Jacques Rousseau (1712–1778), in his recommendations for private tutorial education, set the stage for later "progressivist" and "libertarian" themes in modern education. In his epigrammatic writings, principally in *Emile,* he conceptualizes a naturalistic form of education in which the individual would be in harmony with his natural environment, literally at peace with himself, without substantial reliance on social structures. For Rousseau, only corrupting layers of civilization could emasculate the essential goodness in human nature.

Rousseau's model of education was a transaction between tutor and pupil in which the former would only *indirectly* prepare the latter for a gradual unfolding of naturalistic, experiential perceptions through the careful education of the senses and human sentiments. Indeed, the pupil would be taught only when he was "ready" and ripe for learning in a rural setting apart from the corrupting influences of society and urban strife.

For the young student, Rousseau recommended a bountiful period of playful activity, gymnastics, and equally ample periods in which he would simply observe nature. In particular, Rousseau admonished the tutor to observe one cardinal pedagogic principle: permit the pupil "to do what he desires so long as that is within his power."[1] Thus, the indirect nature of tutorial pedagogy was characterized by Rousseau as a kind of "negative education" in which the tutor avoids any undue frustration of the student. More specifically, Rousseau warned against any pedagogic appeal

> to the student's desire to excel over others: this will lead to jealousy and hatred. The student should compete for excellence in learning; but his rival should be his own earlier record, not the activity of those few others with whom . . . he may associate.[2]

Indeed, the student should learn "to take into account wider matters than his own immediate interest if he is to gain cooperation from others, and he learns that public and private interests are linked."[3]

Thus, early child-centered romanticists such as Rousseau leaned toward a view of student freedom as "freedom from."[4] This version of freedom is conceived as an absence of restraint or coercion so that any restrictions on the student would be an abrogation of that pupil's freedom. That is, the greater the area of noninterference, the greater the individual's freedom. Rousseau's recommendations arose as a reaction against what he believed to be the philosophy of traditional education. This older education, he claimed, forced children to learn subject matter isolated from the child's daily experience, exercised authoritarian control, and employed stern discipline that failed to consider the vital needs and interests of the child.

On Rousseau's new terms, the child would be freed from stringent rules and regulations and could be permitted to develop naturally, to explore and create. In turn, the teacher's role changed from disciplinarian and task-master to facilitator of learning activities.

PROGRESSIVISM

Unlike Rousseau's more limited, isolated example, Progressivism was a reform movement that attempted to institutionalize alternatives to traditional education. It was part of a larger progressive movement in modern American society that sought to improve the lives of people. Yet the pedagogical thrust of progressivism sustained some of Rousseau's earlier admonitions. "The good teacher is now the one who puts friendliness in place of authority, who secures enthusiasm in place of obedience."[5] For those who practiced early twentieth-century progressivism, children were not governed by fear of teacher disapproval or motivated by classroom competitiveness, but were "happily busy." Instead of military discipline and competition, cooperation was substituted where the students subordinated themselves for larger social goals considered worthwhile.[6]

"Progressivism," according to Lawrence Cremin, "implied the radical faith that culture could be democratized without being vulgarized . . . "[7] The progressive movement initially consisted of child-centered educators (such as Francis Parker), pragmatist philosophers (such as John Dewey), and social reformers (such as Jane Addams); but by the 1930s, the Progressive Education Association, founded in 1919, consisted mainly of child-centered educators with few reformers. The movement reached its peak in the 1930s and by 1955 the Progressive Education Association closed its doors. By then progressivism, though dispersed, had a considerable impact on American life and education.

Like Rousseau, progressives believed that the "whole child" should be educated, not just the mind. This meant that the social, moral, and physical aspects of the child would be given equal weight with the cognitive (the spiritual side would be developed in parochial schools, the home, and the church). It greatly expanded the responsibility of the school, because progressives believed that education involves the total person: it is not just a mind that comes to school, but the entire person who must be nurtured.

The needs and interests of children should be met, according to progressive educators. That means teachers should assess needs and interests of students in their classes and be knowledgeable about the latest findings in learning and human development. One can also ask students about their felt needs and their interests. The teacher's role is to guide learning and provide the resources needed, but not to lecture, promote drill or memorization, or be authoritarian. Harold Rugg and Ann Shumaker proclaimed, for instance, that in the progressive activity school, children would be free from rigid schedules, coercion, and lockstep methods; children would be active and engaged in self-expression; and they would not study subjects but real life interactions. Children would no longer be passive or merely responsive to what is being taught, but would learn how to learn by themselves. Presumably, the teacher would no longer have to worry about discipline because the child would become self-directed and self-disciplined. For the concept of discipline, activity, or child-centered, progressives substituted the concept of growth.[8]

Similarly, the curriculum would seek to fulfill students' needs and interests by focusing on what children are interested in and using this material to fulfill their needs. If, for example, children are interested in boats, they can work together on projects making boats; in so doing, they can learn arithmetic by calculating dimensions, geography by learning where boats travel, meteorology by studying weather conditions for sailing, fine arts by drawing sketches of boats, literature by reading stories about boats, and the like. Moreover, children would also learn to fulfill social needs by learning to work together cooperatively on projects.

The progressive curriculum may be an activity or experience curriculum based on the assumption that children learn best through experiential units, rather than subject matter, that are constructed from a knowledge of their needs and interests. The curriculum also calls for teacher-pupil planning in which teachers ask children about their needs. In working together, a problem-solving approach is used to determine tasks.

The progressives experimented with many different types of curricula, all of which broke with the subject curriculum. The life functions curriculum was organized around persistent life situations: protecting life and health, engaging in recreation, satisfying the desire for beauty, securing education, improving material conditions, and the like. By studying persistent life situations and how these tasks are performed in society, specific plans for learning could be designed. Health needs, as an example, consisted of satisfying physiological, emotional, and social needs plus learning to avoid and care for illness and injury.

In terms of the central issue of competition versus cooperation, John Dewey (1859–1952) was vitally interested in the formation of participative, "face-to-face," educative communities that would ideally link the individual with his or her social environment. Indeed, Dewey's educational theory is profoundly opposed to atomistic individualism. His conception of the Laboratory School which he founded at the University of Chicago in the 1890s favored arrangements of "cooperative integration":

> It was held that the *process* of mental development is essentially a social process of participation; traditional psychology was criticized on the ground that it treated the growth of the mind as one which occurs in individuals in

> contact with a merely physical environment of things. And . . . the *aim* was ability of individuals to live in cooperative integration with others.[9]

More fundamentally, Dewey conceived of the close interplay among communication, cooperation, democracy, and education as a lifelong process of growth:

> To learn to be human is to develop through the give-and-take of communication an effective sense of being an individually distinctive member of a community; one who understands and appreciates its beliefs, desires and methods, and who contributes to a further conversion of organic powers into human resources and values. But the translation is never finished.[10]

For the schoolteacher, this means that she must be continuously engaged in critical reflection and activity that addresses key questions for forging cooperative, democratic modes of education: "How full and free are the various forms of association? How numerous and varied are the interests consciously shared?"[11]

Ultimately, Dewey sought to harmonize individual and social interests in a complex world that was sloughing off an "old individualism" no longer relevant to its needs. The "old individualism" fostered laissez-faire attitudes akin to Spencer's competitive version of social Darwinism. Dewey's "new individualism" would instead necessitate the cooperative application of creative imagination. Furthermore, this new individualism would require increased *political action* on the part of both individuals and government, i.e., larger intervention in a wide array of social problems. In essence, Dewey was calling for synergistic societal efforts in such diverse areas as industry, law, politics, medicine, religion, art, philosophy, and, most of all, education. In fact, education would become the "fundamental method" for his progressive vision of social reform.[12]

Progressive education would come under severe attack by the 1950s. Generally, the critique against progressivism could be viewed as an essentialist attack. The essentialist tradition emphasizes the values of transmitting the cultural heritage to all youth, of seeing that they are soundly grounded in "the fundamentals," and that they study the basic disciplines. Only in this way, essentialists contend, will students become educated persons and good citizens. Students cannot study what meets their immediate interest but must study what they need in order to fulfill their adult responsibilities.

The essentialists argued that progressives had tended to discredit exact studies in the disciplines, were failing to teach basic skills effectively, and had abandoned rigorous standards of scholastic achievement. Rather than study subjects in terms of a logical, chronological, or causal approach, progressives had substituted activities and projects based on the immediate interests of students. Essentialists contended that discipline was no longer being stressed, resulting in a failure to develop sound study habits and an inadequate mastery of the basic disciplines. Arthur Bestor, for instance, believed that the public schools of the 1950s were not as effective as the schools even in the first decade of this century in teaching the fundamental disciplines.[13] On the other hand, Admiral Hyman Rickover, who also believed that schools had failed, looked to European education for new models.[14]

Much of the criticism against progressivism was aimed at the child-centered group of progressives. Some of this criticism was warranted, while other facets of it seemed to be founded largely on ideological and personal predilections. Progressives did, indeed, adopt a more cooperative model of learning. They rejected ability grouping and did not compare children except in relation to their own abilities. Extrinsic rewards were usually eliminated in favor of learning based on interest and motivation. "Readiness" was carefully considered so that whatever was introduced into the curriculum was based on the learners' maturational and developmental levels. Pressure on students was avoided, grades de-emphasized, and systematic modes of cooperation encouraged.

The child-centered progressives were also influenced by sense realism and romanticism. Drawing on sense realism, learning activities were usually approached inductively and were based on concrete experience before any generalizations were drawn. Progressive classrooms usually had many sensory objects—children's drawings, photographs of historical figures, bulletin boards, and science displays. In addition, progressives believed in first-hand experiences that included frequent field trips.

Akin to Rousseau's romanticism, child-centered progressives held that the child was born basically good; and, therefore, there is no need to place many restrictions on the child's self-expression. Although they did not educate the child away from society as Rousseau advocated, they did believe in nature study and readiness for learning. Pupil-teacher planning was promoted as not only a democratic procedure, but one that would improve learning outcomes. Essentialism rejected romanticism and the romantic view of the child.

Yet Dewey himself, during the 1930s, warned child-centered educators that they cannot develop a philosophy by merely doing just the opposite of traditional education, i.e., by opposing external imposition to self-expression; external discipline to free activity; and learning from textbooks and teachers to learning from experience. Thus, child-centered progressivism is in danger of developing its philosophy negatively rather than positively and constructively.[15]

In fact, both Dewey and the essentialists criticized child-centered progressives about student interest, but for different reasons. Where child-centered educators believed that the teacher should focus and build on the child's interest, the essentialists claimed that interest is a function of effort, i.e., that one first had to exert considerable effort to gain knowledge of a subject before interest could be aroused, as students could not become interested in something that they knew little about. Dewey, instead, agreed with the child-centered educators that teachers should begin with student interests; yet that is only the starting point, for the teacher should then attempt to expand student interests through organized bodies of knowledge.

Although in the progressive model a serious attempt is made to meet the child's needs and interests, and discipline is more closely related to instruction and the social life of the school, other problems remain. Progressives may have overemphasized "freedom from" prior to sufficient development of "freedom to." The latter form of freedom holds that one is not fully free to do something without the ability to perform an act; that is, to be free to do *X* not only means an absence of restraint but includes the ability, power, and means to do *X*. Thus, an individual needs opportunity to choose among available alternatives, the ability to understand the character of the alternatives, and the ability to arrive at any informed choice.

In other words, in some forms of progressivism students were released from the restraints of traditional education to express themselves and develop naturally; yet many students had not developed the requisite abilities to perform the expected acts and to employ needed skills and judgment. Not only is it legitimate to curb "freedom from" when it causes others harm, suffering, or interferes with their rights; such freedom could also be justly curtailed when the student exercising it may be harmed.

This brings us to the role of paternalism in education. A paternalistic act is one which "the protection or promotion of a subject's welfare is the primary reason for attempted or successful coercive interference with an action or state of another person."[16] Such an act is done in the person's best interest whenever the person is incapable of performing the act for herself.

In terms of immaturity, perhaps some education authorities have been overly rigid in assuming the student must reach a certain chronological age before certain decisions can be made; they generally believe that a certain level of cognitive development must occur. A combination of cognitive, social, and experiential measures needs to be applied and each student should be looked at individually before a particular paternalistic practice is undertaken. And in situations where the evidence is not compelling, the student should be given the freedom to act independently of education authorities so long as serious injury or harm is not likely to result.

Finally, some progressives also overestimated the child's ability to use a discovery approach in gaining basic knowledge. The use of an experience curriculum where the child must initiate learning and gain knowledge first-hand may be a welcome change from expository presentations but, when used exclusively, it could be fallacious and dangerous. It assumes that the immature child should learn from scratch what it has taken civilization thousands of years to discover, develop, and refine. Since there are not enough lifetimes for any student to discover knowledge experientially, it is necessary to combine experiential learning with expository learning.

LIBERTARIANISM

In the broad sweep of contemporary history, school reform has been marked by cyclical tides that seem to ebb and flow toward either "academic content" orientations (as with the essentialists in the 1950s and from the mid-1970s to the present) or concern for economic, social, and psychological issues (as with the progressives in the earlier part of this century and in the 1960s).[17] Libertarianism was a prevailing reform movement of the 1960s that exhibited some outward, if superficial, similarities with early progressivism; it was also a direct reaction to the dominant practices of essentialism during the 1950s.

As a political philosophy, libertarianism has become a small but growing movement in the United States and brings with it an educational philosophy with distinctive programmatic ideas. Its roots lie in political anarchism, a movement and philosophy that emerged in France during the nineteenth century. Anarchism opposes the coercive power of the modern state and seeks the maximum possible freedom compatible with social life.

In the nineteenth century, William Godwin, the English political reformer, believed that the state would use schools to inculcate an ideology based on nationalism, monarchism, or militarism. At the same time, Francisco Ferrer, a Spanish educator, claimed that the schools reflect values of a capitalist society. Historically, such libertarians have sought to liberate students by offering an "integral education" that would develop all aspects of a person's potential and, according to Pierre-Joseph Proudhon, equip him with a range of entry skills into various crafts and occupations. Practical processes were viewed as examples of theoretical problems. Since the worker should not be restricted to one industrial task, he should participate in a variety of workshop settings. Intellectual education complemented manual and physical training by encouraging the child to seek principles underlying the training. The teacher's role was a complementary one: correcting the pupil's misapprehensions and explaining principles.[18]

For example, Ferrer insisted that pedagogy be noncoercive and that children not be compelled to attend class, while Sébastian Faure was in favor of promoting the child's autonomy. The Russian master Leo Tolstoy found that pupils can eventually develop their own order, an order based on mutual adjustment rather than hierarchy. Related to this principle was a belief in natural motivation: by removing impediments to motivation, the pupil can gain meaning for herself because there is a natural disposition to structure experience in terms of meaning.

Modern-day libertarianism holds that all people have the right to make their own choices so long as they do not interfere with the choices of others. Thus, all individuals have rights to their own life and property and a duty to refrain from violating the same rights of others. Rights are violated through the use of force, and government is the principal culprit. Therefore, the role of government should be limited to the protection of life, liberty, and property (in contradistinction to the wider interventions permitted by many progressives). In general, libertarians believe that the coercive power of government in public education has usurped the rights of parents and students. They claim that public schools have largely been unsuccessful and that the rights of parents have been abrogated in their children's education. Their central contention, therefore, is that parents, rather than the state, should have primary responsibility for education.

The basis of freedom, according to the nineteenth-century German schoolmaster Max Stirner, is free will. The individual should work to develop and strengthen free will and let her values be an expression of it. Motivation is a psychological concept, but will is a moral one.

Philosopher and 1972 Libertarian Party presidential candidate, John Hospers, has promulgated some specific Libertarian principles.[19] Rearticulating some of the libertarian tenets outlined above, Hospers argues that it is through property rights that the individual's work is rewarded, goals can be achieved, and future plans can be confidently made. Therefore, Libertarians would reject laws that require people to help one another, such as unemployment compensation, social security, minimum wages, rent ceilings, and the like. And they would oppose laws regulating pornography, alcohol, and drugs. Libertarians also consider the state's role to be detrimental to private education and offer legislation and plans for reducing what they consider to be government interference and for granting parents principal authority in the formal education of their children. This education might be conducted exclusively in the home or in public, private, or parochial schools. The main point is: parents (or guardians) would choose the education best for their children.

At the same time, such libertarians as John Holt and Richard Farson believe that children should be granted the same rights as adults.[20] Thus, children would have the right to do what adults legally do. But, says Holt, what we have done instead is to create an army of people to tell the young what they have to learn and to make them learn it. Compulsory education, he asserts, "is such a gross violation of civil liberties that few adults would stand for it. But the child who resists is treated as a criminal."[21] Farson, too, opposes compulsory school attendance and claims that schools function not to educate but to maintain the system through indoctrination and other coercive techniques.[22] Thus, Farson would abolish compulsory schooling and with it indoctrination, while Holt would allow young people "to decide if, when, how much, and by whom, they want to be *taught* and the right to decide what they want to learn in a school and if so which one and for how much of the time."[23]

While seeing a need for compulsory education in the primary grades, Paul Goodman, another contemporary libertarian, is opposed to its extension to the high school.[24] He recommends that the funds for compulsory secondary education be turned over to youth to establish their own learning communities and enable them to be free to experiment with their own life styles and seek their own self-identity. The funds could also be used to promote apprenticeship programs and travel opportunities.

Ivan Illich, in his *Deschooling Society* (1971), goes further by recommending that compulsory schooling be abolished, the whole system be dismantled, and society itself be deschooled.[25] He proposed instead that everyone will have free access to information and tools needed in their lives. They would have access to museums, laboratories, and libraries; to apprenticeship programs; and to peer matching where each person with a particular skill could teach another in exchange for the person taught to reciprocate by teaching the skill that he or she knows.

Still other libertarians have extended the dicta of Rousseau's early Romanticism and the progressives' views against forcing children to learn subject matter isolated from the child's daily experience, the exercise of authoritarian control, and the use of stern discipline that failed to consider the vital needs and interests of the child. At Summerhill, a boarding school in England, A. S. Neill used play, children's own interests, and their capacity to work and live with peers in a cooperative arrangement by means of developing their own rules and regulations and seeing that they were enforced. In dealing with children who had failed to receive love and approval, it is important, he believed, to take their point of view and not try to channel them toward certain ends, which the child would only associate with disapproving adults. Neill tried several measures to combat childhood neurosis: sublimation (the release of instinctual energy to creative activities), direct analysis to uncover the roots of the neurosis, and the development of an accepting permissive environment.

If a child threw mud on a door that Neill had just painted, Neill would swear at him; but if the child had done this act after just transferring from a hateful school, Neill would help the child sling mud so that the child could get back at the authority. Neill insisted that he observed a distinction in his policies between liberty and license: that license may be necessary for a cure, but ordinary children should respect others' rights.[26]

In the system of self-government that Neill established at Summerhill, he retained responsibility for overall administrative matters, diet and health, but turned the rest of the operations over to students, who met weekly to discuss rules and determine action to be taken against violators. Everyone was encouraged to express his/her views, and each student older than eight had one vote. Neill claimed that self-government is good civic education. It is therapeutic because it releases tensions. Children are more likely to abide by rules that they, rather than adults, make. And since peers impose punishment, better relations are promoted between teachers and students because the teacher is no longer a disciplinarian.[27]

Despite their sometimes refreshing pleas for a nonrepressive, more individualistic form of educational alternatives, there are a host of conceptual and practical problems attending the various recommendations of the above libertarians.

It may well be that, in their enthusiasm to emancipate children, libertarians such as Holt and Farson may sacrifice the welfare of children for their presumed rights because they overlook the developmental differences between children and adults. Adult constraint, says Diana Baumrind, is a precondition for self-determination.[28] No child psychologist would contend that the child is equal to the adult in experience, intelligence, and moral competence. And not even the child liberators can deny the immense differences in knowledge, experience, and power separating the child from the adolescent, the adolescent from the adult. These differences, Baumrind adds, do not stem from adult exploitation but from laws of nature that are not revokable. Thus, the child liberators ignore the fact that children are inferior to adults in their ability to survive, and that self-determination is a product of growth and maturation which is fostered by adult authority exercised in early years. This sense of paternalism may be warranted because of the immaturity of children and youth as well as their relative inability to judge soundly what is in their best interest and to protect themselves from needless harm and suffering.

Goodman and other libertarians may also have misinterpreted the coercive characteristics of compulsory attendance laws. Laws create obligations and embody standards. The standards justify demands for compliance; therefore, compulsion is a secondary rather than a primary factor in the way that laws function. Persons tend to speak about the state's coerciveness only in connection with laws of which they disapprove; since most Americans accept compulsory schooling, they would use the standard built into the law to criticize those who deviate from it.[29] It is a mistake to ascribe a connection between compulsory school attendance and the substantive results of schooling, because the legal requirement itself does not tell us anything about the content of education, the operation of programs, and teaching practices. There is no logical connection between the two and, if there is an empirical connection, libertarians have not shown it.

If compulsory attendance laws were to be abolished, certain social outcomes would be probable. Some who have profited from advanced schooling may favor the repeal of these laws, because the benefits of schooling would be less widely distributed, and competition would be reduced.[30] The poor and disadvantaged would likely suffer the most should compulsory schooling be abolished.

As for Illich's deschooled society, he has no assurance that it will provide learning environments that he proposes because the larger society itself remains essentially unchanged. Schools are largely a reflection of their societies, and the objectionable features that Illich found in the established educational system are not extirpated by disestablishing schools: they still exert their influences over youth through other institutions and agencies. Illich's own criticism of educational systems largely fails to distinguish the different levels of development and concomitant problems in educational systems in other countries. Thus, he has essentially the same prescription for all.

More generally, libertarian proposals for improving education seem to be less connected to specific criticisms of public education than to fears about government coercion and the consequent abrogation of parental and student freedom. Thus, the libertarians' case is based more on philosophical grounds rather than specific empirical claims. In other words, libertarians attempt to show what a more ideal education would look life, in view of their principles and assumptions about human nature and the good society.

In recent years, the chief concern of the Libertarian Party's educational agenda has been to increase parental choice. The Libertarian Party has tended to oppose the state's coercive powers and its alleged monopoly over education, especially its fiscal power. The most significant consequence of the state's powers is the restrictions placed on parental choice in educating their children. Parents, Libertarians contend, are responsible for choosing food, shelter, and clothing for their children, but not their children's education. Protection of children against malnutrition or starvation is as important as protection against ignorance, but laws are not passed for compulsory and universal eating. Not all parents are expert dieticians, but they can get advice and instruction, if necessary, and choose appropriate foods for their children. Similarly, with the help of expert advice, parents could choose wisely their children's education.

Complex decisions about food, rest, and other important matters are left to parents. According to John Coons and Stephen Sugarman, "Only when it comes to education has the state, deliberately or otherwise, virtually emasculated the family's option."[31]

Since the argument by analogy is frequently made by libertarians and much is made of it, let us look momentarily at analogical arguments to see if libertarians have established their case. Analogical arguments are not valid in the sense that the conclusions follow from the premises with logical necessity; rather, *probability* is all that can be claimed. One pertinent criterion for assessing analogical arguments is the number of respects in which the things involved are said to be analogous. Parents, we are told, make the final decisions regarding their children's food, shelter, clothing, hours of rest, and other important matters. But in what way are these functions similar to education, other than their obvious importance, and that adults—parents or educators—usually choose for children? Educational functions are more complex than the other functions enumerated, greater expertise is required, and more parents are competent to fulfill the other functions than educational ones. This is substantiated by the relatively few parents who qualify to educate their children at home.[32] The other functions that parents fulfill do not require them to understand cognitive processes, how learning occurs, or how to develop instructional objectives, select content, structure learning experiences, and evaluate learning outcomes. Thus, there are many dissimilar tasks between education and the other functions; therefore, the analogical argument has a *low probability* of being sound.

Libertarians might want to claim, however, that they are not actually advocating that most parents take over the day-to-day responsibility of educating their children. Instead, they want parents to be vested with final authority for choosing the education best for their child—whether public, private, or parochial school or home education—and to be granted the necessary financial support to exercise control effectively. The original argument, with the above modification, is now weaker. It holds that parents, with access to sufficient information, expert advice, and adequate funding, could and should make the decisions as to how their children can best be educated.

Coons and Sugarman have perhaps developed the grounds for family control of education more thoroughly than any other libertarians.[33] They seek to discover what is in the best interests of the child. Beyond the acquisition of a few basics, they find a lack of consensus and no agreement on the means to achieve these objectives. Despite this lack of consensus, public schools have a certain sameness that emphasizes technology, uncontroversial information, and neutrality. For Coons and Sugarman, the question is converted into whom the state shall empower to decide the best interests of the child. The agent best qualified to decide should be willing to listen, have appropriate knowledge about the child, and have sufficient concern for the child's interests. Educators have knowledge about classes of children, but parents have intimate knowledge about particular children. There is a question whether anyone (other than parents) really cares about children. Even for those teachers who are altruistic and caring, the nature of their role causes their caring to remain "cool and abstract." The child is usually with a teacher no more than a year, but she is with the family for many years. The family is in the best position to observe the outcome of educational decisions over long periods of time.

Ultimately, Coons and Sugarman posit autonomy as the most crucial goal in educating the child. The autonomous person is intellectually and morally independent, a coordination of intellect and responsible action. The public schools, they believe, tend to develop the "conditioned man" rather than the "autonomous man"; such schools promote the "true American," a person without distinctive and independent qualities. Since most faculties are comprised of teachers of similar socio-economic background, students are not confronted with a range of different views and values. Under a family choice system, Coons and Sugarman contend that the average child of twelve should be able to participate with parents in school choices and thereby promote personal autonomy and independence.

Many of the statements that Coons and Sugarman make about family choice seem plausible. However, they tend to overlook the value of impartiality, objectivity, and expertise in decisions about a child's education. History is filled with cases of parents who sought to fulfill their own frustrated ambitions through their children or who failed to recognize the significance of dormant talents and punished their children for expressing them. The American family is also going through a turbulent period of increased violence, high divorce and desertion rates, lack of parental supervision, and a host of other problems. It does not appear that the family would be prepared to assume these greater responsibilities. However, even if families were capable of doing so, they still may not be the logical choice. For instance, it is not clear why some families would be willing for children to participate in decisions about their education and other families would not be.

While libertarians should be commended for their attention to the child's interest, they are amazingly silent about the public interest. Public schools were established, not only to fulfill the child's interest, but the public interest as well. *Public,* as opposed to *private,* is that which has no relation to a particular person or persons, but concerns all members of the community without distinction. Thus, a hall is said to be public, not because every member of the community chooses to visit it, but because it is open to any person who chooses to enter.

The public interest can be supported by either positive or negative actions. Positive actions would provide goods and services; negative actions would be taken to prevent harm. Public schools would be an example of the former and police acts of the latter. Indeed, public schools are public in terms of purpose, control, support, access, and commitment to civic unity.[34] A public school serves a public rather than a private purpose; it is not maintained for the personal advantage of teacher, proprietor, student, or parents. The public schools are designed to serve the welfare of a democratic society by assuring the imparting of knowledge and understanding needed for citizenship responsibilities.

Thus, the libertarian formula for freedom is workable only in a world in which human desires and choices rarely conflict. To apply the formula in our complex world, where conflict and rivalry are obdurate facts, would result in greater freedom for the strong than the weak, and no very stable freedoms for anyone.

However, this set of circumstances does not mean turning one's back on the child's interest, because it is in the child's interest—at least in the larger, longer view—to have a strong system of public education. All too often an artificial opposition is erected between individual and public interests. In many cases, individual and public interest coincide, but the life chances of each person depend upon more than just increasing options. Life chances—opportunities for individual growth and realization of talents—are a function of two elements: *options* and *ligatures.*[35] Options are possibilities for choice in the social structure on which personal choice depends. These could be choices in terms of occupation, living conditions, goods and services, and the like. On the other hand, ligatures are bonds and linkages, e.g., forefathers, nation, and community. Ligatures give meaning to the place the individual occupies; they create an anchoring and a foundation for action. Although ligatures without options would be oppressive, options without ligatures would be meaningless.

A critical problem facing American society is the erosion of ligatures, which carries with it a loss of values and a sense of pointlessness. Although public schools have usually been thought of as functioning to increase options, an overlooked function is its preservation of ligatures. In other words, schools transmit certain values, traditions, and principles of citizenship; and there is less assurance that family control of education would offer the ligatures needed in a balanced combination with options to maximize life chances. Thus, neither life chances nor the public interest is likely to be served best by the plan of libertarian family control.

MARXISM

As a competing theory to competition in education and society, Marxism stems from a conflict view of social, political, and economic relationships, in contrast to a functionalist view of social behavior. The functionalist, or social disorganization, approach explains human behavior in light of understanding how the social system seeks to maintain itself. A social system is organized through a consistent set of norms and values that foster orderly and predictable social interaction among its members. Leaders of society try to foster a normative consensus. Social disorganization results whenever orderly social interaction breaks down and normative consensus fails to be achieved. Disorganization stems from *anomie* (literally, "a state of normlessness"), or, to be more precise, from a lack of consensus on norms since some norms, even when society is disorganized, can always be found. Social disorganization is expressed in inadequate institutionalization of goals, inappropriate procedures for achieving goals, weakened social control, and deficient socialization practices.[36]

The functionalist approach has the advantage, for those who believe in the worth of the ongoing social system, of explaining how the system can be maintained and those factors likely to bring about various forms of societal unrest and upheaval. However, the functionalist theory does not recognize that what may appear to the dominant groups as normlessness and disorganization may not be so perceived by more powerless groups because they adhere to different norms and points of view, especially given their less powerful positions in society.

In contrast, the conflict approach views society as a struggle of contrasting and opposing groups. Each group pursues its own values, which may be in conflict with the values of other groups. This does not necessarily mean that the other groups are disorganized or that the overall social organization is threatened. Society is not an integrated system in which normative consensus is typical; rather, it tends to be a balance of contending groups. In any group conflict the dominant groups are the definers of power, status, and control. Those belonging to groups considered less dominant may suffer alienation and a feeling of illegitimate control and exploitation. Conflict develops whenever groups holding different values live in the same society, and laws and norms of the dominant groups are extended to cover the other groups. Social disorganization, even violence, may likely erupt from such conflicts.

The conflict approach is a corrective to the functionalist approach insofar as it affords greater recognition to cultural pluralism, diverse values, and inevitable conflict in a complex society. It also contends that those who are called "powerless" and who feel alienated and exploited by the establishment are actually cases of the establishment's failure to recognize divergent values and the needs of alienated groups. But one problem with this theory is that, even though society is heterogeneous, it is actually constituted by more than various conflicting groups—otherwise it could not persist. Moreover, the conflict approach does not explain why some people deviate from their own group norms. In essence, the theory is much more suited as an explanation of political and ideological conflict.

The Marxist theory of dialectical materialism is probably the most influential linear conflict theory of history in this century. It was advanced by Karl Marx (1818–1883), German economist and philosopher and the leading theorist of modern socialism and communism, and his collaborator, Frederich Engels (1820–1895). Marx borrowed from Georg W. F. Hegel (1770–1831), the German philosopher, the notion of dialectic, which attempted to account for the unfolding of events in nature as a result of the conflicts of opposites and the development of negations leading to a new synthesis. For Hegel, every state, condition, or proposition calls forth its own negation, which provokes the negation of the negation, leading to a new synthesis. For example, Hegel started with Being. But, since Being makes no distinctions, it reveals its emptiness, turning into its opposite, Nothing. But the passage of Being into Nothing is what is meant by Becoming. Marx, while keeping the Hegelian dialectic, reversed it by eliminating the idealistic content of Spirit and self-consciousness and by substituting a "materialistic" content, the basis of which he borrowed from Ludwig Feuerbach (1804–1872). Thus, by doing so, Marx developed the fundamental structure for his philosophy of history that he called "dialectical materialism."

Marx contends that the mode of production of the material means of existence predominantly affects and conditions the whole of social, intellectual, and political life. Religion, art, education, and morality do not develop first with the mode of production emerging from those factors; instead, they are largely determined by the mode of production. Human social existence determine's one's consciousness rather than the converse. Thus, the mode of production conditions all other factors in society and becomes the key for understanding societies at different historical periods. Engels provides a sketch of historical evolution by using Marx's thesis as an explanatory principle. He finds production on a small scale in medieval society. The fruits of production are used for immediate consumption by the producer or feudal lord; and it is only when production exceeds consumption that the excess is offered for sale. However, the seed of "anarchy in the production of society at large" may already be found.

Capitalism emerges, without affecting the form of exchange, when the development of manufacturing replaces scattered workshops. The capitalist seeks to control the means of production by appropriating the products and turning them into commodities for his personal profit. Unrestrained competition develops in the market and antagonism arises between the proletariat (working class) and the bourgeoisie (middle class and capitalist). As human beings change the way they earn their living, they change their social relations. Thus, a sense of alienation from labor and from one's fellows develops. As a consequence, the development of capitalistic controls over the mode of production leads to class conflict, alienation from labor, and overall dehumanization. Class conflict stands in the center of Marx's conception of history because, other than class conflict, history is a record of insignificant trivialities.

As history moves to more advanced stages shifting from feudal to capitalistic society, exploitation increases and alienation from labor, the source of creative relations with others and the world, becomes more acute. The seeds of its own destruction can be found in the competitive capitalistic system with its overproduction, cyclical crises, and its unemployed workers. The capitalist waits to turn his products into capital before circulating them. However, circulation is limited due to overproduction. And the bourgeoisie are indicted for their incapacity to manage the productive forces of society.

The next historical stage is represented by socialism wherein the proletariat revolt against and overthrow the bourgeoisie, leading to the "dictatorship of the proletariat," in which the agencies of production would be organized first by joint-stock companies, later by trusts, and then finally by the state. Socialized production, which has presumably eliminated the abuses of capitalism, constitutes an interim stage that will give way to communism, the final historical stage, in which the state will "wither away" and classes will no longer exist. Thus, whereas the capitalistic state sought to perpetuate itself and maintain its power structure, the dictatorship of the proletariat deliberately prepares for its own demise by striving to abolish the class system. The alienation of labor endemic in capitalism will cease to exist when communism is reached. And the division of labor, which is the ultimate reason for the existence of classes, will be eliminated. Productive labor will become a creative and pleasurable activity by giving the individual the opportunity to develop his abilities, both physical and mental. Since no division of labor would exist in an ideal communist society, there would be no one sphere of activity to which the individual would be limited; for he could perform one activity today and another tomorrow, hunting in the morning, fishing in the afternoon, and raising cattle in the evening, if he so desires.

In short, dialectical materialism is partially deterministic, teleological, and utopian. Its sense of determinism issues in a form of historical inevitability in which the different historical stages will well-nigh necessarily occur (though precipitated by revolution), leaving only certain avenues for human choice. It is teleological insofar as there is an end toward which history is moving (communism) and that end once again restricts human choice and other options. It is utopian insofar as history moves toward and results in an ideal society. Utopian societies have sometimes been criticized for being unrealistic, unattainable, sterile, static, and tedious. Nevertheless, dialectical materialism has had enormous influence due to its comprehensive perspective, its appeal to the Enlightenment (beliefs in the use of reason, empiricism, and the idea of progress), and, ultimately, its passionate demand for cooperation, social justice, and equality.

In educational and economic terms, present-day Marxists and neo-Marxists argue that schooling tends to *reproduce* dominant class structures of competitive, capitalistic exploitation by those who hold power, status, and control over the social system. Under state control, public schools

> will serve to reproduce the relations of production that are essential to maintaining the dominance of the capitalist class. This means that schools will produce workers who are able to work at the different levels of the capitalist enterprise. They produce managers and janitors, as well as an array of people in between.[37]

As an arm of the state, schools, moreover, form part of that vast system of cultural apparatus which restricts individual freedom and sustains existing relations of power and control. According to Louis Althusser, a prominent neo-Marxist theoretician, these Ideological State Apparatuses (ISAs) are huge, indeed; they include most all means of media and communication, literary and art forms, religion, the family, political parties, labor unions, and even sports.[38]

More traditional Marxist interpreters, such as Robert Cohen, have criticized the shortcomings of capitalism in its failure to achieve the "promise of material and spiritual abundance," its frequent economic crises, its seeming incapacity to harmonize class and racial interests, and its "inability to fulfill our educational heritage."[39] Instead, Cohen envisions schools that are wonderfully equipped, pervaded by cooperation among all constituents, classless in their economic divisions and spiritual distinctions, and persistently regardful of the holistic totality of human existence in mind, heart, and hand. In many ways, Cohen weaves a kind of utopian educational model in much the same manner as Marx did for larger societal frames of reference.

Other critics of competition and capitalism have been sensitive to the overriding theme of individualism that has, in fact, permeated American society and its schools, including many of their progressive and libertarian reformers. Steven Lukes captures the power of individualism in the main currents of American thought and culture:

> It became a symbolic catchword of immense ideological significance, expressing all that has at various times been implied in the philosophy of natural rights, the belief in free enterprise, and the American dream. It expressed, in fact, the operative ideals of the nineteenth and early twentieth-century America (and indeed continues to play a major ideological role), advancing a set of universal claims seen as incompatible with the parallel claims of the socialism and communism of the Old World.[40]

Transposing such admonitions to the arena of civic education, Samuel Bowles and Herbert Gintis warn that

> Democracy—particularly economic democracy—involves both authority and an intrinsically social consciousness on the part of the individual. Above all, [democratic] socialism involves the will to struggle as well as the capacity to cooperate. A realistic educational philosophy must reflect this.[41]

Instead of a program of excessive competition and individualism, Bowles and Gintis proffer an educational agenda based on cooperative learning and the personal integration of communal skills and perspectives.

According to Elizabeth Cagan, "Collectivist character development as a goal for socialist education is a reflection of the values and ideals of more than a century of socialist thought and derives from a Marxist analysis of the relationship between individuals and society." Rather than portraying Marx as a mere deterministic, reductionist thinker, she sees him as invoking a new form of consciousness—one which will issue "a collectivist entity, requiring the unified participation of all for the good of all." This kind of education, Cagan argues, will require the deliberate inculcation of cooperative values and modes of behavior, as in the recent cases of educational and economic development in China and Cuba, if repressive layers of excess capitalism and competition are, indeed, to be transformed. In the process, Cagan is silent about the distinct possibilities for indoctrination that usher from her educational recommendations.[42]

Cagan's analysis introduces the pivotal role of human agency in any interpretation of neo-Marxist forms of schooling. The philosophical problem of agency, which assumes the power of self-conscious determination in human affairs, is a vexing one for Marxist ideology. As mere superstructural institutions, schools would appear to play rather minimal roles within the massive array of reproductive relations which already constrain human beings in the social system.[43] Neo-Marxist theoreticians Stanley Aronowitz and Henry Giroux articulate this quandary in stark fashion:

> Marxism claims that history replaces ethics, that class analysis precludes reform and that the language of possibility must address only the project of global social transformation. Lacking an immediate prospect for the latter, Marxist educational theorists are constrained, at a certain point, to shut up.[44]

Some recent cultural neo-Marxist educators have attempted to mitigate the overly deterministic thrust of social reproduction theory by claiming that "the cultural sphere has a degree of relative autonomy."[45] Rather than stressing social reproduction, they emphasize *ideological* production as a conscious method for actively constituting social meaning and social change in schools and society. In a certain sense, cultural neo-Marxism revises orthodox Marxism by recasting social contradictions and complexities beyond those that Marx himself had originally formulated or thought about. Yet, in minimizing economic determinism and dialectical materialism (at least in comparison to Marx), these same neo-Marxists have been accused of a kind of "trivialization" of the purity of Marxism:

> ... in [the cultural neo-Marxists'] hands the contradictions in schooling are "liberated" from Marx's view of history and Marx's notion of class. They do not seem to result from the development of the technological base. Nor do they characterize the fundamental antagonisms inherent in the class structure generated by the social relations of production of capitalism. ... To claim that an institution is contradictory is to claim that that institution has a set of functions that cannot be simultaneously realized. This is a perfectly sensible notion of contradiction. ... But it is not, in any way, uniquely Marxist. Modern sociology, economics, and political science are full of discussion of such "contradictions."[46]

In addition, some cultural neo-Marxists have themselves rejected the notion of social reproduction for its reductionism in explaining how students behave and react to internalized social and psychological pressures. According to Michael Apple, a prominent spokesperson for the cultural school of thought, social reproduction theses tend to "view students as passive internalizers of pregiven social messages."[47] Since neo-Marxist educators such as Aronowitz, Giroux, and Apple call for schools to be *transformative* social agencies, they implicitly assume that teachers and students are, indeed, capable, under certain conditions, of surmounting the harsher realities that often beset them. That is to say, they can sometimes rebel against, and resist, what are often deemed to be ineluctable social circumstances. This arena for resistance, under ripe social conditions, thus assumes a degree of personal autonomy and self-determination. In the end, then, we may not be so doomed by the seemingly inexorable laws of social reproduction, after all.

Finally, Marxist and neo-Marxist critics of schooling have not been exceptionally notable for their contributions toward the improvement of internal classroom practices.[48] Given their emphasis on the need to overhaul larger social, political, and economic systems, they tend to stress, in their critiques, those *external* conditions which impede educational progress. Nevertheless, they have been influential, with other critics, in pointing out those elements of the "hidden curriculum" in schools that often prepare students, usually unconsciously and willy-nilly, for their roles and functions in capitalist society. Examples of the hidden curriculum are legion: competitive systems of grading and evaluation; the textbooks that foster the acceptance of the political and economic status quo; the passivity involved in rote memorization; the rituals of punctuality, cleanliness, and politeness which punctuate classroom pedagogy; and the practice of putting students in straight lines as they parade to the lavoratory. All these practices instill in students certain habits that will carry over into the work force, in their personal lives, and in their roles as citizens. To that extent, Marxists and neo-Marxists can rightly speak of the individual freedom that is mitigated by school practices and of the overarching components of competition that are endemic to those practices.

FEMINISM

Competition and inequality between the sexes have been part of the defining features of Western political and educational theory since its birth. In recent decades, wide-ranging, sensitive scholarship in feminist thought has shown that women have been largely denied full and equal access to the re-creation of shared societal understandings. On a broad cultural level, feminist thinkers such as Susan Moller Okin have attempted to demonstrate that conventional functionalist translations of role-distribution and role-patterns are not necessarily basic and imperative for the ongoing survival and growth of civilized social and political life. Okin clarifies how certain given assumptions have served to solidify sexism, competition, and inequality within dominant functionalist paradigms: (1) the premise of "familial primacy," which has tended to link state and family interests; (2) gender dualism, with its attendant unequal differentiations in sex roles and political participation; and (3) the centrality of patriarchy, which has extended unequal sexual differentiation to the legal and social disfranchisement of women.[49]

Each of the above primary assumptions may be explained through the lens of Herbert Marcuse's critical analysis of "basic" versus "surplus" repression. Extrapolating on Freud's cultural paradigm, Marcuse defines "basic" repression as that modification of the "instincts necessary for the perpetuation of the human race in civilization," e.g., provision of food and shelter and combating of disease. By contrast, "surplus" repression refers to those "restrictions necessitated by social domination," i.e., additive forms of constraint over and above that which is vital to civilized life. Surplus-repression has been a result of sociohistory, not one of necessity; as such, it is amenable to social change. In feminist terms, the primacy of the family, patriarchy, and gender dualisms amounts, in practice, to an elaboration of the principle of surplus-repression.[50]

In his characterization of female physiology, for example, Freud appears to extend a *prima facie* case of biological circumstances (the famous dictum, "anatomy is destiny") into an extra-layered case of societal surplus-repression. As Elizabeth Janeway points out:

> Freud himself occasionally warned . . . against the "superimposition" of unjustified significance on the facts of physical differences between the sexes. But these differences are just what he cites to account for the social roles of men and women, even though anyone reading him today can follow his arguments perfectly well (indeed better) by taking these differences as symbolic of assigned gender roles . . . of the socialization process of learning and accepting norms of behavior and expression.[51]

Likewise, Okin claims that dominant Western thinkers from Aristotle, in ancient Greece, through Talcott Parsons, in mid-twentieth century American sociology, have presented theories "about a particular historical set of institutions as a dictum for human behavior throughout eternity."[52] Similarly, Carole Pateman has analyzed some dominant ethical conceptions of justice which run through the works of other central figures in Western thought, especially those of Rousseau and Freud. She delineates the role of theories of the "state of nature" and "social contract" (Rousseau) as well as distinctions between "private" and "universal" spheres of interest (Freud). For Pateman, each of these theoretical developments serves to illustrate how women have been misplaced and misappropriated in that "scheme of things" which constitutes civilization. Their misplacement—and mistreatment—afford countless further examples of surplus-repression.

In the realm of educational theory, the contemporary philosopher of education Jane Roland Martin has offered a particularly pointed challenge to dominant modes of discourse on what constitutes the "ideal of the educated person." In her own discipline, Paul Hirst's analytic treatment of liberal education as "a form of education knowing no limits other than those necessarily imposed by the nature of rational knowledge" has been widely acknowledged and accepted.[54] At the same time, R. S.

Peters, another highly respected analytic philosopher of education, has persuaded many of his colleagues to accept certain educational "aims" as well-nigh self-evident and beyond reasonable doubt.[55] His aims resemble those of Hirst. Yet Hirst and Peters also leave other critics to wonder whether their educative goals are as "obvious" as they would make us believe.[56] Martin is a direct critic of both Hirst and Peters. She broadly questions the whole notion of liberal education as developed in the "rational" tradition of Western political thought from Plato to Rousseau.[57]

According to Martin,

> the educated person . . . coincides with our cultural stereotype of a male human being. According to that stereotype men are objective, analytic, rational; they are interested in ideas and things; they have no interpersonal orientation; they are neither nurturant nor supportive. According to the stereotype, nurturance, supportiveness, empathy and sensitivity are female attributes. Intuition is a female attribute too.[58]

Sensing a "male bias" in the treatment of educational aims, Martin calls for a "gender-sensitive" and "gender-just" ideal which might yield more equitable, and thus identical, educational results. Indeed, her powerful argument has engendered a new controversy among her brethren and sisters in analytic educational philosophy over issues which had been seemingly long laid to rest by Hirst and Peters.

As with the history of educational theory and practice, the focal point for the history of moral development theory has also been the study of men rather than women. Freud typically insisted on viewing women through stained glass, referring to them as "a dark continent for psychology."[59] Piaget tested his cognitive development theory by utilizing the game of marbles and story-telling techniques with young boys.[60] More recently, Lawrence Kohlberg omitted women from the original sample which became the basis for his pioneering longitudinal survey of developmental modes of moral reasoning.[61] In even more recent years, some bold, and equally pioneering, feminist scholars have attempted to recast moral development by unearthing hidden dimensions of feminine experience and perspectives.

A colleague of the late Kohlberg at Harvard University's Center for Moral Education, Carol Gilligan has challenged his theories in light of her own research on women. Gilligan's model, though still unfinished, counterposes a rich tapestry of particular social and personal context alongside Kohlberg's more abstractly "rational," contemplative universe of discourse. While Kohlberg's thesis speaks of individual liberty and a cognitive hierarchy of stages, Gilligan's argument underscores a language of care, responsibility, cooperation, and not wanting to hurt others in women's presumably unique moral thema and moral vision.[62]

Gilligan also notes that Kohlberg found women, in his studies, to favor an intermediate, "conventional" stage of moral development, i.e., a "nice girl" orientation whereby one earns approval and maintains strong interpersonal relations.[63] Kohlberg held that such a stage of development was functional and adequate for women. (He also argued that once women take on the same social roles as men, women's moral development will likely be the same as that of men.) Gilligan laments that the traits that have conventionally defined the "goodness" of women—their care and sensitivity to the needs of others—are those that mark them as deficient in Kohlberg's schema for moral development. She suggests that Kohlberg's scoring system may be biased against women because of the disproportionate number of males in research samples and that the developmental theories themselves tend to be formulated by men.

According to Gilligan, women speak "in a different voice" than men. Extrapolating on Kohlberg's studies, she hypothesizes that women's language is substantially one of caring and interpersonal responsibility whereas men's dialect seems to be framed in terms of individual rights, duties, and their attendant protection. Indeed, some critics have argued that the preeminence of Kohlberg's paradigm may be explained, in part, by its tendency to "reinforce current dominant views about pluralistic democracy and justice as fairness."[64] In other words, Kohlberg's model of justice may be part and parcel of that strong core of "liberal individualism" so popular in Western culture.

How does Gilligan conceptualize the development of "self" and "other"? She takes an evolutionary stance attuned to the subjective passages of those women she interviews in her studies. For Gilligan, the fluid growth sequence in women's ethic of care appears to follow: (1) "an initial focus on caring for the self in order to ensure survival" [a more competitive mode]; (2) "a transitional phase in which this judgment is criticized as selfish"; and (3) a new understanding of the connection between self and others which is articulated by the concept of responsibility [a more interdependent mode]."[65]

Gilligan further contends that this "new understanding" of relatedness would be vitiated if one were to gauge women's moral development solely with reference to Kohlberg's theoretical interpretations. In her interviews with 11-year-old children, Amy and Jake, Gilligan tries to show how Amy's evident moral virtues would be minimized if she were judged by Kohlberg's categories. Using Kohlberg's classic Heinz case (stealing from the druggist to save the life of one's spouse), Gilligan's interviews reveal different responses from Amy and Jake. The latter solves the Heinz dilemma in a manner akin to the algebraic gymnastic he performs in mathematics class: who has the property right and what is fair for the individual? Amy, on the other hand, is more intent on making sure that Heinz and his wife do not suffer in their relationship as a result of any theft. On Kohlberg's scale of values, Amy's compassionate logic would be insufficiently informed by principles of moral *reasoning*, which presumably emphasize fairness, justice, and rights.

Gilligan admits that her samples are "small and nonrepresentative," including mostly upper-middle class children and Radcliffe-Harvard students.[66] Of the three studies referred to in her seminal work, *In a Different Voice,* the total sample size is 144 (8 males and 8 females at varying ages at nine points across the life cycle, i.e., ages 6–9, 11, 15, 19, 22, 25–27, 35, 45, and 60); this sample includes a "more intensively interviewed subsample of 36 (2 males and 2 females at each age)."[67] Other critics have raised more substantive philosophical questions concerning Gilligan's distinctions on assumed male versus female ethical differences. As one writer has observed, ". . . the ethical differences that emerge in interviews with males and females documented by Gilligan might better be summarized as variations in expressions of care and responsibility."[68]

Nor do Gilligan's sensitive explorations of androgyny and moral boundaries directly address wider social and political concerns. She tends to postulate social relationships which are largely restricted to personal relations among family members, friends, and colleagues. Indeed, Gilligan's "new maps of moral development" do not precisely touch on "the possibility of aspiring beyond liberal goals of distributive justice and the satisfaction of private interest" which might form cooperative social bonds dedicated to "the ideals of affective, productive, and rational community."[69] In this shortcoming, Gilligan joins hands with Lawrence Blum, who has also articulated a "two-streamed" portrait of morality: one of Kantian rights and impartiality, the other of primary human feeling—"sympathy, compassion, and human concern."[70] Though Gilligan and Blum are interested in a morality of cooperative interaction, theirs is one "that is prerequisite to the fulfillment of . . . individual goals."[71] Yet recent empirical evidence tends to confirm that engagement in actual social interaction, particularly interactions of relative equality, may in fact be the most effective way to develop a morality a tolerance for a truly moral community.[72]

Repercussions from Gilligan's studies have recently begun to generate sustained dialogue and further exploration in women's studies and beyond. In *Caring* (1984), the educational philosopher Nel Noddings bases her theoretical argument on principles of "natural caring," as in the case of a mother's concern for her child. Noddings maintains that the powerful stream of "natural caring" has been largely neglected in most traditional philosophic approaches to ethics. By positing such an ethic as foundational, Noddings holds out as a wider task that of forging a future agenda for fuller moral education—one which she contends would benefit men as well as women.[73]

Noddings' thesis resembles, in part, the more global world-view of another contemporary feminist scholar, Sara Ruddick. In her work entitled "Maternal Thinking," Ruddick views the concept "maternal" as a social category:

> Although maternal thinking arises out of actual child-caring practices, biological parenting is neither necessary nor sufficient. Many women and some men express maternal thinking in various kinds of working and caring with others.... It is an attitude elicited by the work of "world-protection, world-preservation, world-repair."[74]

For Ruddick, maternal thinking represents the virtue of humility, "a selfless respect for reality"; the virtue of "clearsighted cheerfulness," which is a "willingness to continue, to give birth and to accept having given birth, to welcome life despite its conditions"; and the virtue of love as a growth-enabling power:

> The recognition of the priority of holding over acquiring once again distinguishes maternal from scientific thought, as well as from the instrumentalism of technocratic capitalism. In recognizing resilient good humor and humility as achievements of its practices, maternal thought takes issue both with contemporary moral theory and with popular moralities of [competitive] assertiveness.[75]

At the same time, Ruddick cautions against "cheery denial" of the harsher realities of life as well as the more subtle restraints, such as consumerism, that pervade late twentieth-century life styles.[76]

Particularly since the mid-1970s, the feminist world-view has reverberated in the classroom as well. Yet there is a long way to go. Both scholars and practitioners have sought to minimize sex-role stereotyping, e.g., the macho visage that society stamps on young boys and the "Miss Cute" image that it imposes on little girls.[77] For example, textbooks have been scrutinized more fully for such images, as has the mass media for its indulgences in violence, anti-Gay bashing, and pornographic excesses. Indeed, the feminist critique has made us all more acutely aware of how social structures, including the family and schools, can become subtle purveyors of stunted forms of socialization, of lessons that run counter to complete human development.

ENDNOTES

1. Price, Kingsley: *Education and Philosophical Thought.* Boston, Allyn and Bacon, 1962, p. 316. Cf. Rousseau, Jean-Jacques: *Emile,* Barbara Foxley (Tr.). London: J. M. Dent and Sons, 1911, pp. 38–39, 97–121.

2. *Ibid.,* p. 318. Cf. Rousseau: *Emile,* pp. 128–30, 133–35, 139–40, 142, 147.

3. Pateman, Carole: *Participation and Democratic Theory.* Cambridge, Cambridge University Press, 1970, pp. 24–25. Cf. Rousseau: *The Social Contract,* Maurice Cranston (Tr.). Harmondsworth: Penguin, 1968.

4. Cranston, Maurice: *Freedom: A New Analysis.* London: Longmans, 1953, pp. 4–6.

5. Morton, Snyder: What is progressive education? In Cubberley, Ellwood P. (Ed.): *Readings in Public Education in the United States.* Boston: Houghton Mifflin, 1934, p. 420.

6. Bachman, F. P. and Flexner, A.: Merits of the Gary plan. In *Ibid.,* p. 418.

7. Cremin, Lawrence: *The Transformation of the School.* New York: Knopf, 1961, p. ix.

8. Rugg, Harold and Shumaker, Ann: *The Child-Centered School.* New York: World, 1928, pp. 102, 314.

9. Mayhew, Katherine C. and Edwards, Anna C.: *The Dewey School.* New York: D. Appleton-Century, 1936, p. 467. Cf. Dewey, John: *Democracy and Education.* New York, Macmillan, 1916, pp. 295, 297: "When knowledge is regarded as originating and developing within an individual, the ties which bind the mental life of one to that of his fellows are ignored and denied. . . . Every individual has grown up, and always must grow up, in a social medium. . . . Through social intercourse, through sharing in the activities embodying beliefs, he gradually acquires a mind of his own. The conception of mind as a purely isolated possession of the self is at the very antipodes of truth."

10. Dewey, John: *The Public and Its Problems.* New York: Henry Holt, 1945, p. 154. Cf. Dewey: *Democracy and Education,* p. 5: "There is more than a verbal tie between the words common, community, and communication. Men live in a community in virtue of the things which they have in common; and communication is the way in which they come to possess things in common."

11. Popp, Jerome A.: If you see John Dewey, tell him we did it. *Educational Theory,* 37: 149, Spring, 1987.

12. For a systematic analysis of these reform issues, see Dewey, John: *Individualism Old and New.* New York, Minton, Balch, 1930.

13. Bestor, Arthur E.: *Educational Wastelands: The Retreat from Learning in Our Public Schools.* Urbana: University of Illinois Press, 1953.

14. Rickover, Hyman G.: *Swiss Schools and Ours: Why Theirs Are Better.* Boston: Atlantic-Little, Brown, 1962.

15. Dewey, John: *Experience and Education.* New York: Macmillan, 1938.

16. Carter, Rosemary: Justifying paternalism. *Canadian Journal of Philosophy,* 7: 133, March, 1977.

17. Brandwein, Paul: *Memorandum: On Renewing Schooling and Education.* New York: Harcourt Brace Jovanovich, 1981.

18. For an interesting account of the European origins of libertarian pedagogy, see Spring, Joel: *A Primer of Libertarian Pedagogy.* New York: Free Life Editions, 1975.

19. Hospers, John: What Libertarianism is. In Machan, Tibor R. (Ed.): *The Libertarian Alternative.* Chicago: Nelson-Hall, 1974, pp. 3–20. Also see Hospers, John: *Libertarianism.* Los Angeles, Nash, 1971.

20. Holt, John: *Escape from Childhood.* New York, E. P. Dutton, 1974; and Farson, Richard: *Birthrights.* New York: Macmillan, 1974.

21. Holt, John: *Escape from Childhood,* pp. 241–242.

22. Farson, Richard: *Birthrights,* ch. 7.

23. Holt, John: *Escape from Childhood,* p. 240.

24. Goodman, Paul: What rights should children have? *New York Review of Books,* 17: 20–22, September 23, 1971.

25. Illich, Ivan: *Deschooling Society.* New York: Harper & Row, 1971.

26. Neill, A. S.: *The Problem Child.* New York: McBride, 1927.

27. Neill, A. S.: *Summerhill: A Radical Approach to Child Rearing.* New York, Hart, 1960.

28. Baumrind, Diana: Reciprocal rights and responsibilities in parent-child relations. *Journal of Social Issues,* 34: 182–184, Spring, 1978. For an incisive critique of libertarian pedagogy in the 1960s and 1970s, see Vogel, Alfred T.: *The Owl Critics.* University, AL: University of Alabama Press, 1980.

29. Katz, Michael S.: Compulsion and the discourse of compulsory school attendance. *Educational Theory,* 27: 179–185, Summer, 1977.

30. Reagan, Gerald M.: Compulsion, schooling, and education. *Educational Studies,* 4: 1–7, Spring, 1973.

31. Coons, John E. and Sugarman, Stephen D.: *Education by Choice: The Case for Family Control.* Berkeley, University of California Press, 1978, p. 10. The same argument is also presented by other libertarians. See West, E. G.: *Education and the State.* London, The Institute of Economic Affairs, 1965, p. 13; and Cunningham, Robert L.: *Education: Free and Public.* Wichita, Center for Independent Education, n. d., p. 2.

32. Bumstead, Richard A.: Educating your child at home: the Perchemides case. *Phi Delta Kappan,* 61: 97–100, October, 1979.

33. Coons and Sugarman: *Education by Choice,* chs. 3–5.

34. Butts, R. Freeman: The public schools: assaults on a great idea. *The Nation,* pp. 553–560, April 30, 1973.

35. Dahrendorf, Ralf: *Life Chances.* Chicago: University of Chicago Press, 1979, pp. 30–39.

36. Some examples of the functionalist, or social-disorganization, approach: Parsons, Talcott: *The Social System.* Glencoe, Ill., Free Press, 1951; Merton, Robert: *Social Theory and Social Structure.* Glencoe, IL: Free Press, 1957; and McGee, Reece: Social Disorganization in America. San Francisco, Chandler, 1962.

37. Feinberg, Walter and Soltis, Jonas F.: *School and Society.* New York: Teachers College Press, 1985, p. 56.

38. Althusser, Louis: *Lenin and Philosophy and Other Essays.* New York: New Left Books, 1971, pp. 123–173.

39. Cohen, Robert S.: On the Marxist philosophy of education. In Henry, Nelson B. (Ed.): *Modern Philosophies and Education.* Chicago, National Society for the Study of Education, 1955, pp. 196–197.

40. Lukes, Steven: *Individualism.* New York: Harper & Row, 1973, p. 26.

41. Bowles, Samuel and Gintis, Herbert: *Schooling in Capitalist America.* New York: Basic Books, 1976, p. 252.

42. Cagan, Elizabeth: Individualism, collectivism, and radical educational reform. *Harvard Educational Review,* 48: 236–238, May, 1978. Cf. Marx, Karl: *Capital,* vol. 3. Chicago: Charles H. Kerr, 1909, p. 954: "What we have to deal with here is a communist society, not as if it *had developed on a basis of its own,* but on the contrary as *it emerges from capitalist society,* which is thus in every respect tainted economically, morally and intellectually with the hereditary diseases of the old society from whose womb it is emerging."

43. Strike, Kenneth A.: *Liberal Justice and the Marxist Critique of Education: A Study of Conflicting Research Programs.* New York: Routledge, 1989, pp. 136–138.

44. Aronowitz, Stanley and Giroux, Henry: *Education under Siege.* South Hadley, MA: Bergin & Garvey, 1985, p. 6.

45. Apple, Michael W.: Reproduction and contradiction in education: an introduction. In Apple, Michael W. (Ed.): *Cultural and Economic Reproduction in Education.* London: Routledge & Kegan Paul, 1982, p. 11.

46. Strike, Kenneth A.: *Liberal Justice and the Marxist Critique of Education,* p. 158.

47. Apple, Michael W.: *Education and Power.* London: Routledge & Kegan Paul, 1982, p. 14.

48. A notable exception to this rule is Norton, Theodore Mills and Ollman, Bertell (Eds.): *Studies in Socialist Pedagogy.* New York: Monthly Review Press, 1978.

49. Okin, Susan Moller: *Women in Western Political Thought.* Princeton: Princeton University Press, 1979.

50. Marcuse, Herbert: *Eros and Civilization: A Philosophical Inquiry into Freud.* New York: Vintage, 1962, pp. 32–34.

51. Janeway, Elizabeth: *Cross Sections: From a Decade of Change.* New York: William Morrow, 1982, pp. 78–79. See also Freud, Sigmund: *Three Essays on the Theory of Sexuality,* J. Strachey (Tr.). New York: Basic Books, (1905), 1962.

52. Okin, Susan Moller: Women's place and nature in a functionalist world. In DeVitis, Joseph L. (Ed.): *Women, Culture and Morality: Selected Essays.* New York: Peter Lang, 1987, p. 57.

53. Pateman, Carole: The "disorder of women": women, love, and the sense of justice. *Ethics,* 91: 20–34, October, 1980.

54. Hirst, Paul: In Archambault, R. D. (Ed.): *Philosophical Analysis and Education.* London: Routledge & Kegan Paul, 1965, p. 127.

55. Peters, R. S.: *Authority, Responsibility and Education,* 2d ed. London: Allen & Unwin, ch. 7.

56. See Beck, Clive: *Educational Philosophy and Theory: An Introduction.* Boston: Little, Brown, 1974, ch. 1.

57. Martin, Jane Roland: The ideal of the educated person. *Educational Theory,* 31: 97–109, Spring, 1981. For a more recent synthesis of Martin's ideas, see her *Reclaiming a Conversation: The Ideal of the Educated Woman.* New Haven: Yale University Press, 1985.

58. Martin, Jane Roland: The ideal of an educated person, p. 102.

59. Freud, Sigmund: The question of lay analysis. In Strachey, J. (Ed.): *The Standard Edition of the Complete Psychological Works of Sigmund Freud,* vol. 20. London: Hogarth, 1955, p. 212.

60. Piaget, Jean: *The Moral Judgment of the Child* (1932), Marjorie Gabain (Tr.). New York: Collier, 1962.

61. Kohlberg, Lawrence: The development of modes of moral thinking and choice in the years ten to sixteen. Unpublished doctoral dissertation. University of Chicago, 1958.

62. Gilligan, Carol: *In a Different Voice: Psychological Theory and Women's Development.* Cambridge, Mass.: Harvard University Press, 1982. Cf. also Gilligan, Carol; Lyons, Nona P.; and Hanmer, Trudy J. (Eds.): *Making Connections: The Relational World of Adolescent Girls at Emma Willard School.* Cambridge, MA: Harvard University Press, 1990.

63. Kohlberg, Lawrence: *The Philosophy of Moral Development: Moral Stages and the Idea of Justice.* New York: Harper & Row, 1981.

64. Sichel, Betty A.: Moral development and education: men's language of rights and women's language of responsibility. *Contemporary Education Review,* 2: 34, Spring, 1983.

65. Gilligan, Carol: *In a Different Voice,* p. 74.

66. Murphy, J. M. and Gilligan, Carol: Moral development in late adolescence and adulthood: a critique and reconstruction of Kohlberg's theory. *Human Development,* 23: 84, 1980.

67. Gilligan, Carol: *In a Different Voice,* p. 3.

68. Prakash, Madhu Suri: Review of *In a Different Voice: Psychological Theory and Women's Development.* In *Educational Studies,* 15: 194, Summer, 1984.

69. Wolff, Robert Paul: *The Poverty of Liberalism.* Boston, Beacon, 1968, pp. 183–184. Also see Rawls, John: *A Theory of Justice.* Cambridge, MA: Harvard University Press, 1971.

70. Blum, Lawrence A.: *Friendship, Altruism and Morality.* London, Routledge & Kegan Paul, 1980, p. 8.

71. *Ibid.,* p. 98.

72. See Serow, Robert C.: *Schooling for Social Diversity: An Analysis of Policy and Practice.* New York, Teachers College Press, 1983, especially chs. 2 and 3. For a recent empirical analysis which directly challenges Gilligan's findings, see Walker, Lawrence J.: Sex differences in the development of moral reasoning: a critical review. *Child Development,* 55: 677–691, 1984.

73. Noddings, Nel: *Caring: A Feminine Approach to Ethics and Moral Education.* Berkeley: University of California Press, 1984.

74. Ruddick, Sara: Maternal thinking. *Feminist Studies,* 6: 350, 1980.

75. *Ibid.*

76. *Ibid.,* pp. 354–361.

77. For example, see Best, Raphaela: *We've All Got Scars: What Boys and Girls Learn in Elementary School.* Bloomington: Indiana University Press, 1983; and Schniedewind, Nancy and Davidson, Ellen: *Open Minds to Equality: A Sourcebook of Learning Activities to Promote Race, Sex, Class and Age Equity.* Englewood Cliffs, NJ: Prentice-Hall, 1983.

Chapter Nine

NONCOMPETITIVE EDUCATIONAL PROGRAMS AND PRACTICES

Throughout the history of society and schooling, there have been countless examples of programs and practices that bring persons together as interacting agents in joint educative ventures. According to the old German proverb, "What is new is seldom true; what is true is seldom new." Much the same could be said of many of the programs and practices that emphasize cooperation among students and teachers. Perhaps they only appear to be "new" because they inhabit a subterranean realm within a wider array of educational structures that have been perennially and persistently individualistic and competitive in nature. This chapter seeks to unearth and discuss some important modes of education that embody noncompetitive ideas and practices to a rather considerable degree: peer tutoring, peer collaboration, and cooperative learning. In addition, we will examine such curricular innovations as nongraded schools, open education, alternative schools, and the whole language movement.

PEER TUTORING AND PEER COLLABORATION

The historical roots of peer tutoring, i.e., cooperative interactions involving cross-age and same-age peers, appear to be at least as old as ancient Greece. Aristotle (384–322 B.C.) was said to have relied on student helpers (archons) for some of the organizational work necessitated by his peripatetic teaching.[1] In his *Institutio Oratoria* (93 A.D.), the Roman educator Quintilian (35–97 A.D.) pointed out that older peers could be appropriate tutors for younger peers, particularly since they could be, at times, more exuberant and inventive than adult mentors.[2] John Amos Comenius (1592–1670), an influential Moravian schoolmaster, wrote in his *Didactica Magna:* "The saying 'He who teaches others, teaches himself,' is very true . . . because the process of teaching in itself gives a deeper insight into any subject taught."[3] Johann Heinrich Pestalozzi (1746–1827), a Swiss pedagogical disciple of Rousseau, reported in *How Gertrude Teaches Her Children* that he trained peer assistants to teach most of the 80 children under his care.[4] (Pestalozzi's experiment was very short-lived, however.)

On American soil, the most wide-sweeping transfusion of peer tutoring came from the British educators Joseph Lancaster (1778–1838) and Andrew Bell (1753–1832). Both instituted *monitorial* forms of instruction. In Lancaster's model, the schools were, for all intents and purposes, run by the students. In them, older pupils were tutored by the schoolmaster; in turn, they monitored and drilled the younger students. An older pupil (monitor) was assigned to each class in order to keep track of student decorum and progress. Bell had one master teacher in each of his schools, but a wider assortment of peer tutors and pupils (whom he designated as "ushers" and "sub-ushers") who largely taught one another and were responsible for school administration. Bell's program was an early example of peer collaboration.

Lancaster eventually came to the United States in 1818. By that time, there were more than 150 monitorial schools as far east as Baltimore, Philadelphia, and New York and as far west as Detroit, Cincinnati, and New Orleans. By the 1830s, Lancaster's influence had also been established in monitorial schools in the South, most notably in Tennessee, Georgia, Kentucky, and Mississippi. Monitorial methods were employed especially in one-room schools in the rural countrysides.[5]

In 1917, T. J. Woofter published *Teaching in Rural Schools*, a manual which described how older student peers could be used as teaching assistants.[6] Some of the assumptions of peer tutoring and peer collaboration appear to presage basic tenets in progressivism.

In contemporary times, there have been numerous studies on the impact of peer teaching at all levels of education. Perhaps the most significant of these studies were those conducted by researchers at the University of Michigan in the 1960s and 1970s. Lippitt and Lohman examined a series of pilot projects in Michigan during that time and reported the following findings about peer tutoring: (1) it affords definite opportunities for cross-age interaction; (2) it provides closer means of cooperation between students and teachers; (3) it generates peer attitudes of noncompetitiveness; (4) it helps students and teachers prepare for their functions as helpers; and (5) it offers instantaneous feedback on the teaching-learning process. In addition, it was found that both older and younger pupils improved in academic achievement and exhibited growth in social skills.[7] In 1971, Gartner, Kohler, and Riessman summarized peer teaching practices in various programs across the country and concluded that they assist in individualizing classroom instruction and, indeed, were more effective in general than more traditional, teacher-dominant pedagogical models.[8] In the affective domain of education, a whole host of research studies have pointed to the manner in which peer teaching can positively influence student self-esteem and socialization skills in the process of reinforcing academic preparation.[9]

Apparently, peer tutoring fosters the development of internal mechanisms of self-efficacy and control when applied to many different schools of thought on teaching and learning. In role-theory analysis of pedagogy, which stresses the function of roles in changing attitudes and behavior, "in the case of the child who enacts the role of teacher for another child, the role represents prestige, authority, and feelings of competence."[10] In sociolinguistic theory, which emphasizes the impact of socialization patterns on speech and self-perception, M. C. Ratti has observed that peer teachers can help peer students since they literally speak on each other's own terms.[11] In developmental psychology, B. M. Greenspan has adumbrated a psychophilosophical justification for encouraging adolescent peers to become tutors by incorporating the work of Piaget and Kohlberg.[12] For Greenspan, peer tutoring allows adolescents to assume adult roles, to reach toward higher-level cognitive thought processes, and to heighten social participation and global awareness and thus navigate toward more postconventional moral development. From the perspective of behavioral psychology, some studies have also found that accompanying external rewards with peer tutoring can further stimulate peer-tutor involvement in classroom activities.[13]

A substantial basis for both psychological and philosophical rationales for peer collaboration can be discovered in the underlying assumptions surrounding debates on child development, in particular the classic debate between Emile Durkheim (1858–1916), the famous French sociologist, and Jean Piaget (1896–1980), the equally illustrious Swiss psychologist. A significant portion of Piaget's *The Moral Judgment of the Child* (1932) is devoted to a revisionist critique of Durkheim's social theory. By definition, Durkheim viewed education and development as the proper exercise of adult influence on "those that are not yet ready for social life."[14] Piaget, on the other hand, gave much greater play to the child's *own* transformation of inner perception and external reality. He implied that Durkheim had carried the traditional adult-role model of human development to such an extent that he had become blinded to youth's potentialities:

> Durkheim thinks of children as knowing no other society than adult society or the societies created by adults (schools), so that he entirely ignores the existence of spontaneously formed children's societies, and of the facts relating to mutual respect.[15]

Once the child resolves some of the difficulties inherent in distinguishing his own "reality" from the givens in external reality, Piaget foresees a more or less natural process of gradually unfolding human development (much in the manner of Rousseau's "ripe tomato" analogy). Unless one is somehow deprived of social experiences, particularly with peers, Piaget assumes that such growth will occur. To a significant degree, he argues that *peer interaction* is vital because it is the only legitimately *equal* form of social participation. As such, he implies, on a broader level, that peer equality may likewise be the most legitimate testing ground for morality in general.[16]

Nevertheless, the interactional "give-and-take" that Piaget postulates as the *sine qua non* of social and moral development has not been conclusively substantiated in the research literature. Urie Bronfenbrenner has observed that peer interaction in American youth often leads to excessive dependence on peer approval.[17] Thus, the maturing child may simply be relinquishing one form of authority for another, i.e., adult authority gives way to peer authority.

Despite the above admonitions, Piaget's powerful themes regarding children's interactions with others have been further elaborated in more recent times by such cognitive theorists as L. S. Vygotsky and William Damon. The latter offers a penetrating synthesis of Vygotsky's argument on the potency of peer interaction:

> Children are introduced to new patterns of thought when they engage in dialogues with peers. This is because peer dialogue is by nature a cooperative exchange of ideas between equals and therefore emulates several critical features of rational thinking. In particular, the verification of ideas, the planning of strategies in advance, and the symbolic representation of intellectual acts are enacted through peer communication. Eventually, after repeated exposure to cooperative peer exchange, the child's own thinking becomes influenced. That is, the child takes on or "internalizes" the very communicative procedures that the child experiences when interacting with a peer. In this manner, the child's intellectual abilities are permanently modified for the better.[18]

Indeed, Vygotsky uses the term "zone of proximal development" to signify the difference between individual and social problem-solving. He conceptualizes the zone as "the distance between actual developmental level as determined by independent problem solving and the level of potential development through problem solving under adult guidance or in collaboration with more capable peers."[19] Another influential cognitive theorist, Jerome Bruner, has articulated this theme in similar fashion in his portrait of the child's world:

> That world is a symbolic world in the sense that it consists of conceptually organized, rule-bound belief systems about what exists, about how to get to goals, about what is to be valued. There is no way, none, in which a human being could possibly master that world without the aid and assistance of others for, in fact, that world *is* others.[20]

At this point, it now seems appropriate to distinguish between the principal forms of peer interaction that we have been discussing, and will discuss further, in this chapter. Damon and Phelps have afforded us some helpful ways in which to differentiate such concepts as "peer tutoring," "peer collaboration," and "cooperative learning." They focus on two major fulcrums of peer interaction: "equality" and "mutuality of engagement." Equality refers to a definite and definable attribute of a peer relationship, e.g., equivalence in age, cognitive development, or problem-solving skills held by the interacting peers. Mutuality of engagement signifies the manner and depth of "connection" or "synchronization" each peer has in working with other peers on the same activities in a problem-solving situation. Damon and Phelps contend that "peer tutoring is relatively low on equality and high on mutuality; cooperative learning is high on equality and low on mutuality; and peer collaboration is high on both."[21] In peer tutoring, for example, a dyadic power relation is still assumed between peer mentor (superordinance) and peer pupils (subordinance). In light of these distinctions, we can now turn to the task of describing and analyzing what we mean by "cooperative learning."

COOPERATIVE LEARNING

Educators who decry the excessively competitive structure of traditional classrooms that sort students into "winners" and "losers" have formulated alternative approaches known as "cooperative learning." Like peer tutoring and peer collaboration, cooperative learning methods have been practiced informally for several millenia. Shlomo Sharan, a prominent proponent of cooperative learning, traces its roots at least as far back as Jewish pedagogy in the ancient Yeshiva, where pupils could

> make knowledge their own, not by repeating what they heard, but by exploring ideas through intense conversations with others with whom they quite often disagree. These discussions [could] afford the participants the opportunity to think and rethink, formulate and reformulate their ideas, using what they know, what they think and what they hear, until they reach some sense of completeness about their own thoughts and understanding.[22]

In modern times, particularly since the 1970s, cooperative learning methods have incorporated lessons from both progressivist and behavioral streams of educational thought, as will be noted.

In the late 1940s, Morton Deutsch amplified Kurt Lewin's notions on motivation and developed a theoretical paradigm for the study of competitive, individualistic, and cooperative modes of learning. In *competitive* goal structures, learners are situated in such a way that they are separate from one another; indeed, by definition, if one person achieves a goal, the others cannot. This places the learner in a position of seeking her goals at the expense of others. In *individualistic* learning situations, the pupil carries out her goals irrespective of the educative aims of other participants; her accomplishment has no real effect on the others' goal attainment. In *cooperative* modes of learning, however, student goals are linked in a fashion that necessitates that one person's aims can only be accomplished through the goal achievements of all other group members. Consequently, the cooperative learner tries to effect outcomes that are mutually rewarding to all participants in the learning process.[23]

Basically an extension of peer collaboration, but more formal and structured, cooperative learning in present-day pedagogy has become highly systematized and includes the following generic components: (1) *face-to-face interaction* among peer students; (2) *evaluational criteria and procedures* that are explicit for all pupils; (3) *individual mechanisms of accountability* which permit the teacher to monitor student progress; (4) *group cohesion* that fosters teamwork and the full cooperation of all students; (5) *social skills development* such that students learn to cooperate and solve problems together; (6) *teacher monitoring* so that adult mentors know whether students are performing cooperatively and attaining requisite academic and social skills; and (7) *pedagogical processing* in order to ensure immediate feedback to students about their daily learning activities and results.[24] Needless to say, cooperative learning calls for extremely careful and continuous monitoring, processing, and assessment by the instructor if it is to be worthwhile. It should also be noted that points one and four are largely progressivist in principle; that points two, three, and six are substantially behavioral; and that point five combines both behavioral and progressivist interests.

Knight and Bohlmeyer have schematized various models of cooperative learning methods which assist in distinguishing different facets of each model.[25] Each of these models will be briefly described and analyzed.

Circles of Learning (Learning Together)

Developed by David W. Johnson and Roger T. Johnson, this model entails both social and academic group goals: the cooperative setting of aims, face-to-face communication of ideas and materials, effective division of tasks and functions, and group reinforcements. As such, it is an amalgam of behavioral and progressivist notions on the teaching-learning process. Customarily, in Circles of Learning, students work on a single group project, assist one another with their responses, monitor each other's progress for clarity and understanding, request teacher feedback only when necessary, and come to expect teacher rewards for their products.[26] Johnson and Johnson's studies seem to indicate that explicit task-orientation and the assistance of peer helpers can be potent motivational tools for both elementary and secondary school students.[27] They can create a cooperative environment in which "a fellow student's knowledge can be a source of interest, stimulation, and information rather than a threat to one's own sense of competence."[28]

Jigsaw Methods

Designed by Elliot Aronson and his associates, this model supports a "required" interdependence among students by granting each student in a learning group only limited information to a particular portion of a lesson or learning activity. Originally, the Jigsaw was created specifically for ethnic and multiracial student groups, but its use has proliferated beyond those groups. Cooperativeness is taught as a *skill,* again in both the academic and social senses of that term. Other important components of the method include teambuilding, heterogeneous grouping, an emphasis on communication and listening skills, and group brainstorming. The teacher is seen as a facilitator who prepares explicit learning environments and carefully explains learning procedures. Again, the Jigsaw classroom incorporates both progressivist and behavioral elements in its overall design. Its motivational structure is primarily individualistic in that grades are based on each person's performance. Students in one Jigsaw group are expected to teach their specific section of the lesson or activity to the other members of the Jigsaw group. Thus, in order to master the "whole picture," students must rely on one another.[29] Research tends to confirm that Jigsaw methods affect the ways in which students relate to each other, help them in accepting others' perspectives, and strengthen academic attitudes and achievement, especially among ethnic and racial minorities.[30]

Student Team Learning

Formulated by Robert Slavin, this method of cooperative learning emphasizes competition among groups through the use of peer tutoring in the form of drill and practice and the deployment of group sanctions and group rewards. Slavin's method also employs heterogeneous grouping in terms of pupil achievement levels, sex, and racial and ethnic background. The teacher transmits material to the student teams in lecture or discussion format and then hands out study worksheets. Team members use the material with each other until mastery is presumably achieved. Students are instructed to learn the concepts in the material and are not considered to have completed the study until they have understood it. Team practice follows, after which pupils are examined on the material studied. Slavin argues that it is critically important to establish particular group rewards for any individual learning involved; only in that way will students make efforts toward the fulfillment of peer norms and goals. Pupils are then given group rewards through recognition in the class newsletter.[31]

Variations on the Student Team Learning model have also been developed. The Teams-Games-Tournaments (TGT) method of cooperative learning involves pairing students of similar ability levels from different teams so that they might compete in tournaments. "Winners" compete with pupils of higher ability in subsequent tournaments, and "losers" compete with students of lesser ability. Examinations are used to establish individual grades.[32] Slavin has devised another alternative strategy, which he terms "Team-Assisted Individualization or Team-Accelerated Instruction" (TAI).[33] In TAI, each pupil is assigned an individualized unit of instruction in mathematics. Team peers check over each other's work, do practice tests, and prepare each other for examinations. Certificates are awarded to those teams whose grades meet an objective criterion. Again, the teacher acts mainly as a facilitator and resource person for the learning groups. Elements of both behavioral and conceptual learning buttress the Student Team Learning models, though they seem more heavily driven by the former.

Group Investigation

Sharan and his collaborators have designed the Group Investigation (GI) method, which traces its intellectual roots to Dewey's social progressivism and the approach to group dynamics developed by field psychologist Kurt Lewin in the 1930s and 1940s. The GI model places more emphasis on peer governance over learning activities and social interactions. Interest groups are formed out of peer interests by way of pupils' identifying subsets of a larger topic formulated initially by the teacher. The class is then divided into small groups along the lines demarcated by those interests. As with Slavin's models, GI consists in cooperative methods of group control and cooperative means for establishing group goals. Once a division of labor is organized, the groups gather information, analyze their data, and formulate how their work will be combined into a single group product. Advised to eschew lectures, teachers serve as aides in group planning and as resource personnel in assisting students with appropriate sources of study and exploration (e.g., books, interviews, site visits, etc.). Such group studies eventuate in final group reports. Students are "encouraged to use innovative and interactive forms of reporting, such as skits, demonstrations, experiments, learning centres where their classmates carry out various tasks, simulations, exhibitions, models, quiz shows, dramatizations, mock TV programmes, etc." Pupils contribute to the evaluation process in the form of preparing exam questions and submitting them to the instructor and by giving feedback to their student colleagues. The GI approach has been used especially in desegregated school settings and multiethnic classrooms.[34]

What are we to make of these various characterizations of cooperative learning? Is it the answer to many of our educational maladies? We should be wary of any approaches that proffer "quick-fix" solutions or ultimate panaceas because such efforts have often tended to exacerbate existing educational problems. Indeed, any ill-conceived, precipitate rush for "innovation," without careful consideration of basic underlying assumptions and likely and potential consequences, would seem to be fraught with possibilities for unintended mistakes and adverse outcomes. In fact, "competition" and "cooperation" may themselves be exaltatory or pejorative terms, depending on one's frame of reference and one's personal and ideological proclivities. And innovations which are introduced with great fanfare and promise often fade or crumble under close scrutiny. Thus, we shall now scrutinize the theory and practice of cooperative learning for what it stipulates, what it leaves unsaid, and where it might lead us.

Many forms of cooperative learning, particularly Slavin's dominant model, seem to embody a rather technicist, *technocratic rationality*—"a mode of reasoning, investigation, or planning that gives priority to considerations of procedure or technique."[35] That is to say, they appear to take for granted that their aims and purposes are "good" without question. Thus, since there is presumably no need for debate on substantive ends, we can quickly proceed to implement the goals of cooperative learning. The means and methods become the ends of inquiry, not the ends-in-view themselves. Ironically, even though some proponents of cooperative learning invoke John Dewey to support their cause, they fail to acknowledge that, in Dewey's philosophy of education, ends and means are always to be considered in consonance.[36]

Secondly, such technized versions of cooperative learning may not address questions central to the role of the teacher as a critically reflective practitioner.[37] Mara Sapon-Shevin poses this issue in stark terms:

> How do we move from talking about and teaching about cooperative learning as an effective teaching strategy (which it is), to asking teachers to reflect about the ways in which schools are organized, the reward structures which guide our behavior, beliefs about how and why people learn which shape our current practices, and the possible broad-ranging political, economic, and structural changes which might follow our thoughtful implementation of principles of cooperation, mutual empowerment, shared decisionmaking, and respect for diversity and heterogeneity?[38]

Following prescriptive recipes does not make for reflective practice.

Relatedly, Sapon-Shevin and others have urged researchers and practitioners of cooperative learning to "go beyond superficial evaluations of effectiveness to more serious explorations of the many choices which practitioners make."[39] For example, advocates of cooperative learning often focus on classroom management and pupil achievement while neglecting prior—and fundamental—questions of aims, goals, and purposes, as has been noted earlier. Some of these submerged educative purposes might well speak to the wider aims of critically reflective education in ways which transcend the pat, and limited, formulae of teamwork, team building, group sanctions, and group rewards which are typically employed in existing models of cooperative learning.

Proponents of cooperative learning tend to express their educational objectives rather strictly in terms of their *instrumental* value. Aims can be justified on either extrinsic or intrinsic grounds. An object, quality, or act has extrinsic value when it is derived from the value of something else. For instance, advocates of cooperative learning believe that it develops social skills and promotes interdependence. Cooperative learning would have extrinsic value, then, because its value is drawn from the value of fostering such joint social interactions. This is an *instrumental* value. Thus, *X* is instrumentally valuable if it leads to *Y* (which is valuable) or if it leads to the avoidance or weakening of *Z* (which has negative value). In the case of cooperative learning, competition, as such, would appear to constitute a more negative value.

One difficulty with an instrumental value is the danger of an infinite regress. For example, if learning to cooperate is thought to be desirable, one might ask why and be told that it enables one to get along better with people, which, in turn, will help in obtaining and maintaining a good job. But why does one want a good job? Because one needs to support oneself and his or her family. But why? Sooner or later, the answer will have to be that it is valuable for its own sake, not for what it leads to. The fact of the matter is that often it is simply easier to persuade persons to do what is "good" for them by appealing to short-term instrumental values, rather than speaking of such activities as critical reflection or such qualities as transcendence and aesthetic fulfillment.

A thing that has *intrinsic* value is something that has value in and of itself; its value is not derived from anything else. Is "cooperation" alone a self-sufficient activity? As complex organisms, most of us would probably not fully assent to that question. Disagreement over whether a thing has intrinsic value can result from genuine philosophical differences or from differing definitions for the same term. Have the advocates of cooperative learning adequately defined and defended what they mean by "cooperation"? Without substantial examination and definition of that term, one might not want to use it as a justification for an aim, educational or otherwise.[40]

Finally, there are also some practical concerns about cooperative learning. For example, might some students become distracted, frustrated, or bored in concentrating primarily on group activities? And what becomes of the pupil who does not contribute more or less equally to the group's tasks, functions, and goals? Since students vary in their learning styles, it seems more appropriate to diversify classroom activities in order to ensure a wide variety of alternative methods, e.g., individual and group work.[41] It is quite noteworthy that some cooperative learning models (e.g., Slavin's Student Team Learning) cannot avoid making use of *competitive* formats and *competitive* frames of reference, i.e., teams compete against other teams.

OTHER NONCOMPETITIVE OPTIONS

Along with the noncompetitive approaches already focused on in this chapter, there have been a number of other curricular innovations during recent decades, some of which have been widely used, others of which have been less common but still influence educational thought and practice today. The remainder of this chapter will provide summaries of some of these additional noncompetitive options and alternatives.

Nongraded Schools

The principal feature of nongraded schools is that grade levels and all expectations associated with separate grades are eliminated. In theory, nongraded schools offer individualized instruction and permit pupils to learn at their own rate of speed. The problems associated with promotion and retention are presumably minimized, instruction no longer has to be geared to the hypothetical "average" student, and pupils are no longer delayed by other classmates. Different age groups work together and learn from one another, thus partaking of some of the concepts alluded to in previous sections of this chapter. For example, a child may be advanced in arithmetic but less advanced in social studies; consequently, she is placed with others who have similar abilities in the subjects and works with them in large and small groups. The students also spend time working alone. Nongraded schooling fosters some decidedly progressivistic notions.

Teachers, however, need special preparation to teach in these programs; and the demands can be greater than the demands in traditional graded plans. Most curricular materials are designed for graded schools and, therefore, teachers have to rely on programmed materials and related self-instructional devices. Again, such practices may not lend themselves to the model of the teacher as reflective practitioner. Furthermore, many schools that *claim* to have made the transition to nongraded programs have not really done so. Instead, they merely have substituted homogeneous grouping within the same grade and left vertical curriculum organization and teaching practices unchanged.

Open Education

This innovation arose in England with the Plowden Report (1967) and was adapted in the United States in the 1970s; it drew upon the findings of such psychologists as Susan Isaacs and Jean Piaget. In "open education," the teacher instructs and guides learning in small groups or individually rather than instructing the class as a whole. Scheduling is flexible and many activities progress simultaneously. The abolition of a required curriculum enables students to make some decisions about their work. Grading is de-emphasized, students learn at their own pace and in terms of their own learning style, and the teacher is more of a facilitator, diagnostician, and stimulator of learning activities. Above all, the "whole child" is recognized. Although open education shares similarities with progressive education, it differs in that it is used more in public than private schools, provides an active role for the teacher, and offers more of a planned environment than do child-centered progressive schools.

The Vermont Design for Education (1968) affords a basic rationale and cardinal tenets for one model of open education: acceptance of the personhood of the student; recognition of her individuality and originality; emphasis on experimental, exploratory learning; self-pacing relevant to individual needs; the role of the teacher as guide and partner in learning; an expansion of the total learning environment to include the larger community; provision of multiple modes of cooperative learning; and the development of commitment and social responsibility.[42]

Some learning environments have been designed around flexible architectural arrangements, i.e., "open-space" schools. Research into open-space schools has not found significant improvements in learning or teaching outcomes.[43] Any type of innovative program can exist in open-space or traditional classrooms. Merely changing the architectural design does not really make a difference. Open education, however, does seem to have a positive influence on self-concept, attitude toward school, independence, creativity, and curiosity. In a study of ten schools, researchers found higher achievement in schools that used traditional methods and higher self-concept in schools that used open education approaches.[44] However, the different definitions of open education and the varied evaluative criteria make it difficult to arrive at conclusive evidence about its overall effectiveness.[45]

Free Schools

One of the alternative forms of schooling which sprang up across the country in the late 1960s was the *free school.* Though varying from place to place, it was usually small, private, and based on a belief in liberating the child. Its impetus was parents' attempts to create new types of learning environments for their children. Using city storefronts, old barns, barracks, abandoned churches, and people's homes, they tried to bring greater freedom of learning through humanistic principles. "Freedom" became a watchword among free-school advocates, even though the term was not always clearly defined or examined. While the majority of these schools were organized by middle-class white parents and attended by their children, integrated school settings could occasionally be found. Free schools mix progressive and libertarian methods, borrow child-development ideas from Piaget, and add some practices from English infant schools, i.e., those that influenced open-classroom approaches. School atmospheres range from free and easy to structured, but, generally, children are not pushed to acquire basic skills before they show a readiness to learn.

George Dennison's vivid description of his First Street School introduces us to the rich fabric of one such freeschool environment:

> We made much of freedom of choice and freedom of movement; and of reality of encounter between teachers and students; and of the continuum of persons, by which we understood that parents, teachers, friends, neighbors, the life of the streets, form all one substance in the experience of the child. We abolished tests and grades and Lesson Plans. We abolished Superiors, too—all that petty and disgusting pecking order of the school bureaucracy which contributes nothing to the wisdom of teachers and still less to the growth of the child. We abolished homework (unless asked for), we abolished the category of truant. We abolished, in short, all of the things which constitute a merely external order; and in doing this, we laid bare the deeper motivations and powers which contribute to . . . "internal order," i.e., a structuring of activities based upon the child's innate desire to learn, and upon . . . the needs of children, the natural authority of adults, the power of moral suasion . . . and the deep attachment and interest which adults inevitably feel toward the lives of children.[46]

Embodied in Dennison's teachings are some long-standing progressivist and libertarian lessons drawn from such figures as Dewey, Neill, Tolstoy, and nineteenth-century anarchist educators.

Most free schools have had difficulty raising funds to keep going, and the average school closes down after about eighteen months. Financial instability and the more independent, idiosyncratic personalities of those who are drawn to establish free schools combine to offer further possible explanations for their transience. Free schools have also been criticized for being accessible mainly to middle-class whites and for putting little emphasis on basic skills and political education:

> Free Schools, by and large, begun by upper-class white people, have been not merely nonpolitical but, in many instances, conspicuously and intentionally anti-political.... The issue is of particular importance when we speak of schools that serve primarily children of rich people. It is not just honest to lead children, by deceptive processes, to "experience" freedom if they are not free. In an unjust nation, the children of the rich and powerful and upper classes are not free in any way that genuinely matters if they are not free to know the price in pain and exploitation that their lives are built upon.[47]

With these serious problems and the increased availability of alternatives in the public schools, free schools declined sharply in the 1970s.

Alternative Public Schools

Alternative schools in the public sector seek to provide options to the traditional model in order to serve diverse educational needs within the community. Such alternative public schools tend to have more comprehensive goals than traditional schools, offer greater curriculum flexibility, and usually are smaller and less bureaucratic than traditional schools.

Alternative public schools have several forms, many of which rely upon progressivist and/or libertarian models. "Open schools" feature individualized learning activities organized around interest centers. "Schools without walls" use the entire community for learning. In a large urban area, learning resources might be concentrated in educational parks that are accessible to every student in the city. "Magnet schools" promote desegregation and special programs not offered in the traditional high school. Street academies and "drop-out centers" organize programs for a specific population. Multicultural schools stress ethnic and racial awareness and cultural pluralism. Science academies and schools for the performing arts appeal to students with special talents. Any of these alternative programs can be organized as a unit within a more traditional school.

The rules in alternative schools are usually fewer and clearer, and there are higher levels of order and organization than in traditional schools.[48] Studies also have found that students in these programs have more favorable attitudes toward themselves, their teachers, and their schools than do students of traditional schools.[49] Nevertheless, much of the research on alternative schools is of limited value because it typically uses case studies focused on only one or two schools and few studies have compared the academic achievement of students in alternative schools with that of students in traditional schools.

Magnet Schools

During the 1970s magnet schools were established to promote integration. They were designed to offer different types of programs that would stem "white flight" from the public schools and attract students of different racial and ethnic backgrounds. Magnet schools can be found in many areas of the country, offering programs to students who meet admission criteria regardless of the neighborhoods in which they reside. The 1976 Amendments of the Emergency School Act (ESAA) provided funding for magnet-school programs, and the Reagan administration used magnet schools for out-of-court settlement of desegregation cases.

Magnet-school programs have continued to proliferate. In high schools, they can be built around any one of a number of themes: academies, the performing arts, special needs of the gifted and talented, vocations, communications and mass media, health professions, foreign languages, and commercial arts. Elementary magnet schools tend to focus on a particular teaching-learning style: open classroom, Montessori methods, or emphasis on basic skills.

The Houston Independent School District, for example, has created an extensive network of magnet schools, ranging from Petro-Chemical Careers Institute to a High School for Law Enforcement and Criminal Justice. This network has been instrumental in reducing segregation of African-American and Hispanic youth and in attracting white suburban students to city schools. Magnet schools have also promoted desegregation in Milwaukee. And magnet schools for the performing arts have been established in such places as Philadelphia, Cincinnati, and Baltimore.

While the quality of magnet schools varies widely, some studies show that these schools can be effective.[50] They seem to foster a positive climate for learning and a commitment by faculty and students to the school's mission. Magnet schools offer voluntary desegregation, but cannot, by themselves, overcome segregation problems. Some studies indicate that school districts that implement mandatory desegregation plans achieve more than three times the racial balance of districts implementing voluntary plans.[51] Other research makes the case that voluntary magnet plans tend to generate more *durable* desegregation than does mandatory busing.[52] On the other hand, a lack of support for magnet schools in some districts from school board members, faculty, and especially parents have led to unimpressive results.[53] Criticisms also come from administrators of neighborhood schools who see magnet schools siphoning off the brightest students and isolating students by promoting elitism. In terms of admissions and evaluational policies, some magnet programs (especially those involving students with special talents) are indeed quite competitive and selective.

Whole Language Movement

During the last several decades, the "whole language" movement has begun to sweep across myriad fields of knowledge, incorporating research findings in such diverse areas as linguistics, psycholinguistics, anthropology, sociology, philosophy, child development, curriculum studies, composition, literary theory, and semiotics. Rather than offering prescriptions and recipes for learning, whole language represents a distinctive philosophic stance that is grounded in the above disciplines. Abandoning segmented, mechanistic, and linear views of knowledge and experience, whole language focuses on the creation of *situational meaning* through the *actual, lived* use of language in all manner of incidental ways.

A major philosophical rationale for the whole language movement can be found in the influential linguistic theories of Noam Chomsky. His notion of "generative-transformational grammar" has redefined linguistics as a field and forged new approaches to interdisciplinary scholarship which strongly oppose narrow behavioristic arguments that depict language and behavior as basically subject to the principles of operant conditioning.[54] Chomsky poses a mentalistic, naturalistic portrait of cognition. For him, the acquisition of language is an innate activity which assumes that human beings have the capacity for linguistic creativity: "Anyone concerned with the study of human nature and human capacities must somehow come to grips with the fact that all normal humans acquire language."[55]

Chomsky claims that human beings possess a "language information device" (LAD) which stores the mental data and processes needed for language development. Thus, he hypothesizes a kind of universal linguistic mechanism which generates structural rules for the growth of grammar, syntax, and semantics.[56] According to Chomsky, the human possession of such innate mental apparatus allows young children to learn language rapidly, informally, and incidentally. Of course, no one has really *proven* the existence of such innate mechanisms, though Chomsky's speculations have provided ample grounds for further inquiry and exploration.

Like Deweyan progressivists, whole-language advocates speak to the interests of the "whole child" in those multifacted forms of dialogue, dialect, and voice that each child presents. Fostering an interactive approach to learning, they promote cooperative activity among students and between teacher and pupils. Students are given varied opportunities to listen, speak, read, write, and think in multiple contexts. Authentic texts, such as actual letters from one pupil to another, form the foundation of whole-language experience. Any revisions in language are appropriated by the students themselves in settings which stress support and acceptance for all concerned. The teacher's role is that of helper and facilitator in the mutual creation of "meaning-voyages."

Thus, whole language emphasizes "the constructive, generative, and transactive nature of learning, and . . . acknowledges that language is not only endemic to human experience but also meaningful, integrated, empowering, emergent, social, owned, and useful."[57] Furthermore, it underscores the primacy of critical reflection on the part of all participants in the learning process.

Linda Irwin-DeVitis describes the basic assumptions of the whole-language philosophy: "(1) children learn language by using language; (2) the focus in language learning should be on meaning in real situations, not on form; (3) language learning occurs best when children are in a secure environment that encourages risk-taking; (4) children learn to use and vary their language in an ever-expanding variety of contexts; (5) the learning of language rules is intuitive, largely self-directed and is dependent upon certain universal prerequisite conditions."[58] Many of the latter conditions assume the kinds of prerequisites implicit in the theories of Chomsky and Vygotsky.

Orsyia Hull and other teachers in Manitoba have developed an effective and creative example of whole language in action:

> The teachers choose one sample of student writing (in which the student had a reasonable degree of autonomy in topic choice and development) early in the year. Several times throughout the year, the teacher dictates the sample composition to the child. The dictated copies are compared to the original, allowing

> documentation of progress in conventions of print, orthography, spelling, punctuation and relation of form to clause structure. The students themselves examine their progress, become self-evaluators, and become more aware of their own growing command of written language.[59]

In their enthusiasm for their cause, some doctrinaire devotees of whole language have been known to cut off debate and dialogue on controversial issues in language development. Yet others have welcomed open-ended discussion: "Whole language teachers themselves have different definitions and viewpoints . . . there are as many manifestations of whole language instruction as there are whole language teachers."[60] Although whole language should not be taken as a panacea for all our educational ills, it does afford rich possibilities for genuine noncompetitive alternatives which incorporate some of the best elements of progressivism and interdisciplinary studies.

POSTSCRIPT

As the preceding discussion makes evident, human beings differ in their learning styles and preferences. It would thus seem appropriate to expose students to a wide variety of classroom practices, including individualistic, competitive, and cooperative modes of pedagogical arrangements. Though systems of mass schooling tend to discourage a diverse set of programs and practices, "with careful planning, it should be possible to meet the unique needs of all students within one unified system of education—a system that does not deny differences, but rather a system that recognizes and accommodates for differences."[61]

Such an educational system, if it is to be made practicable, would require school reforms which acknowledge that students "must learn to curtail as well as to express, to fulfill obligations as well as to claim rights."[62] At the same time, such a system would have to ensure ultimate respect for persons so that all people are treated justly by promoting just rules and practices, whether they are individualistic, competitive, or cooperative.

ENDNOTES

1. Wise, J.: *The History of Education.* New York: Sheed & Ward, 1964.
2. Kennedy, George A.: *Quintilian.* New York: Twayne, 1969.

3. Keatinge, M. W.: *The Great Didactic of John Amos Comenius,* part 2. London: A. & C. Black, 1923.

4. Pestalozzi, Johann Heinrich: *How Gertrude Teaches Her Children,* L. E. Holland and F. C. Turner (Tr.). London: George Allen & Unwin, 1915.

5. Wagner, Lilya: Social and historical perspectives on peer tutoring in education. In Foot, Hugh C., Morgan, Michelle J., and Shute, Rosalyn H. (Eds.): *Children Helping Children.* New York: John Wiley & Sons, 1990, pp. 21–42. (This essay has been particularly useful in preparing this portion of our discussion.) On the growth of monitorial schools in specific sections of the United States, see Fowle, William Bentley: *The Teacher's Institute,* 2nd ed. Boston: William B. Fowle, 1847; McCadden, J. J.: *Education in Pennsylvania, 1801-1835.* New York: Arno Press, 1969; Palmer, A. E.: *The New York Public School.* New York: Macmillan, 1905; and Eggertsen, C. A.: The monitorial system of instruction in the United States. Unpublished doctoral dissertation, University of Minnesota, 1939.

6. Woofter, T. J.: *Teaching in Rural Schools.* Boston: Houghton Mifflin, 1917. See also Tyler, Ralph: Wasting time and resources in schools. *Viewpoints,* 52: 59–73, 1975; Thelen, Herbert A.: Tutoring by students. *The School Review,* 77: 229–243, 1969; and Martin, J. H.: The grade school came from Prussia. *Educational Horizons,* 51: 28–33, 1972.

7. Lippitt, P. and Lohman, J. E.: Cross-age relationships—an educational resource. *Children,* 12: 113–117, 1965; Lippitt, P. and Lippitt, R.: Cross-age helpers. *NEA Journal,* 57: 24–26, 1968; and Lippitt, P. *Students Teach Students.* Bloomington, Ind., Phi Delta Kappa Educational Foundation, 1975.

8. Gartner, A., Kohler, M. C., and Riessman, F.: *Children Teach Children: Learning by Teaching.* New York: Harper & Row, 1971.

9. For insights into the affective dimensions of peer teaching, see Bloom, Benjamin S.: *Human Characteristics and School Learning.* New York: McGraw-Hill, 1976; Allen, V. L. (Ed.): *Children as Teachers: Theory and Research on Tutoring.* New York: Academic Press, 1976; Melaragno, R. J.: *Tutoring with Students.* Englewood Cliffs, NJ: Educational Technology Publications, 1976; and Buckholdt, D. R. and Wodarski, J. S.: The effects of different reinforcement systems on cooperative behaviors exhibited by children in classroom contexts. *Journal of Research and Development in Education,* 12: 50–68, 1978.

10. Allen, V. L. and Feldman, R. S.: Studies in the role of tutor. In Allen, V. L. (Ed.): *Children as Teachers.* Cf. also McWhorter, K. T. and Levy, J.: Influences of a tutorial programme upon tutors. *Journal of Reading,* 14: 221–225, 1971; and Ehly, S. W. and Larsen, S. C.: *Peer Tutoring for Individualized Instruction.* Boston: Allyn and Bacon, 1980.

11. Ratti, M. C.: Comrades in distress. *Links,* 5: 19–22, 1980.

12. Greenspan, B. M.: Facilitating psychological growth in adolescents through a child development curriculum. Unpublished doctoral dissertation, Harvard University, 1976. Of course, as D. P. Paolitto notes, the kind of complex development that Greenspan has in mind will call for a rather lengthy period of human development. See Paolitto, D. P.: The effect of cross-age tutoring on adolescence: an

inquiry into theoretical assumptions. *Review of Educational Research,* 46: 215–237, 1976.

13. Strodtbeck, F. L., Ronchi, D., and Hansell, S.: Tutoring and psychological growth. In Allen, V. L. (Ed.): *Children as Teachers.* Cf. also Sharpley, A. M. and Sharpley, C. F.: Peer tutoring: a review of the literature. *CORE,* 5: 3, 1981. More generally, see Imich, Andre J.: Pupil tutoring: the development of internality and improved school attendance. In Foot, Hugh C., Morgan, Michelle J., and Shute, Rosalyn H. (Eds.): *Children Helping Children,* pp. 93–115, which has been helpful in framing this section of our chapter.

14. Durkheim, Emile: *Education and Sociology* (1922), S. D. Fox (Tr.). Glencoe, IL: Free Press, 1956, p. 71.

15. Piaget, Jean: *The Moral Judgment of the Child* (1932), Marjorie Gabain (Tr.). New York: Collier, 1962, pp. 343, 356.

16. *Ibid.,* pp. 346, 348, 371.

17. Bronfrenbrenner, Urie: *Two Worlds of Childhood: U.S. and U.S.S.R.* New York, Sage Foundation, 1970. See also Hogan, Robert: Moral conduct and moral character: a psychological perspective. *Psychological Bulletin,* 79: 227, 1973.

18. Damon, William: Peer education: the untapped potential. *Journal of Applied Developmental Psychology,* 5: 333–334, 1984.

19. Vygotsky, L. S.: *Mind in Society.* Cambridge, MA: Harvard University Press, 1978, p. 86.

20. Bruner, Jerome S.: Vygotsky: a historical and conceptual perspective. In Wertsch, J. V. (Ed.): *Culture, Communication and Cognition: Vygotskian Perspectives.* Cambridge: Cambridge University Press, 1985, p. 32.

21. Damon, William and Phelps, E.: Peer collaboration as a context for cognitive growth. Paper presented at the Tel Aviv University School of Education Annual Symposium on Human Development and Instruction, June, 1987, as cited in Foot, Hugh C., Morgan, Michelle J., and Shute, Rosalyn H.: Children's helping relationships: an overview. In Foot, Hugh C., *et al.: Children Helping Children,* pp. 8–9.

22. Sharan, Shlomo: The group-investigation approach to cooperative learning: Theoretical foundations. Unpublished paper, University of Tel Aviv, 1988.

23. Deutsch, Morton: Cooperation and trust: Some theoretical notes. In Jones, M. R. (Ed.): *Nebraska Symposium on Motivation.* Lincoln, University of Nebraska Press, 1962, pp. 275–319. Cf. also Garibaldi, A.: The effective contributions of cooperative and group goal structures. *Journal of Educational Psychology,* 71: 788–795, 1979.

24. Rottier, Jerry and Ogan, Beverly J.: *Cooperative Learning in Middle-Level Schools.* Washington, DC: National Education Association, 1991, pp. 13–15.

25. Knight, George P. and Bohlmeyer, Elaine Morton: Cooperative learning and achievement: Methods for assessing causal mechanisms. In Sharan, Shlomo (Ed.): *Cooperative Learning: Theory and Research.* New York: Praeger, 1990, pp. 1–7.

26. *Ibid.,* pp. 2–3. Johnson, David W. and Johnson, Roger T.: Type of task and student achievement and attitudes in interpersonal cooperation, competition, and individualization. *Journal of Social Psychology,* 108: 37–48, 1979; Johnson, David W.,

Johnson, Roger T., and Skon, L.: Student achievement on different types of tasks under cooperative, competitive, and individualistic conditions. *Contemporary Educational Psychology,* 4: 99–106, 1979; Johnson, David W., Johnson, Roger T., Tiffany, M., and Zaidman, B.: Are low achievers disliked in a cooperative situation? a test of rival theories in a mixed ethnic situation. *Contemporary Educational Psychology,* 8: 189–200, 1983.

27. Johnson, David W. and Johnson, Roger T.: Motivational processes in cooperative, competitive, and individualistic learning situations. In Ames, R. and Ames, C. (Eds.): *Research on Motivation in Education: The Classroom Milieu,* vol. 2. New York: Academic Press, 1985, pp. 249–286.

28. Nicholls, John G.: *The Competitive Ethos and Democratic Education.* Cambridge, Mass.: Harvard University Press, 1989, p. 169. Cf. also Johnson, David W., Johnson, Roger T., and Scott, L.: The effects of cooperative and individualized instruction on student attitudes and achievement. *Journal of Social Psychology,* 104: 207–216, 1978; and Smith, K., Johnson, David W., and Johnson, Roger T.: Can conflict be constructive? Controversy versus concurrence-seeking in learning groups. *Journal of Educational Psychology,* 73: 651–663, 1981.

29. Aronson, Elliot, Blaney, Nancy, Cookie, Stephen, Sikes, Jev, and Snapp, Matthew: *The Jigsaw Classroom.* Beverly Hills: Sage, 1978.

30. Ziegler, S.: The effectiveness of cooperative learning teams for increasing cross-ethnic friendship: Additional evidence. *Human Organization,* 40: 264–268, 1981.

31. Slavin, Robert E.: *Student Team Learning: An Overview and Practical Guide.* Washington, DC: National Education Association, 1983, pp. 6–7.

32. DeVries, D. and Slavin, R.: Teams-games-tournaments: a research review. *Journal of Research and Development in Education,* 12: 28–38, 1978.

33. Slavin, R.: Team-assisted individualization: Combining cooperative learning and individualized instruction in mathematics. In Slavin, R., Sharan, S., Kagan, S., Hertz-Lazarowitz, R., Webb, C., and Schmuck, R. (Eds.): *Learning to Cooperate, Cooperating to Learn.* New York: Plenum, 1985, pp. 177–209.

34. Sharan, Shlomo: Cooperative learning and helping behaviour in the multiethnic classroom. In Foot, Hugh C., *et al.: Children Helping Children,* pp. 156–158. Cf. also Sharan, S., Kussell, P., Hertz-Lazarowitz, R., Bejarano, Y., Raviv, S., and Sharan, Y.: *Cooperative Learning in the Classroom: Research in Desegregated Schools.* Hillsdale, NJ: Lawrence Erlbaum, 1984.

35. Cornbleth, Catherine: Knowledge in curriculum and teacher education. *Social Education,* 51: 514, 1987.

36. Dewey, John: *Democracy and Education.* New York: Macmillan, 1916, pp. 102–103, 106, 323, 346–347.

37. See Schon, D. A.: *The Reflective Practitioner: How Professionals Think in Action.* New York: Basic Books, 1983; and Schon: *Educating the Reflective Practitioner: Toward a New Design for Teaching and Learning in the Professions.* San Francisco: Jossey-Bass, 1987.

38. Sapon-Shevin, Mara: Cooperative learning: Liberatory praxis or hamburger helper. *Educational Foundations,* 5: 9, 1991. See also Schniedewind, Nancy: *Cooperative Learning, Cooperative Lives.* Dubuque: IA, William C. Brown, 1987; Sapon-Shevin,

Mara and Schniedewind, Nancy: Cooperative learning as empowering pedagogy. In Sleeter, Christine (Ed.): *Empowerment Through Multicultural Education*. Albany: State University of New York Press, 1991, pp. 159–178; Ellsworth, E.: Why doesn't this feel empowering? Working through the repressive myths of critical pedagogy. *Harvard Educational Review*, 59: 297–324, 1989; and Kohn, A.: *No Contest: The Case Against Competition*. Boston: Houghton Mifflin, 1986.

39. Sapon-Shevin, Mara: Cooperative learning: Liberatory praxis or hamburger helper, pp. 6–7. See also Bigelow, W.: Inside the classroom: Social vision and critical pedagogy. *Teachers College Record*, 91: 437–448, 1990.

40. For discussions on the justification of educational aims, see Dupuis, Adrian (Ed.): *Nature, Aims, and Policy*. Urbana: University of Illinois Press, 1970; Brown, L. M. (Ed.): *Aims of Education*. New York: Teachers College Press, 1970; and White, John: *The Aims of Education Restated*. Boston: Routledge & Kegan Paul, 1982.

41. On some theoretical and practical difficulties in applying cooperative learning models, see Miller, S. A. and Brownell, C. A.: Peers, persuasion, and Piaget: Dyadic interaction between conservers and nonconservers. *Child Development*, 46: 992–997, 1975; and Koestner, R., Ryan, R. M., Bernieri, F., and Holt, K.: Setting limits on children's behavior: the differential effects of controlling vs. informational styles on intrinsic motivation and creativity. *Journal of Personality*, 53: 233–248, 1984; and Schultz, James L.: Cooperative learning: Refining the process. *Educational Leadership*, 47: 43–45, 1989/1990.

42. Vermont Department of Education: Vermont design for education. In Nyquist, Ewald B. and Hawes, Gene R. (Eds.): *Open Education: A Sourcebook for Parents and Teachers*. New York: Bantam, 1972, pp. 55–62.

43. Armstrong, D. G.: Open space vs. self-contained. *Educational Leadership*, 32: 291–295, 1975.

44. Lukasevich, A. and Gray, R. F.: Open space, open education, and pupil performance. *Elementary School Journal*, 79: 108–114, 1978.

45. Chittenden, Edward A. and Bussis, Anne M.: Open education: Research and assessment strategies. In Nyquist, Ewald B. and Hawes, Gene R. (Eds.): *Open Education*, pp. 360–372.

46. Dennison, George: *The Lives of Children*. New York: Random House, 1969, p. 6. See also Graubard, Allen: *Free the Children: Radical Reform and the Free School Movement*. New York: Vintage, 1972; and Kozol, Jonathan: *Free Schools*. Boston: Houghton Mifflin, 1972.

47. Kozol, Jonathan: *Free Schools*, pp. 95–96. Kozol continues his argument: "The heart of the deception is the pretense of free choice within a carefully constructed framework of contrived and managed possibilities. The children can 'choose' for Herman Hesse, for Richard Brautigan or Tolkien, for Mexican sandals, Polaroid cameras or brown rice with mushrooms; but they cannot 'choose' for starving and malnourished kids in Harlem . . . " (pp. 96–97)

48. Trickett, E. J.: Toward a social-ecological conception of adolescent socialization: Normative data on contrasting types of public school classrooms. *Child Development*, 49: 408–414, 1978.

49. Duke, D. L. and Muzio, I.: How effective are alternative schools? a review of recent evaluations and reports. *Teachers College Record,* 79: 461–483, 1978.

50. Doyle, Denis P. and Levine, Marsha: Magnet schools: Choice and quality in public education. *Phi Delta Kappan,* 66: 265–269, 1984.

51. Smylie, Mark: Reducing racial isolation in large school districts: the comparative effectiveness of mandatory and voluntary strategies. *Urban Education,* 17: 77–83, 1983.

52. Rossell, Christine H.: *The Carrot or the Stick for School Desgregation Policy: Magnet Schools or Forced Busing.* Philadelphia: Temple University Press, 1990.

53. Lowry, James Associates: *Survey of Magnet Schools.* Washington, D.C., National Institute of Education, 1984.

54. For an incisive critique of behavioral approaches to language development, see Rhodes, Lynn K. and Dudley-Marling, Curt: *Readers and Writers with a Difference: A Holistic Approach to Teaching Learning Disabled and Remedial Students.* Portsmouth, N.H., Heinemann, 1988, p. 67: "Behavioral objectives are well motivated. They presume to ensure maximally efficient instruction by focusing on well-defined, easily achievable 'building blocks' of learning. But they depend on a technology which does not exist. Precise descriptions of cognitive, social, and linguistic behavior, including reading and writing, are not possible and probably not desirable. Higher forms of human learning are not reducible to their component parts."

55. Chomsky, Noam: *Language and Mind.* New York: Harcourt, Brace & World, 1968, p. 59.

56. Chomsky, Noam: *Syntactic Structures.* The Hague, Mouton, 1957; and Chomsky: *Aspects of a Theory of Grammar.* Cambridge, MA: M.I.T. Press, 1965.

57. Mickelson, Norma I.: Roots and wings: Whole language theory and practice. *Prime Areas,* 31: 3, 1988. Cf. also Goodman, Kenneth S.: *What's Whole in Whole Language?* Portsmouth, N.H., Heinemann, 1986; Goodman, Kenneth S., Goodman, Yetta M., and Hood, Wendy J. (Eds.): *The Whole Language Evaluation Book.* Portsmouth, NH: Heinemann, 1989; Newman, Judith M. (Ed.): *Whole Language: Theory in Use.* Portsmouth, N.H., Heinemann, 1985; Rich, Sharon J.: Restoring power to teachers: the impact of "whole language." *Language Arts,* 62: 717–724, 1985; Altwerger, Bess, Edelski, Carole and Flores, Barbara M.: Whole language: What's new? *The Reading Teacher,* 23: 144–150, 1987; Johnson, Terry D.: What is whole language? *a working response. Prime Areas,* 31: 6–12, 1988; Smith, Frank: Demonstrations, engagement and sensitivity: the choice between people and programs. *Language Arts,* 58: 634–642, 1981; and Wells, Gordon: *The Meaning Makers: Children Learning Language and Using Language to Learn.* Portsmouth, NH: Heinemann, 1986.

58. Irwin-DeVitis, Linda: Review of Rhodes, Lynn K. and Dudley-Marling, Curt: *Readers and Writers with a Difference: A Holistic Approach to Teaching Learning Disabled and Remedial Students.* In *Educational Studies,* 20: 185, 1989.

59. Irwin-DeVitis, Linda: Review of Goodman, Kenneth S., Goodman, Yetta M. and Hood, Wendy J. (Eds.): *The Whole Language Evaluation Book.* In *Educational Studies,* 21: 310, 1990.

60. Gunderson, Lee: *A Whole Language Primer.* New York: Scholastic, 1989. As Judith Newman further points out, "As with all theoretical arguments, each of us is obliged to explore the practical ramifications in his own way." Newman, Judith M. (Ed.): *Whole Language: Theory in Use,* p. 1.

61. Stainback, W. and Stainback, S.: A rationale for the merger of special and regular education. *Exceptional Children,* 51: 109, 1984.

62. Feden, Preston D. and Clabaugh, Gary K.: Developmental education: La Salle's rationale and program for integrative teacher education. In DeVitis, Joseph L. and Sola, Peter A. (Eds.): *Building Bridges for Educational Reform: New Approaches to Teacher Education.* Ames: Iowa State University Press, 1989, p. 155.

Chapter Ten

THE PLACE OF COMPETITION IN EDUCATION

This chapter summarizes and synthesizes findings from previous chapters and offers policies for augmenting healthier competition in education. What is the place of competition in education? As seen in previous chapters, it has a large and growing place in American education; however, it may assume undesirable or noxious forms, and some of the more positive arrangements it could possibly take have yet to occur. Our approach to summarizing and synthesizing is to organize these ideas into two sections focusing on concepts and theories and on common issues before turning attention to specific policy recommendations.

CONCEPTS AND THEORIES

Competition is found in many spheres of education. It is found in testing, grading, class rankings, and scholastic awards. And it can be observed in the quest for college admissions, admission to graduate and professional schools, and fellowships, scholarships, and grants. It is manifested in games, sports, interscholastic and intercollegiate athletic competition, and in numerous other activities.

Yet these are outward manifestations of a deeper ideological level undergirding American culture and education. At this ideological level, competition is embedded in social, political, and economic theories about American life that shape the values of its citizens. Hobbesian political thought provided a model of struggle in a state of nature based on severe conflict and competition. Freud envisioned the demands of civilized life required the repression of natural aggressiveness and sexuality to be sublimated into creative cultural forms to avoid imperiling cultural cohesion. Social Darwinism offered a rationalization for the rapid expansion and rapacious policies of corporate titans in an emerging industrial age. It promoted the political belief that individuals, left to their own devices without government interference, would advance or fall according to their own abilities. Yet American ideals historically preserved a place for the doctrine of "fair play"; and, more recently and less influential, "fair shares," which emphasizes an equality of results. Sociobiology, an interdisciplinary field, drew upon population biology and evolution in conceptualizing humans as continuous with the animal kingdom; it contrasts with social Darwinism, among other ways, by emphasizing altruism in the evolutionary process. Sociobiology recognizes not only struggle and competition for survival for humans and animals but cooperation and altruism as well.

Some influential thinkers countered the elevation of competition in social life by viewing the individual in a more cooperative mode. For Alfred Adler, egocentric striving for power was seen as neurotic and counterproductive to the development of social interest and cooperative community life. Social interest encompasses communal feeling and empathy for other and leads to cooperative, democratic relations based on equality. Jean Piaget, in his developmental studies, found cooperation to be necessary to eliminate infantile behavior. It is in mutuality through peer relations that older children and adolescents learn a democratic value system.

The competitive model in economics utilizes a perfect competition notion that usually fails to realistically describe actual market behavior; therefore imperfect competition more accurately describes what occurs and accounts for oligopolies and monopolies. Order and efficiency—two qualities valued in business and industry—were imposed on public education through business leaders on local school boards and in other influential positions. It took the form of a bureaucratic model that sought greater efficiencies while following Frederick Taylor's principles of industrial management based on time-studies of tasks, leading to a standard time for each job and payment of wages according to output. Yet not all aspects of bureaucratization have been harmful to schools, as it has kept schools free from corrupt patronage, helped centralize and standardize schools, and reduced disorganization during periods of rapid change and cultural conflict.

Accountability, a watchword since the 1970s, emphasizes measurement, efficiency, system models, and competitiveness, with outputs in terms of standardized achievement test scores the principal measure for determining quality. The program and instructional goals must be stated in measurable terms in order that outputs can be appraised and costs assessed. The accountability model has been criticized for utilizing educational engineering that applies cost accounting to education and thereby emphasizes means and techniques rather than ends and fails to consider the full range of educational outcomes but is limited to those readily measurable.

As in economics, an attempt has been made in sports to relate the Protestant ethic to the expansion of sports activities. This hypothesis, however, is not supported internationally because of the achievement level of sports in non-Protestant nations. But what can be observed in any society where sports holds an important place is that the achievement motive is basic. The achievement motive is greatest in the upper-middle class. Other value orientations are the exertion of power, obedience in team sports, and asceticism in individual sports.

Functionalism, interactionism, and neo-Marxism have sought to explain sport. But probably the most potent ideology in both sport and American life, especially for the middle class, is the American Dream. Americans generally believe in the values of achievement, success, materialism, equal opportunity, ambitiousness, and hard work as the bulwark of the American Dream. Sport is an accessible means to understand the American Dream because of its open and largely unrestrained expression and wide media coverage of sport exemplars and failures. Sport dramatizes and ritualizes the quest for achieving respectability in a society obsessed with status, advancement, and success. The American Dream, as exemplified in sport, serves as an integrative force in a society that reflects similar values. Though lacking hard evidence for its validity, the ideology nevertheless serves to motivate and compel devotion.

The three types of competition found in sport may also apply outside of sport. One type is direct competition where two opponents (individual or team) confront each other (as in all contact and nearly all court sport). This type also applies to norm-referenced tests, class recitations, musical competitions, and public debate. Second, parallel competition, an indirect form, where contestants take turns competing with one another by taking turns or competing in separate areas (e.g., golf, swimming, bowling). Examples outside of sport include seeking grants, scholarships, and betting. Third, competition which is conducted against a standard (as in archery, figure skating, and diving). Criterion-reference tests would be of this type as well as painting, sculpturing, and gambling.

Meritocracy and competition are connected insofar as competition is a necessary feature of all meritocratic systems. As systems become more meritocratic, they would likely become more highly competitive. The meritocrat advocates institutions that enable individuals to develop their talents and that distribute such goods as education, specialized jobs, and high income in a manner consistent with demonstrated ability. Since talents are unequally distributed and standards are developed with reference to human abilities rather than a priori, the outcomes will be unequal. A meritocratic system is based on equal access to education so that those students with the abilities most valued by society will be in a better position to develop them.

Egalitarianism, however, rejects meritocratic systems on numerous grounds. Egalitarians believe that meritocracy reinforces inequalities and race differences in educational achievement. The meritocratic process, egalitarians claim, seeks to convince the lower class of their inferiority and that those in high places deserve to be there because they are more talented and work harder. Schools legitimate this view. Class divisions are replicated in school and are found in tracking and other policies. Students are tracked according to curriculum and sorted through various standardized tests and teacher evaluations. The result of tracking in terms of the college preparatory, general, and vocational tracks is that educational credentials can be used to ration access to higher status occupations.

In terms of faculty advancement, it is difficult if not impossible to separate innate abilities from acquired abilities in merit evaluations, even though egalitarians would emphasize acquired ability and effort. Yet effort could not be the primary consideration in faculty advancement because effort alone, without native talent and a nurturing environment, does not assure the acquisition of requisite competencies and high performance standards.

Two meritocratic provisions—merit pay and career ladders—have been employed in public schools, with the latter more favored by today's educators. Though the career ladder is more likely to be widely used than merit pay, the career ladder may flounder because some states and local districts are unable to fund it. A more probable trend in instructional improvement is through reforming teacher education and establishing national standards for teacher certification. Nevertheless, whenever meritocratic criteria are used in faculty advancement, one needs to avoid acting unjustly by recognizing and acting against the principal injustices: invidious discrimination, judgmental injustice, and exploitation.

Chapter Six demonstrated that testing has exerted an enormous influence on American education. Today's proponents of testing generally appeal to meritocratic criteria whereas opponents cite egalitarian principles.

The expansion of testing in education emerged with the growth of industrialization, urbanization, and immigration during the early 20th century and led to the development of intelligence, aptitude, and achievement tests. Some psychologists at that time believed that intelligence tests would show that some races are inferior and should not intermingle with other races (Carl Brigham), and other psychologists (Robert Yerkes) claimed to find immigrants of limited intelligence and sought the relations of such limitations to crime and delinquency. Still others (Edward L. Thorndike) held that those of superior intellect have higher character and therefore he advocated eugenics. The rationale underlying today's testing movement, however, is articulated in terms of meritocratic criteria and/or national preparedness.

Testing poses some troublesome problems and raises controversial issues. Some critics claim that grades fail to achieve their stated objectives. As a result, more institutional-specific and pupil-specific modes of evaluation are being introduced.

Other influences of the testing movement are minimum competency testing and tracking. Although minimum competency testing is employed in 39 states, critics claim that the tests narrow the curriculum, reduce teacher flexibility, might lead to the minimum requirement becoming the maximum, and may restrict the number of minority candidates entering teaching. Tracking has proven controversial and some courts have prohibited its use when there is an intent to segregate. Certain studies show that tracking offers slight advantages to students in the top group, but may be harmful to those in the bottom group. Some critics recommend cooperative learning instead of tracking.

Even though millions of students take standardized admission tests annually, the SAT shows limited ability to predict first-year college grades. This has led critics to question the need for such tests, and some colleges have decided no longer to require them. Critics see the testing movement as limiting the ability of students to think and write effectively; consequently, the critics challenge testing specialists to reconsider the purpose of education.

Those who object to our competitive society and its competitive forms in education have the option of identifying with various theoretical models that formulate noncompetitive approaches to education and noncompetitive programs and practices. These models include romanticism, progressivism, libertarianism, Marxism, and feminism. While the latter two would seek to create a new society, the others would not do so and, consequently, would need to limit the influences of the mass media and other undesirable influences.

Progressive education imbibed a heady dose of romanticism in its deification of the child, its emphasis on natural development, freeing the child from unnatural restraints, readiness for learning, and meeting children's needs and interests. Also carried forward was a notion of "freedom from" various constraints, as found in traditional education, that may interfere with the child's development. Where Rousseau wrote about an ideal education that opposed existing institutions, progressives initiated a reform movement to institutionalize new dimensions and directions for education. Its impact as a movement was diminished by the diverse groups under its umbrella that failed to reach consensus on goals and programs until the 1940s, a period in which the movement was in decline. Yet progressivism showed how children can work cooperatively on projects, share their ideas with one another, and solve problems; it also showed how traditional forms of education could yield to new approaches.

Dewey, a pragmatist and progressive who was critical of what he considered the movement's excesses, sought participative educational communities that harmonize individual and social interests, a position that opposes atomistic individualism based on laissez-faire attitudes. This new form of individualism would require individuals and government to intervene in a wider array of social problems. Education would become the fundamental method for social reform.

Libertarianism exhibits a superficial similarity to progressivism in its concern about freeing the learner from various restraints. But libertarianism's roots lie in early nineteenth century France as a political philosophy known as anarchism. It opposed the coercive power of the modern state and sought the maximum freedom compatible with social life. Modern-day libertarianism views the government as the principal culprit in violating human rights by imposing its coercive powers. Whereas progressives would expect government to play a large role in promoting public education and social conditions that improves the child's welfare, libertarians insist that the government limit its role to the protection of life, liberty, and property. Libertarians also believe that the coercive power of government in public education has usurped the rights of students and parents and are generally in favor of enlarging children's rights; in fact, John Holt would essentially grant the young the same rights as adults. Other libertarians, such as Ivan Illich, would deschool society. Some libertarians would vest parents with final authority over their children—whether in organized schooling or home schooling—and grant them the necessary financial support to exercise control effectively.

Dialectical materialism employs a conflict model and is partly deterministic, teleological, and utopian. Neo-Marxists contend that schooling tends to reproduce dominant class structures of competitive, capitalistic exploitation by those who control education. Thus public schools, they claim, reproduce production relations essential to maintaining the capitalist class. An alternative is to create a new society—either Marxism or democratic socialism—in which schools are classless and pervaded by cooperation. The educational agenda would be based upon cooperative learning and the personal integration of communal skills and perspectives. Some neo-Marxists seek to revise orthodox Marxism by minimizing emphasis on economic determinism and the school's role of social reproduction. They warn of the "hidden curriculum" and its norms. They also call for schools to become transformative social agencies in which teachers gain more personal autonomy and self-determination.

Feminism has attempted to show how sexism, competition, and inequality have long been defining features of Western educational thought. Surplus repression or restrictions necessitated by social domination has led to the primacy of the family, patriarchy, and gender dualism. Some ethical conceptions of justice, as developed by Rousseau and Freud, illustrate the misplacement and misappropriation of women in civilization. Jane Martin claims that the notion of liberal education from Plato to Rousseau and its ideal of an educated person coincides with our cultural stereotype of males. She calls for a more gender-sensitive and gender-just ideal that may yield more equitable educational outcomes. Leading researchers in human development, such as Piaget and Kohlberg, used only males in their original samples. Carol Gilligan's studies in moral education are formulated in terms of a language of care, responsibility, cooperation, and a concern to avoid hurting others. In considering Kohlberg's theory, she hypothesizes that women's language is largely one of caring and interpersonal responsibility whereas men's dialect is stated in terms of individual rights and duties. Feminists have also sought to minimize sex-role stereotyping in textbooks and the media, and stressed the dangers of stunted forms of socialization and incomplete human development.

COMMON ISSUES

Our purpose in this section is to raise common issues about competition that either were not fully addressed or need further analysis and concluding judgments. These issues are suggestive of remaining concerns the reader may entertain at this point and thereby seek clarification and possible resolution.

1. ***Is the competitive urge innate in human nature?***

Andrew Colman perceives competition as "one of the foundation stones for social life" because of its basis in social behavior, whether primitive or sophisticated, simple or complex. Hobbes views the original state as brutish—a war of all against all, and Freud finds basic instincts of sexuality and aggressiveness running rampant prior to organized society. Other thinkers, such as Adler and Piaget, disagree.

An inherent feature of capitalism is its stress on competition. But since alternate economic systems exist that are less competitive and offer more cooperative arrangements, it is not a plausible argument in this context that competition is innate. Societies differ in competitiveness, with American society probably more competitive than many others because of its heritage, economy, and government. Nevertheless, the intensity and extent of competition is mitigated by a number of policies in American life—in business, government, education, and elsewhere—even when competitiveness is being extolled.

Anthropologists find that competition may be culturally learned behavior as a result of inculcation in the young. A culture may adopt a competitive mode in response to scarce resources or products whenever a high social value is ascribed to such materials; subsequently, social stratification may be based on the aggrandizement and conspicuous display of exiguous goods.

2. ***Should competition be more greatly emphasized in American education in order to keep up internationally?***

Greater competition in education arose in 1957 after the Soviet Union's launching of Sputnik and the urgency to compete more effectively with them in the space race. Since the 1980s the alarm is over the nation possibly losing its preeminence as a world leader in industry and commerce by failing to compete effectively. The former development led to the passage of the National Defense Education Act, and the latter concern precipitated a flurry of national reports in the 1980s, including *A*

Nation at Risk, and an attempt in the early 1990s to establish national goals and standards for public education.

Some observers claim that students' standardized test scores are low in comparison with other industrial nations and that the curriculum is less demanding. The figures, however, may be misleading because a larger percentage of students continue in school in the U.S., while in some European countries a majority of students are streamed-off to vocational schools or drop out; thus the two populations compared may differ substantially at both secondary and undergraduate levels. Moreover, the focus on national preparedness neglects education for individual development and education conceived as intrinsically worthwhile activity while blame for the economy's failures is shifted from business, industry, and government to education.

The coordination of national goals by the nation's governors and the Bush administration is a move to provide a more centralized educational system in order to compete internationally at the highest level by the year 2000. The National Assessment of Educational Progress has approved a plan to establish the first national standards for student achievement. Additionally, a movement is underway to create national examinations for elementary and secondary school students, and the Carnegie study, *A Nation Prepared,* has advocated national teacher certification. Critics, however, claim that such plans would undermine the long-standing tradition of local control, diminish curriculum variety, overtest students, and decide on a student's career options at an early age.

3. ***Why do some cultures emphasize competition more than do others?***

The answer might be found in the goals and aspirations of a given people. Such people may adopt practices and institutional forms that promote competition, as in American culture competition is abetted by a capitalistic economy (as seen in Chapter Four). Mannheim holds that historical, ideological, and sociological knowledge is fostered by a particular group that seeks to make its view of the world universal. Different views of the world correspond to the particular positions different groups occupy in their struggle for power. He interprets competition as a stage in historical development that grew out of groups seeking to impose on other groups their interpretation of the world. Each perspective sought to become the universally accepted frame of reference. But this did not occur as anticipated and, as a result of fragmentation, competition, he believes, has resulted in a concentration of competing groups and orientations. Mannheim finds that competition is a basic feature of social life.

Cultural anthropologists have found competitive, cooperative, and individualistic preliterate cultures. Those cultures that experienced shortages of a valued crop or product became competitive (as the Ifugo, as noted in Chapter Two). Many cultures have shortages, but they either do not define it as such or do not value items in short supply and therefore no struggle ensues. Status in some societies is predicated on wealth (e.g., the Kachins in Burma; American society) and therefore one must compete to gain wealth and concomitant social rank. Thus in competitive societies people seek to maximize gains by acquiring more material goods or higher prestige than others and thereby may perceive others as rivals and seek to maximize others' losses. Cooperative societies, in contrast, are less hierarchical, more egalitarian, where people are more altruistic and seek to maximize joint gains.

The economic system greatly influences attitudes toward competition. Central to capitalistic systems are various economic conceptions of competition. Perfect competition occurs when a market for a product has so many buyers and sellers that none can influence the price. Yet in actual markets the number of producers is not so large that no firm has control over price. Some economists object to the perfect competition model of economic activity because it gives excessive attention to price competition. Thus imperfect competition actually prevails and this is represented by oligopolies in which a few large producers divide the market among themselves and set prices that are higher than a pure competition model would enforce. Monopolies also arise in which a single seller controls the entire supply of a good or service that has no substitute. The federal government counteracts some of these tendencies by seeking to maintain competitive markets by enforcing antitrust legislation.

4. ***What are the prospects for creating sound educational programs based on cooperative values?***

Such programs need to be guided by a philosophy or ideological model that espouses some form of cooperative values. These may include romanticism, progressivism, libertarianism, neo-Marxism, and feminism. Each of these models has certain weaknesses (as noted in Chapter Eight), and these weaknesses need to be guarded against and, if possible, overcome.

Deutsch developed a theoretical paradigm for the study of competitive, individualistic, and cooperative modes of learning. In his interpretation of competitive situations, if one person achieves a goal, others cannot do so (which differs from our interpretation of competition in chapter two). With individualistic learning situations, the student carries out her goals irrespective of others' goals and her accomplishment has no effect on others' goal attainment. In cooperative modes of learning, one person's aim can only be accomplished through goal achievement of all group members. Deutsch's paradigm, however, is unrealistic for competitive modes of learning because more than one can succeed in a competitive activity (as in the cast of scholarships, grants, selective admissions, and others). Moreover, it is difficult in some cooperative forms of learning to fulfill his criterion, as one person may be unable to promote the goal achievement of other group members because of different goals, abilities, and needs.

Certain programs also offer considerable promise for instilling cooperative values. Peer tutoring may enable students to develop higher levels of thought, heighten social participation, and foster a cooperative exchange among equals. Yet some observers warn that peer interaction often leads to excessive dependence on peer approval and the child may simply be relinquishing adult authority for peer authority. Cooperative learning comprises various models: circles of learning, jigsaw methods, student team learning, and group investigation. These different models, while offering some promising approaches to learning, are not all strictly cooperative learning, as student team learning emphasizes competition among groups. Moreover, some cooperative learning, especially student team learning, seems to involve technocratic rationality that in its planning gives priority to considerations of procedure or technique. In such cases the means and methods become the ends of inquiry, rather than making judgments about ends. In addition, cooperative learning may not address the teacher as critically reflective practitioner. Since students vary in their learning styles and abilities, it would likely be better for teachers to provide a variety of alternative methods that involve both individual and group work. Thus students should be exposed to competitive, individualistic, and cooperative pedagogical arrangements.

THE SEARCH FOR NEW DIRECTION

We should no longer consider competition and cooperation as logical contradictories but as contraries or, in actual practice, existing side-by-side as in team athletic contests. As for aggression in competitive situations, one would be aggressive in a favorable but not unfavorable sense if one is competing effectively. Thus one would be aggressive by being full of enterprise, bold and active in pursuing ends rather than being hostile, quarrelsome, and starting fights. Competition need not lead to discord; when discord results, it is usually thought that competition has degenerated. Similarly, competition and conflict have different objectives, and the rules of competition seek to prevent the competitive process from degenerating into conflict. Thus those competitive activities that persistently lead to conflict need to be reappraised and modified to avoid such outcomes. Competition may occasionally become violent, but it cannot be intentionally violent; in contact sports, however, force may be used according to the applicable rules, which are expected to have a coercive, but not necessarily harmful, effect on the competitors.

Competition can be both frustrating and anxiety provoking. With insufficient rewards available, there may be many frustrated losers. Even the winner may be frustrated because one's competitor is attempting to thwart or block goal-directed behavior. Anxiety is common in competitive situations, arising as a threat to one's adequacy and a fear of failure.

Frustration and anxiety can be reduced in many ways: having more winners rather than one or a few; entering competitive activities voluntarily rather than as an imposed requirement; being adequately prepared for the competition; and emphasizing fair play and good sportsmanship. Anxiety can also be reduced by rejecting the "winning at all costs" attitude.

The search for more cooperative modes of learning has led to a number of promising new arrangements. Yet with different abilities, backgrounds, and learning styles represented in the student population, no single form is adequate for all and it would therefore be best for teachers to offer a variety of classroom practices that include competitive, individualistic, and cooperative arrangements.

Certain forms of competition should be eliminated or, when not possible, greatly reduced. When rules are formulated, agreed upon, achieve their intended effect, and are fairly applied, then contestants should abide by them rather than evade or violate them or seek to win at all costs. It is important that invidious discrimination, which involves arbitrary unequal treatment in developing and enforcing rules, should be eliminated. The goals of any competitive activity should be desirable rather than illegal or seriously harmful to contestants. And one must also be alert to competition that dehumanizes the participants. Only by so doing will full opportunities for all learners be realized.

INDEX

D